Buzzards and Butterflies

Human Remains Detection Dogs

Buzzards and Butterflies
Human Remains Detection Dogs

By J. C. Judah

ISBN: 978-0-6152-0228-0

Published by Coastal Books
C. 2008 by Joyce C. Judah
All Rights Reserved.

Other books by this Author:

An Ancient History of Dogs: Spaniels through the Ages
Building a Basic Foundation for Search and Rescue Dog Training
Search and Rescue Canine Log & Journal
Search and Rescue Log & Journal
The Faircloth Family History
Brunswick County: The Best of the Beaches
The Legends of Brunswick County: Ghosts, Pirates, Indians and Colonial North Carolina

www.lulu.com/spaniels
www.heritagebooks.com

Contact Information:

carolinakennels@2khiway.net
www.geocities.com/springers2020
(910) 842-7942

Inside Cover Photo of K9 Brenner, handled by Kim Gilmore
Flathead Search and Rescue, Montana.

Printed in the United States of America

Table of Contents

1. Introduction and Equipment 1
   So You Want to be A Cadaver Dog Handler 2
   Burials and the Environment 4
   Soil Composition 5
      Soil pH 5
      How to Determine the pH Level of the Soil 6
      Tools of the Trade 6
      Soil Acidity/Moisture Meter 6
      Magnetometer Maps 7
      Soil Probes 7
      Wooden Stakes 7
      Ground Penetrating Radar 8
      Utility Flags 11
      Flagging Tape 11
      Map of the Area 11
      Sketch Pad 11
      Camera 11
      Additional Equipment 12

2. Burial Customs 13
   Slave Burials 14
   Natural Burials 14
   Preservation of the Body 15
   Caskets 15
   Inclusion of Clothing and Personal Effects 15
   Body Positioning 16
   Bahai Burial 16
   Non Standard Burials 16
   Cremation 17
   The Unburied 17
   American Indian Burials 17
      Blackfeet, Sioux 18
      Navajos 18
      Indians of Costa Rica 19

Inhumation	20
Mohawks of New York	20
Indians inhabiting the Carolinas	20
Wichita Indians	21
Caddoes, Ascena or Timber Indians	21
Persians	21
Klamath and Trinity Indians of the Northwest	21
Pima Indians	22
Coyotero Apache Indians	22
Pennsylvannia Indians	22
Indians of New York	23
Massasauga Indians	23
Central American Indians	23
Muscogulges of the Carolinas	23
Navajo Indians	24
Round Valley Indians of California	24
Burial Mounds	24
Chillicothe Mound	27
Illinois Mounds	27
Mounds near Pensacola, Florida	28
Modern Burial Statistics	29
3. The Decomposition Process	31
Autolysis	31
Factors Affecting Decomposition	32
Mummification	32
Effects of Embalming Upon Decomposition	32
Peat Bog	33
Forensics	33
Skeletonization	33
Buzzards and Butterflies	34
Research Facilities	36
4. Canine Behavior	39
Introduction to the Human Remains Detection / Cadaver Dog	39
Introduction to Reading the Dog	42
How to Read the Search Dog: Natural Communication	43
Canine Ethogram with Interpretation for Search Dogs	44
Categories of Behaviors	45
Behavioral Groups	45

Body Position 45
Head Position 45
Mouth/Nose 45
Ear Position 46
Tail Position 46
Marking Behaviors 46
Vocalization 46
Movement 47
Explanation of Behaviors 47
The Dog Mind and Heart 57
    Reactions to Death 58

5. Land Search 61
    NIMs Compliant Human Remains Detection Training 61
    Introduction 61
    Training Materials - Source Samples 62
    Collecting Scent 63
        Scent Article Collection Method 63
        Reminders and Suggestions Related to Scent Articles 64
    Concrete Samples 66
    Storage of Scent Sources 66
    Release Forms 68
    General Guidelines in HRD Training 68
    Training Scenarios 71
    Proofing 74
    Search Strategies 76
        Buried Searches 76
        Noninvasive Techniques to Locate Graves 79
    Avalanche Searches 81
        Avalanche Training-A Primer 83
        Understanding the Scent Picture 83
        Training methods 85
        Avalanche Search Strategies 87
        Dogs Handler's Avalanche Rescue Pack 88
    Mountain Searches 89
    Disaster Searches 90

Building Searches	92
NIMs Compliant Human Remains Detection Training	93
Flanker Rules	94
6. Water Search	97
Introduction	97
Family Interaction	99
Equipment & Supplies	100
Training Techniques	101
Water Search Techniques	102
Thermoclines	103
Spotters	104
Changing Conditions	104
Personal Floatation Device	105
Canine Floatation Device	105
Scent Machines	105
Marking System	106
Reaching Device	106
Body Recovery Bag	106
Side Scan Sonar	106
Divers	107
Boats and Boat Operators	108
Types of Water	109
Lakes and Quarries	109
Rivers and Creeks	109
Swiftwater	110
Floods	110
Hazardous Materials and other Hazards	111
Critical Incident Stress Management	113
7. HRD and the LAW	115
Introduction	115
Cadaver Dog's Alert as Reasonable Suspicion,	116
Human Scent Detector Dogs: The police service dog, search and rescue dog, tracking dog, trailing dog, scent identification dog, etc.	116

  Contraband Substance Detector Dogs are defined as narcotic detection dogs or explosive detection dogs. 116

Trained, Certified and Reliable 116

Cadaver Dogs 117

Federal and State Appellate Case Law on Cadaver Dogs 117

STATE Case Law 117

Possession of Contraband for K-9 Training Purposes 120
  LETTER of the LAW 120
  Possession of Narcotics 120
  Possession of Explosives 121
  Possession of Cadaver 122
  SPIRIT of the LAW 122

  COMPLIANCE with OTHER STATE LAWS or 123
  SOURCES of CONTRABAND TRAINING AIDS: 123
  POSSESSION SOLUTIONS 124

Crime Scene Preservation 125

Cross-Trained or Not 126

Handler, Protect Thyself 127
  Videotaping Training Sessions and Searches 128

Handler - Know Thy Place 128

8. Searches 131

Search for Drowning Victim at Bear Lake, Utah 131

Search for Drowning victim at 133

Search for Lacey Peterson 135

Plane Crash Recovery 136

Some Days are Like That 145

Some things I wish I had been told 146

Special Victims 148

Small and Rural Streambed 148

Two Winters and One Summer 149

Oceanesque K9 Water Searches 151

Flash Floods 164

The Letter 167

Hurricane Katrina and Ground Zero 169

APPENDIX 184

Sample HRD Evaluation Forms 184
HRD Water Recovery Certification Sample Evaluator 187
Human Remains Detection 190
Evaluation for Human Remains Detection 192
CONSENT AND RELEASE FOR PLACENTA DONATION   196
CONSENT AND RELEASE FOR TEETH & TISSUE DONATION   197
CONSENT AND RELEASE FOR TISSUE, BLOOD and / or FLUIDS DONATION   198
Ground-Penetrating Radar Techniques to Discover and Map Historic Graves   199
Local Heroes 212
Bibliography 217

K9 Rascal, Handler Beckie Stanevich, USAR

Dedication & Thank You

This work is dedicated to all of the volunteers who have so unselfishly given of themselves, their time, their energies, their finances, and talents to provide communities across the globe with search and rescue services. It is from their heart that families can welcome back the lost and missing person.

This book is also dedicated to K9 Agent Scully and Sir Tucker of Judah. Scully was born April l998 and died 9 August 2007. Your temperament was the type most only dream of achieving in their breeding programs. You touched us all. Scully we miss you. Tucker was born on June 12, 1994 and joined Scully at the Rainbow Bridge on the 21st of March 2008. Tucker, certified Therapy Dog, was a model for how to manage adversity, how to tolerate pain and suffering and touched my heart so many times. Tucker and Scully, we know you will be waiting for us on the other side.

This book is dedicated to my father, Herman R. Faircloth, who was a part of a mountain search and rescue team in Alaska in the late 1950s - 1960s. He served with the U. S. Army in Anchorage, Alaska on the search team that was dispatched when a plane went down in the mountains of Alaska or lost hunters didn't return from their expeditions. He was one of a team sent to go where vehicles and planes could not venture to retrieve those who couldn't come home on their own. At 81 years old, he remembers the times when a civilian named Mr. Hans Wagner trained him. Mr. Wagner was employed by the U. S. Army to train this elite team in Anchorage. His strict training regime created a strong and reliable SAR team. That team was still in service in 1963.

I would like to thank my teammates for their support during this project. Thank you, especially to Shelley Wood, Roxye Marshall, and Jim Ware, Laurie Babson and other teammates who contributed articles and support to this work.. I would also like to thank Terry Fleck, Kim Gilmore, Susan Martinez, Julie Hartell-DeNardo, Nancy Culberson, Sharolyn Sievert, Patti Gibson, Carol Sanner, K. T. Irwin, Jim Delbridge, Amir Findling, Bruce Barton, and Dr. Larry Conyers, for contributing their experience and expertise to this manual Each of you stepped out on a limb to write words of wisdom for other handlers. Thank you to all the handlers and photographers who provided the great pictures. They have added a wealth of information as a picture is truly worth a thousand words. Without these contributions, the scope of this book would not have been possible. As most handlers, I continue to learn with each training and mission.

9/11….we shall never forget.

Christy Judah

K9 Denali, 3 March 1996 - 19 March 2007, Handler: Bert Lark, Brunswick Search and Rescue Team

1

Introduction and Equipment

Outline
Introduction
So you want to be a Cadaver Dog Handler...
Historical and Ancient Burials
The Environment
Soil Composition
Soil pH and How to Determine the pH of the Soil
Tools of the Trade - Land Search
Soil Acidity/Moisture Meter
Magnetometer Maps
Soil Probes
Wooden Stakes
Ground Penetrating Radar
Utility Flags
Flagging Tape
Map of the Area
Sketch Pad
Camera
Day Pack
GPS
Additional Equipment

    A husband is missing. A suicide note is found. The family is frantic and cadaver dogs are called to the scene. A teen fails to return home. His two friends had joined him on a canoe trip. One made it to shore. The other two remain in the lake. Two mothers cry for the body of their sons. Such are the scenarios of recovery where bringing home the person is no easy task in terms of a physical job or an emotional experience. Thank heavens for those who feel the need in their heart to undertake this necessary service to bring closure to families. Their role affects so many. They are the quiet heros.

    Human Remains Detection (HRD) by trained canines encompasses a wide variety of scenarios. The dog and handler is asked to locate the "scene" of the crime or accident, locate individual human body parts, find bodies on land, in water, hanging, hidden, or buried in a myriad of mediums. Each of these skills defines a sub-discipline and specialty within itself. Each case involves a dog and handler who have consciously decided to participate and train for this endeavor. They spend countless hours preparing to recover the missing.

There is a debate over the proper terminology for dogs who find deceased persons or portions of them. Formerly, all canines working cases involving the deceased were loosely referred to as *Cadaver Dogs*. Eventually, the term Human Remains Detection became more politically correct and began to refer to cases involving minute amounts of remains, as in forensic-type searches. (The word forensics actually refers to information which leads to solving a crime. Forensics information may be lab reports, lab data, physical evidence, etc.)

During the shuttle Columbia search, the term Human Remains was used. It led the way to the shift from *cadaver dogs* to *human remains detection dogs*. Regardless of the nature of the terminology, this book shall use the terms interchangeably based upon the premise that deceased is deceased regardless of the amounts of the remains.

Buzzards and Butterflies is dedicated to sharing training, search techniques and information that may be useful to search and rescue volunteers. It is dedicated to sharing strategies which have been helpful to those dog handlers who actually work with HRD dogs and respond to real missions. The tips and strategies are based on their experiences and knowledge.

Buzzards and Butterflies is not intended to be a comprehensive collection of the "right" ways to conduct an HRD search. It is not a cookie-cutter description of how the HRD dog should or should not alert. It is not an instruction manual on how to train an HRD dog. It is not a foundation book or one targeted for the novice or expert. Instead it it targeted to any HRD handler desiring to read tips and strategies from other HRD handlers across the nation. Perhaps some of the techniques included will enhance the knowledge or expertise of the handler and help them become more efficient and effective in carrying out an HRD mission.

Each search takes place in a different environment with different environmental conditions (temperature, moisture, etc.) and cannot be streamlined into a "type of search." However, for the ease in presentation, search techniques are divided into major categories commonly denoting types of HRD searches. Techniques and strategies are limited only by the handlers' expertise, experience, and creativity in planning and conducting the search.

So You Want to be A Cadaver Dog Handler......

Deciding to become a cadaver dog handler is not an easy decision. The mind-set of finding deceased persons is not one to be taken lightly. Many teams require the handler to be already certified in another discipline (either trailing or wilderness air scent is common) prior to beginning cadaver dog training. This avenue to enter the field is sound in that it will also require the handler to become a "searcher first and handler second." Skills such as search strategy, map and compass skills, incident command procedures, safety, hazardous materials, GPS use, urban search, first aide, missing person behavior, and other related skills are crucial for all handlers. While many human remains searches occur in relatively small areas, a fair number may encompass large areas requiring these common search skills. First become a good ground-pounder and remember that your skills as a searcher may be needed at times when your dog is not.

Secondly, the cadaver dog handler must be able to operate in *this* type of search. In other words, can *you* handle working a case with a deceased person at the end of the search? Can *you* emotionally handle mutilation, decapitation, or other types of gruesome displays? Are there any unresolved personal or family death issues you need to put to rest before entering this field? The HR or cadaver search is most difficult at best. Handlers need to be in tune to their own emotions and their ability to handle gruesome scenes despite their best efforts to make eye contact with particular details of the scene. One law enforcement officer described her first encounter with a suicide. This particular case involved death by a gun. A suicide to be specific. Scattered remains included those body parts on the wall that stuck to a photograph of the family. This family portrait was forever engrained in her mind. Time dulls the details, but the memories remain. It takes a very special person to be able to deal with the potential of a deceased person at the end of the search. This paticular type of searcher (HRD) places the ability to help the family bring closure above the emphasis placed upon the death scene. At the end of the day, the cadaver dog handler is an angel sent down to help their fellow human beings bring closure to a horrible event resulting in the loss of a family member.

Thomas Lynch wrote of this task in his poem included in its entirety at the end of this book. He wrote,

But here brave men and women pick the pieces up.
They serve the living tending to the dead.
They bring them home, the missing and adrift,
They give them back to let them go again.

The mentally healthy attitude is absolutely necessary to work an HRD dog. While the proper attitude and outlook is necessary, this does not mean that a cadaver dog handler is a robot. They have feelings and emotions and every case is different. Handlers should de-brief at the end of each search to talk about what they have experienced and seen. They should be aware of Critical Incident Stress Debriefing services, which most mental health facilities offer, that can help the handler deal with unusual and extraordinary circumstances. Each handler needs to remember the order of importance....first searcher,

K9 Kaiser, handled by Roy McNeil of NC Search and Rescue Dog Association, demonstrates a "find" of a skull, age unknown, several years ago in this dramatic picture which takes time to digest and identify the actual article the dog is alerting on. Kaiser passed away in 2007 with many finds to his credit.

second team member, and lastly, the victim. Watch out for yourself. Watch out for your team member. Watch out for your canine. Be sure each is handling the situation and task in a mentally healthy fashion.

Buzzards and Butterflies

Technically, handlers should be able to locate less than 15 grams of human remains during disaster operations, capable of sustaining themselves for 24 hours (Type I U.S. Department of Homeland Security), capable of locating a deceased person (greater than 15 grams) in disaster operations (sustaining themselves for 24 hours in Type II), be capable of locating less than 15 grams of human remains buried, hanging, ground level, or in vehicles in a nondisaster situation for Type III, capable of locating less than 15 grams buried, hanging, or ground level in a nondisaster situation for Type IV, or capable of locating deceased persons buried, hanging, or at ground level in a nondisaster situation for other cadaver certifications. In addition, the Department of Homeland Security has identified various training and equipment which should supplement the handlers skills. Handlers should take courses in biohazard environments, scene preservation, documentation, collection, chain of custody and scene security in addition to first aid (for humans and dogs), person and dog safety and radio communications for disaster operations. Teams throughout the United States and internationally may have different criteria for certification in Human Remains Detection or Cadaver dog work. The appendix contains several sample certification forms used by teams in the U. S.

If you are still interested in reading *this book* and *pursuing this skill*, you just may be a candidate for a cadaver dog handler. *Ahem*, Human Remains Detection dog handler. Next step: find a team and mentor. Learn from the experienced. And continue reading....

Historical and Ancient Burials

Tthe Environment

Using search and rescue dogs to locate historical and ancient graves is a relatively new concept. Some have asked, "how long can bones be detected?" "Can a dog actually alert on bones several hundred years old?" "Do bones last that long?" Recent reports in the National Geographic magazine (2008) as well an other research data suggests that if conditions are right, bones may last thousands of years. "A human skull tentatively dating back 80,000 to 100,000 years may shed light on a murky chapter of evolutionary history," its discoverers say. (National Geographic, Feb 2008.)

The Chinese researchers think this skull came from a modern human and was found in China. Other experts say it is a sister or precusor to the modern human. Regardless, both agree on a relative age. Additional skulls dated at over a half - a - million - years old are stored in China and collectively referred to as the Peking Man. These were found in a cave on the outskirts of Beijing. Do human skulls last? Yes they do.

Who was the Peking Man? He lived about 450 million years ago. He was a "cave dweller, tool maker, fire user, gatherer, and hunter. In view of fossil records and cultural remains, he was superb in his capability of adapting himself to the environment with his adaption of physiological structure and technical ability." (National Geographic.) His remains document his legacy.

Historical HRD searches require the dog to be very slow and methodical and keep the nose close to the surface of the ground. The fast moving dog can and will miss a grave. It takes a patient handler to develop the strategies to do historical burial work and differs from generic Human Remains Detection of new or recent burials. HRD handlers have recently begun developing training and search techniques for these historic and older burial searches. These will be discussed later in more detail.

Soil Composition

An understanding of soil composition is helpful in order to recognize when an environment might yield negative results even in the face of known headstones or visible sunken ground sites. *The more acidic the soil, the faster decomposition takes place.* Therefore an area with an acidic soil will be less likely to yield "finds" and an area less acidic will offer a higher probability of bones being detectable. With that said, soil pH will vary even in close proximity.

◆ *Soil pH*

The term "soil pH" refers to the soil water and is based upon a measurement of "pH", a level of activity of hydrogen ions (H+) in a solution. There are several methods to collect soil water, all of which influence the soil pH in one way or another. The soil pH is linked to the concepts of alkalinity and acidity or acid neutralizing capacity. A neutral solution has a pH of 7 while an acid solution is less than 7. A measure of below 3 is uncommon, but not impossible.

Soil pH is an important consideration for farmers and gardeners for several reasons, including the fact that many plants and soil life forms prefer either alkaline or acidic conditions, that some diseases tend to thrive when the soil is alkaline or acidic, and that the pH can affect the availability of nutrients in the soil, all of which affect the rate of decomposition of a body.

The pH is influenced by the kinds of parent materials from which the soil was formed. Soils formed from basic rocks generally have a higher pH than those formed from acid rocks. Rainfall can affect the soil pH as it leaches nutrients from the soil. They are replaced by acidic elements such as aluminum and iron, therefore soils with a lot of rainfall tend to be more acidic.

Pollution can also affect the pH. A higher vehicle traffic area yields a more acid soil. Heavy fertilizing increases the acidity. Additional organic matter increases the acidity.

Most bacteria prefer a pH level of 6.3 – 6.8. Fungi, molds and anaerobic bacteria tend to prefer a lower pH level. More acidic soils tend to increase the degree of souring and putrefaction. A pH level of around 6.3-6.8 is also the optimum range preferred by most soil bacteria, although fungi, molds, and anaerobic bacteria have a broader tolerance and tend to multiply at lower pH values. All of this influences body deteriorioration.

Buzzards and Butterflies

◆ *How to Determine the pH Level of the Soil*

Soils tend to be more acidic on the surface and less so deeper down. Therefore handlers need to be aware of the levels at varying locations and depths. Handlers can generally estimate the pH level of the soil by the following:

Observe the Predominant Flora (Plants that prefer acidic soil include Erica, Rhododendron, nearly all Ericaceae species, many birch, foxgloves, gorse, and Scots pine, Ash, honeysuckle, dogwoods, lilac and clematis.

Observe the Symptoms that may indicate acidic or alkaline soil. (Plant diseases are noted in alkaline soils. The house hydrangea produces pink flowers at a pH value of 6.8 or higher and blue flowers at a pH level of 6.0 or below.

Inexpensive Testing Kits (Based on barium sulfate in a powdered form, where a small sample of soil is mixed with water and changes color according to the acidity or alkalinity.)

Litmus Paper (A small soil sample is mixed with distilled water and a strip of litmus paper is inserted. If the paper turns red it is acid; if it turns blue it is alkaline.)

Use of a Commercially Available Electronic pH Meter (A rod is inserted into moistened soil and it measures the concentration of hydrogen ions.)

Tools of the Trade

Searchers use varying types of equipment dependent upon the environment, type of search (burial, etc.), and availability of the equipment. Few teams can afford to own all of the items listed, however, it does behoove the searcher to be aware of the types of equipment which can be requested that might enhance the effectiveness or confirm the findings of a cadaver dog team. Some of the more common tools of the trade include:

◆ Soil Acidity/Moisture Meter

Various soil acid/moisture meters are available to test the soil. These are convenient and operate without a power source. To obtain a reading, one only needs to insert the probe into moist soil, leave for three minutes or so, then read the pH and moisture levels on the spot. Metal plates on the sides of the meter produce natural electricity when inserted into the soil. It then measures from 3.5 to 8.0 pH on the outside scale of the dial and from 0-100% moisture on the inner scale of the dial. It is considered accurate from plus/minus 0.2 pH and plus/minus 10% moisture level. These units are about 6.5 inches long.

One such Soil pH Meter is an easy-to-use field instrument that works directly in the soil. PH readings should be done at 1", 2", 3" and 4" depth to see the variation of the soil layers. That means that pH can be checked in the thatch layer, in the root zone and directly below the root zone for a complete pH reading of the entire root zone profile. Simply set the adjustable depth foot to the desired depth in the soil profile and insert the meter. Within 60 seconds a soil pH will be available.

Another meter reads from 0 (bone dry) to 10 (saturated). This meter can also be used to check fertilizer leaching. Check catalogs carefully to compare features.

♦ Magnetometer Maps

A magnetometer is a subsurface detection device that measures minor variations in the earth's magnetic field, often revealing archaeological features as magnetic anomalies; it gives readings as it is run over the target area and these are converted into magnetic contour maps. Some cultural features create anomalies in the earth's magnetic field (e.g., iron tools, burned surfaces, walls made of volcanic stone), and can be located wit magnetometers.

♦ Soil Probes

Soil probes can be helpful for two purposes. They can assist the ground to "breathe" (techniques to be discussed later), and help identify possible "voids or anomalies" warranting further investigation. There are several types of probes available on the market. Dependent upon the local terrain, one should select a probe that most easily adapts to the soil composition. Among the good ones is a strong, flexible steel shaft (about 3/8 inch in diameter) attached to a steel handle with a steel tip. A 48 inch "T" bar probe is commonly used in burials. An example is shown below:

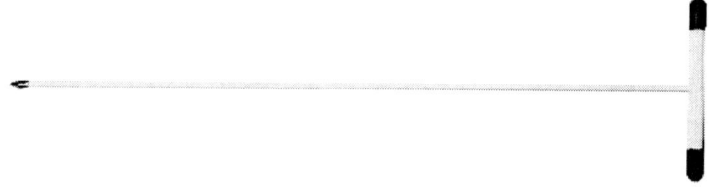

Other fiberglass models are also available. Check forestry supplies suppliers for a variety of models available. For safety purposes, consider using ski pole "tips" to protect the steel tip on the end of the probe when not in use.

The soil probe is one item that is highly recommended to be owned by each cadaver dog handler, as it can be invaluable in allowing the ground to *breathe* during suspected burial searches or historic cemetery searches.

♦ Wooden Stakes

Wooden stakes, untreated, unstained, unpainted in lengths of 24 inches are helpful in helping the ground to breathe. Marking and breathing techniques will be discussed later in this book. They can also be used to mark locations of alerts or remains. Permanent markers easily identify the gravesite number, date, time, team involved, or other pertinent information.

Buzzards and Butterflies

◆ *Ground Penetrating Radar*

Ground Penetrating Radar technology provides critical information concerning anything that lies below the surface. A ground penetrating radar gram can collect reflections indicating the presence of reflectors buried beneath the surface, possibly associated with human remains. GPR is a geophysical method that uses radar pulses to image the subsurface. It can be used in a variety of media including rock, soil, ice, fresh water, pavement, and structures. It can detect objects, changes in material and voids. The depth range of the GPR is limited by the electrical conductivity of the ground and the transmitting frequency. As conductivity increases, the penetration depth decreases. Higher frequencies do not penetrate as far as lower frequencies but give a better resolution in the picture. Optimal depth is achieved in dry sandy soils or massive dry materials such as granite, limestone, and concrete where the depth is up to 15 meters. In moist and/or clay-laden soils, the penetration is sometimes only a few centimeters.

Ground penetrating radar can be useful in locating graves by detecting the buried coffin or vault. It can also detect disturbed soil or other remains of the burial. Remains are easier to locate in sandy soils that do not contain tree roots or stones. It is operated above the ground surface and produces a cross-sectional image of the ground.

The depths of the survey and the detail of the images are determined by the antenna that is used as well as the soil type. A geophysicist demonstrates using some of the equipment in a grave survey in the following photo:

Matthew Turner, Senior Geophysicist for Geo Model, Inc.

An archaeological study in Port Royal, Jamaica, was conducted in 1998-99 to locate the ancient ruins of the city destroyed by an earthquake in 1692. Geophysicists, using the GEO Model, reported interesting results. They examined the subsurface for buildings and remaining walls. public gave considerable attention to the GPR survey due to the importance of the archaeological study. This is but one archaeology project using GPR. Shown are some of the images from other burial projects using GPR:

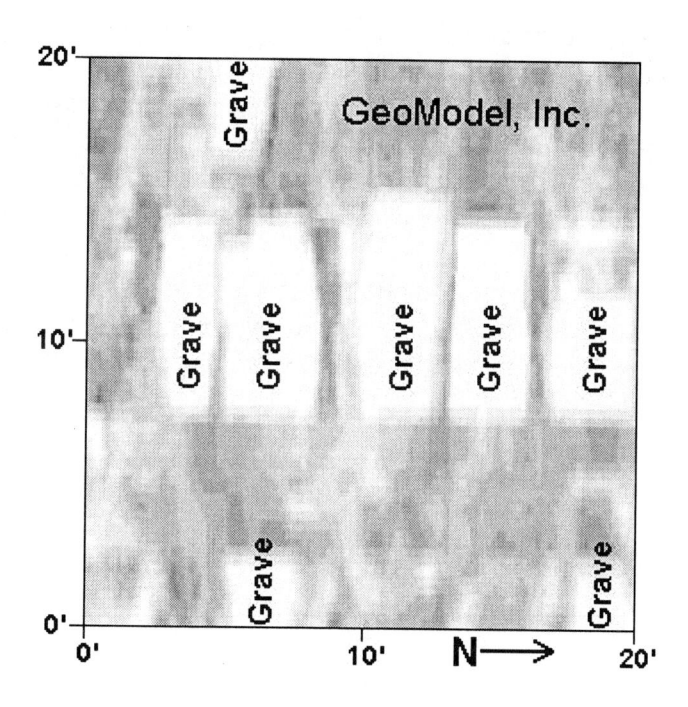

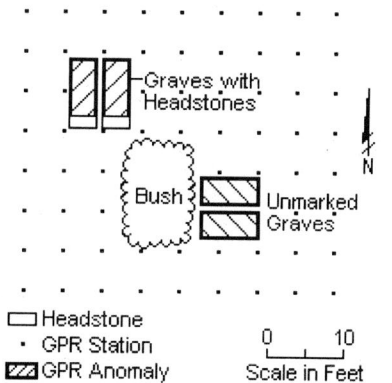

In some special cases, 3-Dimensional imaging can be used to better define graves. This process requires very close spacing of survey lines and the use of special 3-D software. There are many factors that can adversely affect a GPR survey. In unfavorable conditions, the data from a GPR survey may be essentially meaningless. Mud is a poor conductor for GPR. It may be necessary to remove the top few meters of mud

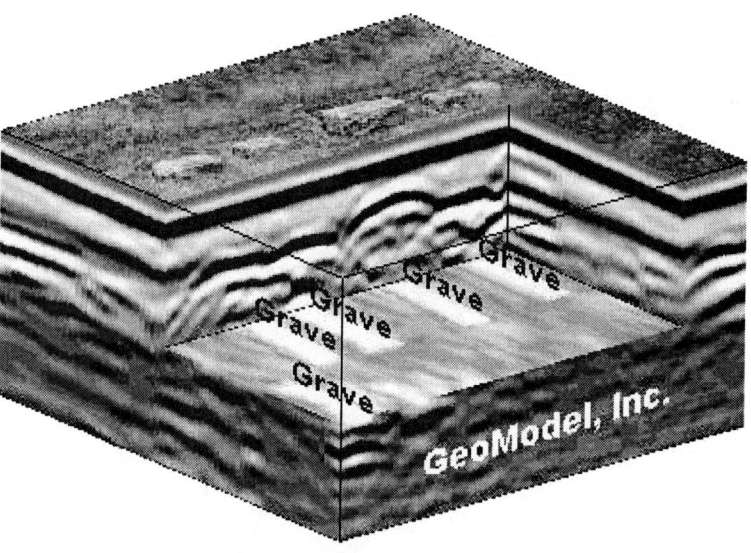

Cemetery with Headstones Showing Cut-Away View of GPR Data Detecting Grave Sites

Buzzards and Butterflies

remove the top few meters of mud before helpful images are achieved. In addition, urban areas present a challenge when metal mesh is used underneath concrete. This takes extra attention in interpreting data under those conditions. Loose snow can also create voids that may be reflected in the data. Heavy rain can cause air pockets that make interpretation of the data difficult. In addition, in ancient burials the soil has already settled to the extent that a GPR cannot detect soil anomalies. The following shows burials in the data. Each hyperbola indicates a burial.

An additional essay on Ground Penetrating Radar and its applications to locate graves is included in the appendix of this book. The article by Dr. Larry Conyers, of the Department of Anthropology, the University of Denver, expounds on the usefulness in locating burials. It is included in this book with his permission.

This photo is a type of GPR showing burials. The darkened gray areas indicate individual burials. The dark square dots indicate surface rocks or possible headstones.

Amplitude Slice Map showing burials and marked tombstones from Kansas.

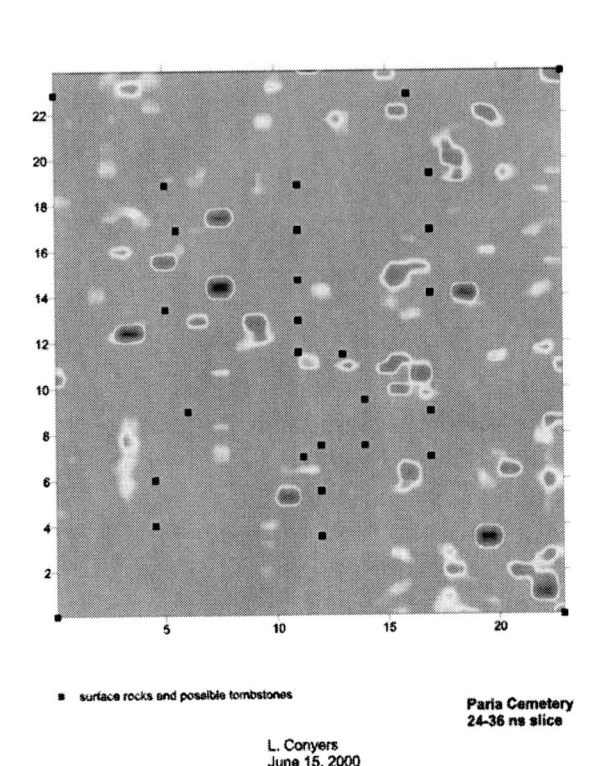

■ surface rocks and possible tombstones

Paria Cemetery
24-36 ns slice

L. Conyers
June 15, 2000

❖ Utility flags to mark alert areas

Standard utility flags (metal stake with plastic flag at the top, easily marks areas of interest or indication/alert areas. They can be easily marked with permanent markers for convenient reference at a later date.

❖ Flagging Tape to identify the search area

Select colors not commonly used in your area by surveyors, if possible. Mark your tape with permanent markers with date and crew number of other identifying data. Consider flagging the outside limits of your search area (if a contained area), and areas of general canine interest, depressions in the ground or alerts/indications. Use tape in addition to utility flags in heavy brush area to help locate the site more easily. Flag at eye level.

❖ Map of the Area

Topographical, street maps, aerial maps, etc. help you identify and provide an overview of the search area. Many water sources are too large or too small for a map to be of much value. However, maps of streams, rivers, coastal waterways, and other water sources are helpful in determining flow of the water or in- and outlets, all of which can have an effect on the movement of the body in the water

❖ Sketch Pad

Sketch paper to draw depressions and approximate burial locations help you reconstruct the layout of burials. Quite often the GPS coordinates are so close it is difficult to chart exact locations on a map. A sketch of the area is a quick method to record wind direction and approximate alert locations referencing landmarks or buoys. Always record the date and time of denotation.

❖ Camera

Never photograph sensitive scenes without permission from law enforcement or other authorities. However, it is helpful to photograph available resources and general terrain for future reference and training purposes.

❖ Day Pack

A basic search daypack is necessary on the boat and land regardless of the proximity to shore or base camp. One cannot anticipate the need for a knife or emergency first aide kit. Drinking water for both searcher and canine is critical. Think search, not distance or shore. Small items like suntan lotion, lip balm, and other comfort items are necessary on the land and water regardless of the time of year, size of the search area, or conditions. Take your pack and train as you search.

Buzzards and Butterflies

◆ GPS

GPS (global positioning system) units will document the location of the find or search site for future reference. A hand held unit is indispensable. It will also allow the handler to compare the "alert" locations with the actual location of the missing person, once recovered. GPS units must be set to locality and type of map. Learning to use a GPS correctly is critical to documentation of HRD cases. More expensive units also allow the handler to download the "track" of the canine.

◆ Additional Equipment

Each team or organization should have a list of what personal equipment is recommended or required to be with the handler at all times. This will vary based upon the terrain and conditions, and whether it is a land or water search. Command staff should be able to make recommendations for required equipment on all searches. The National Association of Search and Rescue requires specific equipment for certification testing, as do some other organizations and teams during their certification procedures and training exercises.

Equipment used in water searches will be discussed in the chapter on water search. In addition, check with mentors and teams that regularly work specialty-type searches such as disaster, cave or avalanche search for a complete listing of suggested equipment and supplies. Better to be prepared.

Skull located by K9 Nia, Handler: K. T. Irwin, Wyoming

2

Burial Customs

Outline
Introduction
Slave Burials
Natural Burials
Preservation of the Body
Caskets
Inclusion of Clothing and Personal Effects
Body Positioning
Bahai Burials
Nonstandard Burials
Cremation
Live Burials
The Unburied
American Indian Burials
Burial Mounds
Modern Burial Statistics

Although man shares the sadness of human loss around the world, his methods of body preparation, burial, and ritual varies. In many cultures, the deceased are usually buried in soil. Search and Rescue (SAR) dog handlers should have an overview and understanding of the types of burials they may encounter in the course of their work. Therefore, extensive descriptions of the most common types of burials that may be encountered in the United States (and elsewhere on the globe) are included. Many souls have gone on before us. Many bones remain.

Since Paleolithic times (about 200,000 years ago), Homo sapiens buried their dead. Our ancestors often used mounds of earth, temples or underground caverns to store the bodies. In modern times, the custom of burying below the ground and marking the site with a stone or monument is common throughout the world. Other means of burial includes cremation that is the norm in Indian burials and is mandatory in Japan. Some burial practices are very ritualized while others are simply practical.

Searches that involve suspected burials might range from recent to prehistoric. Sometimes the dog handler has an idea of the age (length of time considered deceased and buried) of the body. Other times there is a range of probable time the body *could* have been dead and buried. In some situations, the handler may be attempting a much older burial, perhaps from earlier this century to several centuries old. Handlers should preplan techniques and become knowledgeable about factors affecting burial in order to work in the most effective manner.

Burial customs vary by race and country. In some Asian countries, grave sites are purchased by the family for a specific period of time. After that time has elasped (such as forty years), the family must re-purchase it, or the body is exumed, sold or re-located. What may be a common practice in the United States may not be for other countries.

The following descriptions of burial customs and practices are included in order to provide the handler with an overview of information that could be valuable or have an impact on training and search missions. The more information a handler has regarding burial practices, the more likely they may recognize a possible burial location or remains.

Slave Burials

The slave cultures of the late 1700s to the mid 1800s used a more random approach to burying the dead. Extremely large cemeteries held the remains of slaves from many nearby plantations. They were not grouped in families, as the white cemeteries, and the grounds were seldom landscaped or decorated with headstones. Headstones were expensive and most slaves did not place a great deal of emphasis on the burial ground. The soul was in heaven. They did however believe that they should be "laid" in such a manner as to face the nearest water so when they arose during the resurrection, they would be facing Africa.

The slave cemeteries are in contrast to the plantation owners of the same period who had beautifully landscaped graves with handmade stones, bricks and headstones that elaborately marked their final resting places. The materials used to create the décor and the headstones varied from place to place depending upon the availability of materials. Eastern coastal communities might include crushed shells in their composition. Others areas used materials readily available to construct the monuments. Remnants of these walls, crypts and headstones can become a clue to exploring a location. It will behoove the handler to become familiar with the custom of the era or culture targeted for each search. This allows the handler to plan a search strategy using varying and appropriate techniques for each situation. Having a prior knowledge of customs and materials can help the handler avoid contamination or destruction of key elements and preserve the site. While "probing" an area, be attuned to the scraping or texture of the ground, soil and other buried components such as the concrete used in headstones. It if feels different than most of the other soil, it probably *is* something different. (Probing involves using an instrument commonly known as a forestry probe to puncture the ground for a depth of several feet to the length of the probe. Probing allows the buried scent to rise to the surface providing the search dog with a source of scent. Specific probing techniques will be discussed in more detail later in this book.)

Natural Burials

A growing trend involves burial in a "natural way" to protect and restore the natural environment. In this process, a biodegradable coffin or shroud is used and native vegetation is planted near or over the grave to establish a living memorial rather than a conventional cemetery monument. The practice dates back to the late nineteenth century when Sir Francis Seymour

Hayden proposed this method. These natural burial grounds are also referred to as woodland cemeteries, eco-cemeteries, memorial nature preserves, or green burial grounds.

Preservation of the Body

Many cultures use a preservation method, mummification procedure or embalming technique to preserve the body. Bodies are sometimes wrapped in shrouds or placed in a casket or coffin. Sometimes a large container such as a ship is used. Some caskets are also placed inside a burial vault to protect it from collapsing or floating away during a flood. These containers slow down the decomposition process partially by blocking decomposing bacteria and other organisms from gaining access to the body. While we often think of the vault and coffin as totally sealed, this is not always the case.

In other cultures the goal is not to preserve the body but to allow it to decompose or return to the earth. In Orthodox Judaism embalming is not permitted and coffins are constructed of wood, have no metal parts, and even use wooden pegs in place of nails. The Islamic faith prefers to bury their deceased so as not to delay decomposition. The bodies are buried in a shroud, not normally embalmed and use no type of coffin.

The most common embalming fluid is formaldehyde, which is biodegradable and will decompose after normal ground burial except in exceptional circumstances. It oxidizes to form acid, which is a similar toxin such as that found in bee stings and fire ants.

Caskets

Most modern caskets are made from chipboard, a thin veneer. Handles are usually plastic but designed to look like brass. The chipboard requires glue to stick the wood particles together and that causes pollution when cremated or biodegrading. More expensive caskets and coffins are often made using other exotic woods and designed to prevent decomposition.

Inclusion of Clothing and Personal Effects

Some cultures place a favored piece of jewelry, ceremonial clothes or other valued items such as photographs with the body. These grave goods served several purposes. During the funeral services, many cultures feel the deceased should be presented looking at his/her finest. Sometimes the items are viewed as necessary to reach the afterlife. Others believe they will be needed in the afterlife. As a result, archaeologists sometimes find these remains, which provide a glimpse into the life and culture of the person.

Body Positioning

Christian burials normally extended or lie the body flat with arms and legs straight, arms folded on the chest, eyes and mouth closed. Other ritual practices place the body in a flexed position or crouched with the legs folded up to the chest. Many place the body facing east west. In some Christian traditions, the minister is placed in an opposite position, ready to minister to his people during the resurrection.

Warriors in some ancient societies were buried in an upright position. Some religions, such as Islam, place the body so that the head is pointed toward and the face turned toward Mecca, the holy city.

Other cultures place bodies so that when they rise up they will face the east. This is often the case in slave cemeteries, so that the body may raise up to face the water in preparation for the journey back to Africa. The slaves had specific persons assigned to prepare the bodies, build coffins, dig graves, and construct headstones. Slave funerals were typically at night when the workday was over. The master usually attended these ceremonies along with slaves from nearby plantations and communities. The body was wrapped in cloth, hands placed across the chest, and a metal plate placed on top of the hands. The plate hindered the return home by suppressing any spirits in the coffin. Sometimes personal property was buried with the slave to please the spirits. Coffins were nailed closed and carried by hand or wagon to the burial site.

Bahai Burials

Bahai faith burial practices prohibit cremation. They must bury the body within one-hour travel time from the place of death. The body is wrapped in silk or cotton and a ring placed on the finger inscribed with "I came forth from God, and return unto Him, detached from all save Him, holding fast to His Name, the Merciful, the compassionate." The coffin is made of crystal, stone or hard fine wood.

Non Standard Burials

In nonstandard burials such as mass burials, the body may be positioned arbitrarily. This may be necessary in cases of a mass natural disaster, act of terrorism, an epidemic or an accident. This may or may not be a sign of disrespect. Sometimes married couples are buried side-by-side or interred one above the other such that the first burial is placed deeper than the normal burial depth of six feet. In some countries this is the norm with two to three burials on top of each other. A thick layer of earth separates each.

Potter's fields are those burial grounds where burial is at the local government expense. Wolfgang Amadeus Mozart is buried in such a place. Unknown persons are sometimes buried in this manner making future identification unlikely.

Sunken ships are considered mass gravesites. Other mass graves may be war locations such as Douaumont Ossuary, containing over 130,000 soldiers from the Battle of Verdun. Catacombs such as those in Rome or Paris are also designated communal burial places.

Cremation

Cremation, burning the body in a special oven, leaves only a few pounds of bone fragments. Some processes grind those into fine powder which is commonly referred to as ashes. Some cultures choose to keep the ashes close to the heart of the family or at home. Others scatter them in serene locations or bury them underground.

In the cremains, there will be melted metal lumps from jewelry, casket furniture and dental fillings, as well as surgical implants such as hip relacements. Larger items such as titanium hip replacements are usually removed before the bones are ground as they will damage the grinder. After grinding, smaller bits of metal are sieved out and later interred in a designated spot at the local cemetery. Some Human Remains Detection dog handlers have used these titanium hip or knee replacement parts for HRD training. Dogs do seem to "hit" on these items during training.

Live Burials

Live burial, asphyxiation, dehydration, starvation, or exposure in cold climates, cause death. Sometimes these are murders; sometimes accidents; sometimes execution. This can occur deliberately or unintentional in earthquakes, cave-ins, avalanches and other natural disasters.

The Unburied

Humans are not always buried. Some cultures do not bury their dead in every case. Alternatives to burial include *burial* at sea, funerary cannibalism, cremation, ecological funeral decomposition, excarnation, placing them on Towers of Silence, Gibbeting (disiplay of criminals), hanging coffins (on cliffs), Resomation (alkaline hydrolysis), sky burial (mountaintop), space burial (in orbit), or cryonics (preservation until a future date).

American Indian Burials

American Indian burial customs differed by tribe and area of the country. Some Indian burial sites involved placing several bodies, up to a dozen, very near each other, lying on the ground together, and lightly covering with sand. These tribes did not dig a hole or otherwise wrap or place the body in a casket of any sort. In other locales the bodies were laid in a specific direction, or location, and did not touch each other in death. Indian burial grounds were usually little more than three feet high with just enough soil placed on top of the body to cover it. Often they were burned or charred prior to being covered with soil or sand.

Among the burials of the American native Indians, one finds a gamut of rituals. Some of these are included and described in detail to represent the types of artifacts and burial practices which may be found throughout the United States. Several types of Indian burial practices are described to give the reader a variety of examples of burial customs of the American Indian. While many showed similarities, each differed by tribe and locality. Among the rituals were those including

Buzzards and Butterflies

burial above ground inside lodges, particularly in the Valley of the Great Lakes, Utah. In 1852 Stansbury described the Sioux practice:

"I put on my moccasins, and, displaying my wet shirt like a flag to the wind, we proceeded to the lodges which had attracted our curiosity. There were five of them pitched upon the open prairie, and in them we found the bodies of nine Sioux laid out upon the ground, wrapped in their robes of buffalo-skin, with their saddles, spears, camp-kettles, and all their accoutrements piled up around them. Some lodges contained three, others only one body, all of which were more or less in a state of decomposition. A short distance apart from these was one lodge that, though small, seemed of rather superior pretensions, and was evidently pitched with great care. It contained the body of a young Indian girl of sixteen or eighteen years, with a countenance presenting quite an agreeable expression; she was richly dressed in leggings of fine scarlet cloth elaborately ornamented; a new pair of moccasins, beautifully embroidered with porcupine quills, was on her feet, and her body was wrapped in two superb buffalo-robes worked in like manner; she had evidently been dead but a day or two, and to our surprise a portion of the upper part of her person was bare, exposing the face and a part of the breast, as if the robes in which she was wrapped had by some means been disarranged, whereas all the other bodies were closely covered up. It was, at the time, the opinion of our mountaineers that these Indians must have fallen in an encounter with a party of Crows; but I subsequently learned that they had all died of the cholera, and that this young girl, being considered past recovery, had been arranged by her friends in the habiliments of the dead, enclosed in the lodge alive, and abandoned to her fate, so fearfully alarmed were the Indians by this to them novel and terrible disease."

"It might, perhaps, be said that this form of burial was exceptional, and due to the dread of again using the lodges which had served as the homes of those afflicted with the cholera, but it is thought such was not the case, as the writer has notes of the same kind of burial among the same tribe and of others, notably the Crows, the body of one of their chiefs (Long Horse) being disposed of as follows:

"The lodge poles enclose an oblong circle some 18 by 22 feet at the base, converging to a point at least 30 feet high, covered with buffalo-hides dressed without hair except a part of the tail switch, which floats outside like, and mingled with human scalps. The different skins are neatly fitted and sewed together with sinew, and all painted in seven alternate horizontal stripes of brown and yellow, decorated with various life-like war scenes. Over the small entrance is a large bright cross, the upright being a large stuffed white wolf-skin upon his war lance, and the crossbar of bright scarlet flannel, containing the quiver of bow and arrows, which nearly all warriors still carry, even when armed with repeating rifles. As the cross is not a pagan but a Christian (which Long Horse was not either by profession or practice) emblem, it was probably placed there by the influence of some of his white friends. I entered, finding Long Horse buried Indian fashion, in full-war dress, paint and feathers, in a rude coffin, upon a platform about breast high, decorated with weapons, scalps, and ornaments. A large opening and wind-flap at top favored ventilation, and though he had lain there in an open coffin a full month, some of which was hot weather, there was but little effluvia; in fact, I have seldom found much in a burial-teepee, and when this mode of burial is thus performed it is less repulsive than natural to suppose."

Col. P. W. Norris, superintendent of Yellowstone National Park who was an eyewitness in 1876, furnished this account.

"The **Blackfeet, Sioux, and Navajos** also bury in lodges, and the Indians of Bellingham Bay," according to Dr. J. F. Hammond, U. S. A. "They place their dead in carved wooden sarcophagi, enclosing these with a rectangular tent of some white material."

Bancroft [Footnote: Nat. Races of Pac. States, 1874, vol. 1, p. 780.] stated "certain of the *Indians of Costa Rica*, when a death occurred, deposited the body in a small hut constructed of plaited palm reeds. In this it is preserved for three years, food being supplied, and on each anniversary of the death it is redressed and attended to amid certain ceremonies. The writer has been recently informed that a similar custom prevailed in Demerara. No authentic accounts are known of analogous modes of burial among the peoples of the Old World, although quite frequently the dead were interred beneath the floors of their houses, a custom which has been followed by the Mosquito Indians of Central America and one or two of our own tribes."

Although customs vary somewhat, each pays tribute to the life and death of a loved one, relative or community member.   In 1877, a survey was done throughout the U.S. to try to document specific Indian burial rites. Among the information requested from each tribe was:

WASHINGTON, D. C, June 15, 1877.

"SIR: Being engaged in preparing a memoir upon the 'Burial Customs of the Indians of North America, both ancient and modern, and the disposal of their dead,' I beg leave to request your kind co-operation to enable me to present as exhaustive and exposition of the subject as possible, and to this end earnestly invite your attention to the following points in regard to which information is desired:
1st. Name of the tribe.
2d. Locality.
3rd. Manner of burial, ancient and modern.
4th. Funeral ceremonies.
5th. Mourning observances, if any.

"With reference to the first of these inquiries, 'Name of the tribe,' the Indian name is desired as well as the name by which the tribe is known to the whites.
"As to 'Locality,' the response should give the range of the tribe, and be full and geographically accurate.
"As to the 'Manner of burial,' &, it is important to have every particular bearing on this branch of the subject, and much minuteness is desirable.
"For instance:

(_a_) Was the body buried in the ground; if so, in what position, and how was the grave prepared and finished?
(_b_) If cremated, describe the process, and what disposal was made of the ashes
(_c_) Were any utensils, implements, ornaments, & or food placed in the grave? In short, every fact is sought that may possibly add to a general knowledge of the subject.

This was forwarded to every Indian agent, physicians at agencies, to a great number of Army officers who had served or were serving at frontier posts, and to individuals known to be interested in ethnologic matters. A large number of interesting and valuable responses were received, many of them showing how customs have changed either under influences of civilization or altered circumstances of environment.

1st. By INHUMATION in pits, a grave, holes in the ground, mounds, cists, and caves.

2d. By CREMATION, generally on the surface of the earth, occasionally beneath, the resulting bones or ashes being placed in pits, in the ground, in boxes placed on scaffolds or trees, in urns, sometimes scattered.

3d. By EMBALMENT or a process of mummifying, the remains being afterwards placed in the earth, caves, mounds, or charnel houses.

4th. By AERIAL SEPULTURE, the bodies being deposited on scaffolds or trees, in boxes or canoes, the two latter receptacles supported on scaffolds or posts, or on the ground. Occasionally baskets have been used to contain the remains of children, these being hung to trees.

5th. By AQUATIC BURIAL, beneath the water, or in canoes, which were turned adrift.

These might, perhaps, be further subdivided, but the above seem sufficient for all practical needs.
The use of the term "burial" throughout this paper is to be understood in its literal significance, the word being derived from the Anglo-Saxon "birgan," to conceal or hide away.
In giving descriptions of different burials and attendant ceremonies, it has been deemed expedient to introduce entire accounts as furnished, in order to preserve continuity of narrative. (Native American Nations)

His responses allowed the narration of the most complete description of Indian burial by North Americans to date. Summarizing, he said:

Inhumation: interment in the ground; The **Mohawks of New York** make a large round hole in the ground where the body was placed upright, covered with timber, then covered with earth and mounded with a hill. Body was dressed in finery and put wampum and other things into the grave with it. Relatives did not allow grass or weeds to grow above it. [Hist. Indian Tribes of the United States, 1853, part 3, p 183.] This account may be found in Schoolcraft.

Indians inhabiting the Carolinas: (Antiq. of Southern Indians, 1873, pp 108-110) "The expense and formality depended upon the rank of the deceased. The body was first placed on a cane bundle and placed in an outhouse made for that purpose where it remained for one day and night, guarded and mourned by the nearest relatives. The funeral officiates went into town and took blankets from the first young men they met. The bodies were then wrapped in these blankets with two or three mats made of rushes or cane. The coffin was made of woven reeds or hollow canes tied at both ends. The body is then carried from the house into (an) orchard of peach trees. Family members and invited guests sit around the body while the medicine man (or conjurer) pronounces a funeral oration telling of the valor of the deceased, his skill, love of country, property and influence. Those still living are encouraged to walk in his footsteps and remember his everlasting happiness in the land of spirits where he has gone. The body is then brought away from that location to the grave to a sepulcher about six feet deep and eight feet long and has a lightwood or pitch pine fork driven close down the sides of the grave firmly into the ground. (These two forks are to contain a ridgepole.)"

The bottom of the grave is lined with bark and trees; the body is placed there, and then covered again. The Indians then created a roof like pitch over the grave using ridgepoles to hold the logs. Then earth was thrown on top and beaten down on top of the logs. This created a vault like structure for the body. After a time the body was removed from this vault, bones cleaned and deposited in an ossuary called the "Quiogozon."

Wichita Indians: Dr. Fordyce Grinnell, physician to the Wichita Agency, Indian Territory, described their burial practices. "When a Wichita dies the town-crier goes up and down through the village and announces the fact. Preparations are immediately made for the burial, and the body is taken without delay to the grave prepared for its reception. If the grave is some distance from the village the body is carried thither on the back of a pony, being first wrapped in blankets and then laid prone across the saddle, one walking on either side to support it. The grave is dug from 3 to 4 feet deep and of sufficient length for the extended body. First blankets and buffalo robes are laid in the bottom of the grave, then the body, being taken from the horse and unwrapped, is dressed in its best apparel, and with ornaments, is placed upon a couch of blankets and robes, with the head towards the west and the feet to the east; the valuables belonging to the deceased are placed with the body in the grave. With the man are deposited his bows and arrows or gun, and with the woman her cooking utensils and other implements of her toil. Over the body sticks are placed six or eight inches deep and grass over these, so that when the earth is filled in it need not come in contact with the body or its trappings. After the grave is filled with earth a pen of poles is built around it, or, as is frequently the case, stakes are driven so that they cross each other from either side about midway over the grave, thus forming a complete protection from the invasion of wild animals. After all this is done, the grass or other "debris" is carefully scraped from about the grave for several feet, so that the ground is left smooth and clean. It is seldom the case that the relatives accompany the remains to the grave, but they more often employ others to bury the body for them, usually women. Mourning is similar in this tribe as in others, and consists in cutting off the hair, fasting, etc. Horses are also killed at the grave."

Caddoes, Ascena or Timber Indians: Likewise, the Caddoes, "Ascena," or Timber Indians followed a similar burial practice as the Wichitas. However, if the Caddoe was killed in battle, the body was never buried but left to be devoured by beasts or birds of prey.

Persians: Bruhier, in 1740, told us of the Persians and their burial practices. He stated that, "The ancient Persians threw out the bodies of their dead on the roads, and if they were promptly devoured by wild beasts it was esteemed a great honor, a misfortune if not. Sometimes they interred, always wrapping the dead in a wax cloth to prevent odor."

Klamath and Trinity Indians of the Northwest: George Gibbs, in 1853, described the Indian tribe of the Klamath and Trinity Indians of the Northwest:

"The graves which are in the immediate vicinity of their houses exhibit very considerable taste and a laudable care. The dead are enclosed in rude coffins formed by placing four boards around the body and covered with earth to some depth; a heavy plank often supported by upright head and foot stones is laid upon the top or stones are built up into a wall about a foot above the ground and the top flagged with others. The graves of the chiefs are surrounded by neat wooden palings, each pale ornamented with a feather from the tail of the bald eagle. Baskets are usually staked down by the side (of the grave) according to the wealth or popularity of the individual and sometimes other articles for ornament or uses are suspended over them. The funeral ceremonies occupy three days during which the soul of the deceased is in danger from 'O-mah- u' or the devil. To preserve it from this peril a fire is kept up at the grave and the friends of the deceased howl around it to scare away the demon. Should they not be successful in this the soul is carried down the river, subject, however, to redemption by 'Peh-ho wan' on payment of a big knife. After the expiration of three days it is all well with them."

Pima Indians: Capt. F. E. Grossman, of the Smithson Institute in 1871, wrote of the Pima Indians of Arizona. "The Pima tie the bodies of their dead with ropes, passing the latter around the neck and under the knees and then drawing them tight until the body is doubled up and forced into a sitting position. They dig the grave from four to five feet deep and perfectly round (about two feet in diameter), then hollow out to one side of the bottom of this grave a sort of vault large enough to contain the body. Here the body is deposited; the grave is filled up level with the ground, and poles, trees, or pieces of timber placed upon the grave to protect the remains from the coyotes (a species of wolf). Burials usually take place at night, without much ceremony. The mourners chant during the burial, but signs of grief are rare. The bodies of their dead are buried; if possible, immediately after death has taken place, and the graves are generally prepared before the patients die. Sometimes sick persons (for whom the graves had already been dug) recovered; in such cases the graves are left open until the persons for whom they were intended die. Open graves of this kind can be seen in several of their burial-grounds. Places of burial are selected some distance from the village, and, if possible, in a grove of mesquite bushes. Immediately after the remains have been buried, the house and personal effects of the deceased are burned, and his horses and cattle killed, the meat being cooked as a repast for the mourners. The nearest relatives of the deceased, as a sign of their sorrow, remain in the village for weeks and sometimes months; the men cut off about six inches of their long hair, while the women cut their hair quite short."

Coyotero Apache Indians: The Coyotero Apache rituals are described: "In disposing of their dead, (they) seem to be actuated by the desire to spare themselves any needless trouble, and prepare the defunct and the grave in this manner:"

"The Coyotero, upon the death of a member of the tribe, partially wrap up the corpse and deposit it into the cavity left by the removal of a small rock or the stump of a tree. After the body has been crammed into the smallest possible space the rock or stump is again rolled into its former position, when a number of stones are placed around the base to keep out the coyotes. The nearest of kin usually mourn for the period of one month, during that time giving utterance at intervals to the most dismal lamentations, which are apparently sincere. During the day this obligation is frequently neglected or forgotten, but when the mourner is reminded of his duty he renews his howling with evident interest. This custom of mourning for the period of thirty days corresponds to that formerly observed by the Natchez."

Pennsylvania Indians: In Pennsylvania, a similar technique was described by Moses Van Campen: "Directly after the Indians proceeded to bury those who had fallen in battle, which they did by rolling an old log from its place and laying the body in the hollow thus made, and then heaping upon it a little earth."

Indians of New York: Mr. Franklin B. Hough, talking about the Indians of New York in an unpublished journal, wrote in 1794: "Saw Indian graves on the plateau of Independence Rock. The Indians plant a stake on the right side of the head of the deceased and bury them in a bark canoe. Their children come every year to bring provisions to the place where their fathers are buried. One of the graves had fallen in and we observed in the soil some sticks for stretching skins, the remains of a canoe, etc., and the two straps for carrying it, and near the place where the head lay were the traces of a fire which they had kindled for the soul of the deceased to come and warm itself by and to partake of the food deposited near it."

Massasauga Indians: "These were probably the Massasauga Indians, then inhabiting the north shore of Lake Ontario, but who were rather intruders here, the country being claimed by the Oneidas."

"It is not to be denied that the use of canoes for coffins has occasionally been remarked, for the writer in 1875 removed from the graves at Santa Barbara an entire skeleton which was discovered in a redwood canoe, but it is thought that the individual may have been a noted fisherman, particularly as the implements of his vocation, nets, fish-spears, etc., were near him, and this burial was only an exemplification of the well-rooted belief common to all Indians, that the spirit in the next world makes use of the same articles as were employed in this one. It should be added that of the many hundreds of skeletons uncovered at Santa Barbara the one mentioned presented the only example of the kind."

Central American Indians: Among the Indians of the Mosquito coast, in Central America, canoe burial in the ground, was described:

"The corpse is wrapped in cloth and placed in one-half of a pitpan which has been cut in two. Friends assemble for the funeral and drown their grief in 'mushla', the women giving vent to their sorrow by dashing themselves on the ground until covered with blood, and inflicting other tortures, occasionally even committing suicide. As it is supposed that the evil spirit seeks to obtain possession of the body, musicians are called in to lull it to sleep while preparations are made for its removal. All at once four naked men, who have disguised themselves with paint, so as not to be recognized and punished by 'Wulasha', rush out from a neighboring hut, and, seizing a rope attached to the canoe, drag it into the woods, followed by the music and the crowd. Here the pitpan is lowered into the grave with bow, arrow, spear, paddle, and other implements to serve the departed in the land beyond, and then the other half of the boat is placed over the body. A rude hut is constructed over the grave, serving as a receptacle for the choice food, drink, and other articles placed there from time to time by relatives."

Muscogulges of the Carolinas: Bartram, (Bartram's Travels, 1801), described the Muscogulges of the Carolinas:

"The Muscogulges bury their deceased in the earth; they dig a four- foot, square, deep pit under the cabin, or couch which the deceased laid on in his house, lining the grave with cypress bark, (where) they place the corpse in a sitting posture, as if it were alive, depositing with him his gun, tomahawk, pipe, and such other matters as he had the greatest value for in his lifetime. His eldest wife, or the queen dowager, has the second choice of his possessions, and the remaining effects are divided among his other wives and children."

Buzzards and Butterflies

According to Bernard Roman, the "funeral customs of the Chickasaws did not differ materially from those of the Muscogulges. They interred the dead as soon as the breath left the body, and beneath the couch in which the deceased expired."

Navajo Indians: The Navajos of New Mexico and Arizona followed similar customs. "The Navajo custom is to leave the body where it dies, closing up the house or hogan or covering the body with stones or brush. In case the body is removed, it is taken to a cleft in the rocks and thrown in, and stones piled over. The person touching or carrying the body, first takes off all his clothes and afterwards washes his body with water before putting them on or mingling with the living. When a body is removed from a house or hogan, the hogan is burned down, and the place in every case abandoned, as the belief is that the devil comes to the place of death and remains where a dead body is. Wild animals frequently (indeed, generally) get the bodies, and it is a very easy matter to pick up skulls and bones around old camping grounds, or where the dead are laid. In case it is not desirable to abandon a place, the sick person is left out in some lone spot protected by brush, where they are either abandoned to their fate or food brought to them until they die. This is done only when all hope is gone. I have found bodies thus left so well inclosed with brush that wild animals were unable to get at them; and one so left to die was revived by a cup of coffee from our house and is still living and well."

Round Valley Indians of California: Mr. J. L. Burchard, agent to the Round Valley Indians of California, furnished an account of burial somewhat resembling that of the Navajos:

"When I first came here the Indians would dig a round hole in the ground, draw up the knees of the deceased Indian, and wrap the body into as small a bulk as possible in blankets, tie them firmly with cords, place them in the grave, throw in beads, baskets, clothing, everything owned by the deceased, and often donating much extra; all gathered around the grave wailing most pitifully, tearing their faces with their nails till the blood would run down their cheeks, pull out their hair, and such other heathenish conduct. These burials were generally made under their thatch houses or very near thereto. The house where one died was always torn down, removed, rebuilt, or abandoned. The wailing, talks, etc., were in their own jargon; none else could understand, and they seemingly knew but little of its meaning (if there was any meaning in it); it simply seemed to be the promptings of grief, without sufficient intelligence to direct any ceremony; each seemed to act out his own impulse."

Burial Mounds

Prof. F. W. Putnam, curator of the Peabody Museum of Archeology, Cambridge, made the following remarks to the Boston Society of Natural History on October 15, 1878. "It would be of interest to the members, in connection with the discovery of dolmens in Japan, as described by Professor Morse, to know that within twenty-four hours there had been received at the Peabody Museum a small collection of articles taken from rude dolmens (or chambered barrows, as they would be called in England), recently opened by Mr. E. Curtiss, who is now engaged, under his direction, in exploration for the Peabody Museum."

"These chambered mounds are situated in the eastern part of Clay County, Missouri, and form a large group on both sides of the Missouri River. The chambers are, in the three opened by Mr. Curtiss, about 8 feet square, and from 4-1/2 to 5 feet high, each chamber having a passage-way several feet in length and 2 in width leading from the southern side and opening on the edge of the mound formed by covering the chamber and passage-way with earth. The walls of the chambered passages were about 2 feet thick, vertical, and well made of stones, which were evenly laid without clay or mortar of any kind. The top of one of the chambers had a covering of large, flat rocks, but the others seem to have been closed over with wood. The chambers were filled with clay, which had been burnt, and appeared as if it had fallen in from above. The inside walls of the chambers also showed signs of fire. Under the burnt clay, in each chamber, were found the remains of several human skeletons, all of which had been burnt to such an extent as to leave but small fragments of the bones, which were mixed with the ashes and charcoal. Mr. Curtiss thought that in one chamber he found the remains of 5 skeletons and in another 13. With these skeletons there were a few flint implements and minute fragments of vessels of clay."

"A large mound near the chambered mounds was also opened, but in this no chambers were found. Neither had the bodies been burnt. This mound proved remarkably rich in large flint implements, and also contained well-made pottery and a peculiar "gorget" of red stone. The connection of the people who placed the ashes of their dead in the stone chambers with those who buried their dead in the earth mounds is, of course, yet to be determined."

"It is quite possible, indeed probable, that these chambers were used for secondary burials, the bodies having first been cremated."

In the volume of the proceedings already quoted the same investigator gives an account of other chambered mounds. These were mostly adults as the children were buried beneath the dwelling-floors:

"Mr. F. W. Putnam occupied the rest of the evening with an account of his explorations of the ancient mounds and burial places in the Cumberland Valley, Tennessee.

"The excavations had been carried on by himself, assisted by Mr. Edwin Curtiss, for over two years, for the benefit of the Peabody Museum at Cambridge. During this time many mounds of various kinds had been thoroughly explored, and several thousand of the singular stone graves of the mound builders of Tennessee had been carefully opened.... Mr. Putnam's remarks were illustrated by drawings of several hundred objects obtained from the graves and mounds, particularly to show the great variety of articles of pottery and several large and many unique forms of implements of chipped flint. He also exhibited and explained in detail a map of a walled town of this old nation. This town was situated on the Lindsley estate, in a bend of Spring Creek. The earth embankment, with its accompanying ditch, encircled an area of about 12 acres. Within this enclosure there was one large mound with a flat top, 15 feet high, 130 feet long, and 90 feet wide, which was found not to be a burial mound. Another mound near the large one, about 50 feet in diameter, and only a few feet high, contained 60 human skeletons, each in a carefully-made stone grave, the graves being arranged in two rows, forming the four sides of a square, and in three layers.... The most important discovery lie made within the enclosure was that of finding the remains of the houses of the people who lived in this old town. Of them about 70 were traced out and located on the map by Professor Buchanan, of Lebanon, who made the survey for Mr. Putnam. Under the floors of hard clay, which was in places much burnt, Mr. Putnam found the graves of children. As only the bodies of adults had been placed in the one mound devoted to burial, and as nearly every site of a house he explored had from one to four graves of children under the clay floor, he was convinced that it was a regular custom to bury the children in that way. He also found that the children had been undoubtedly treated with affection, as in their small graves were found many of the best pieces of pottery he obtained, and also quantities of shell-beads, several large pearls, and many other objects which were probably the playthings of the little ones while living.

"Near the center of the round fort ... was a tumulus of earth about 10 feet in height and several rods in diameter at its base. On its eastern side, and extending six rods from it, was semicircular pavements composed of pebbles such as are now found in the bed of the Scioto River, from whence they appear to have been brought. The summit of this tumulus was nearly 30 feet in diameter, and there was a raised way to it, leading from the east, like a modern turnpike. The summit was level. The outline of the semicircular pavement and the walk is still discernible. The earth composing this mound was entirely removed several years since. The writer was present at its removal and carefully examined the contents. It contained:

"1st. Two human skeletons lying on what had been the original surface of the earth."

"2d. A great quantity of arrow-heads, some of which were so large as to induce a belief that they were used as spear-heads."

"3d. The handle either of a small sword or a large knife, made of an elks horn. Around the end where the blade had been inserted was a ferule of silver, which, though black, was not much injured by time. Though the handle showed the hole where the blade had been inserted, yet no iron was found, but an oxide remained of similar shape and size."

"4th. Charcoal and wood ashes on which these articles lay, which were surrounded by several bricks very well burnt. The skeleton appeared to have been burned in a large and very hot fire, which had almost consumed the bones of the deceased. This skeleton was deposited a little to the south of the center of the tumulus; and about 20 feet to the north of it was another, with which were…"

"5th. A large mirror about 3 feet in breadth and 1-1/2 inches in thickness This mirror was (made) of isin glass (_mica membranacea_), and on it--"

"6th. A plate of iron which had become an oxide, but before it was disturbed by the spade resembled a plate of cast iron. The mirror answered the purpose very well for which it was intended. This skeleton had also been burned like the former, and lay on charcoal and a considerable quantity of wood ashes. A part of the mirror is in my possession, as well as a piece of brick taken from the spot at the time. The knife or sword handle was sent to Mr. Peal's Museum at Philadelphia."

"To the southwest of this tumulus, about 40 rods from it, is another, more than 90 feet in height, which is shown on the plate representing these works. It stands on a large hill, which appears to be artificial. This must have been the common cemetery, as it contains an immense number of human skeletons of all sizes and ages. The skeletons are laid horizontally, with their heads generally towards the center and the feet towards the outside of the tumulus. A considerable part of this work still stands uninjured, except by time. In it have been found, besides these skeletons, stone axes and knives and several ornaments, with holes through them, by means of which, with a cord passing through these perforations they could be worn by their owners. On the south side of this tumulus, and not far from it, was a semicircular fosse, which, when I first saw it, was 6 feet deep. On opening it was discovered at the bottom a great quantity of human bones, which I am inclined to believe were the remains of those who had been slain in some great and destructive battle first, because they belonged to persons who had attained their full size, whereas in the mound adjoining were found the skeletons of persons of all ages, and, secondly, they were here in the utmost confusion, as if buried in a hurry. May we not conjecture that they belonged to the people who resided in the town, and who were victorious in the engagement? Otherwise they would not have been thus honorably buried in the common cemetery."

Chillicothe Mound

"Its perpendicular height was about 15 feet, and the diameter of its base about 60 feet. It was composed of sand and contained human bones belonging to skeletons that were buried in different parts of it. It was not until this pile of earth was removed and the original surface exposed to view that a probable conjecture of its original design could be formed. About 20 feet square of the surface had been leveled and covered with bark. On the center of this lay a human skeleton, over that had been spread a mat manufactured either from weeds or bark. On the breast lay what had been a piece of copper, in the form of a cross, which had now become verdigrise. On the breast also lay a stone ornament with two perforations, one near each end, through which passed a string, by means of which it was suspended around the wearer's neck. On this string, which was made of sinews, and very much injured by time, were placed a great many heads made of ivory or bone, for I cannot certainly say which."

Illinois Mounds

The mounds of Sterling County, Illinois, were described by W. C. Holbrook, in 1977: "I recently made an, examination of a few of the many Indian mounds found on Rock River, about two miles above Sterling, Ill. The first one opened was an oval mound about 20 feet long, 12 feet wide, and 7 feet high. In the interior of this I found a "dolmen" or quadrilateral wall about 10 feet long, 4 feet high, and 4-1/2 feet wide. It had been built of lime-rock from a quarry near by, and was covered with large flat stones. No mortar or cement had been used. The whole structure rested on the surface of the natural soil, the interior of which had been scooped out to enlarge the chamber. Inside of the dolmen I found the partly decayed remains of eight human skeletons, two very large teeth of an unknown animal, two fossils, one of which is not found in this place, and a plummet. One of the long bones had been splintered; the fragments had united, but there remained large morbid growths of bone (exostosis) in several places. One of the skulls presented a circular opening about the size of a silver dime. This perforation had been made during life, for the edges had commenced to cicatrize. I later examined three circular mounds, but in them I found no dolmens. The first mound contained three adult human skeletons, a few fragments of the skeleton of a child, the lower maxillary of which indicated it to be about six years old. I also found claws of some carnivorous animal. The surface of the soil had been scooped out and the bodies laid in the excavation and covered with about a foot of earth, fires had then been made upon the grave and the mound afterwards completed. The bones had not been charred. No charcoal was found among the bones, but occurred in abundance in a stratum about one foot above them. Two other mounds, examined at the same time, contained no remains."

Buzzards and Butterflies

"Of two other mounds, opened later, the first was circular, about 4 feet high, and 15 feet in diameter at the base, and was situated on an elevated point of land close to the bank of the river. From the top of this mound one might view the country for many miles in almost any direction. On its summit was an oval altar 6 feet long and 4-1/2 wide. It was composed of flat pieces of limestone, which had been burned red, some portions having been almost converted into lime. On and about this altar I found abundance of charcoal. At the sides of the altar were fragments of human bones, some of which had been charred. It was covered by a natural growth of vegetable mold and sod, the thickness of which was about 10 inches. Large trees had once grown in this vegetable mold, but their stumps were so decayed I could not tell with certainty to what species they belonged. Another large mound was opened which contained nothing."

Dr. George Sternbert described the Indian Mounds near **Pensacola, Florida** in 1875:

"Before visiting the mound I was informed that the Indians were buried in it in an upright position, each one with a clay pot on his head. This idea was based upon some superficial explorations, which had been made from time to time by curiosity hunters. Their excavations had, indeed, brought to light pots containing fragments of skulls, but not buried in the position they imagined. Very extensive explorations made at different times by myself have shown that only fragments of skulls and of the long bones of the body are to be found in the mound, and that these are commonly associated with earthen pots, sometimes whole, but more frequently broken fragments only. In some instances portions of the skull were placed in a pot, and the long bones were deposited in its immediate vicinity. Again, the pots would contain only sand, and fragments of bones would be found near them. The most successful 'find' I made was a whole nest of pots, to the number of half a dozen, all in a good state of preservation, and buried with a fragment of skull, which I take from its small size to have been that of a female. Whether this female was thus distinguished above all others buried in the mound by the number of pots deposited with her remains because of her skill in the manufacture of such ware, or by reason of the unusual wealth of her sorrowing husband, must remain a matter of conjecture. I found altogether fragments of skulls and thighbones belonging to at least fifty individuals, but in no instance did I find anything like a complete skeleton. There were no vertebra, no ribs, no pelvic bones, and none of the small bones of the hands and feet. Two or three skulls nearly perfect were found, but they were so fragile that it was impossible to preserve them. In the majority of instances only fragments of the frontal and parietal bones were found, buried in pots or in fragments of pots too small to have ever contained a complete skull. The conclusion was irresistible that this was not a burial place for the bodies of deceased Indians, but that the bones had been gathered from some other locality for burial in this mound, or that cremation was practiced before burial, and the fragments of bone not consumed by fire were gathered and deposited in the mound. That the latter supposition is the correct one I deem probable from the fact that in digging in the mound evidences of fire are found in numerous places, but without any regularity as to depth and position. These evidences consist in strata of from one to four inches in thickness, in which the sand is of a dark color and has mixed with it numerous small fragments of charcoal."

"My theory is that the mound was built by gradual accretion in the following manner. That when a death occurred a funeral pyre was erected on the mound, upon which the body was placed. That after the body was consumed, any fragments of bones remaining were gathered, placed in a pot, and buried, and that a layer of sand brought from the immediate vicinity for that purpose covered the ashes and cinders. This view is further supported by the fact that only the shafts of the long bones are found, the expanded extremities, which would be most easily consumed, having disappeared; also, by the fact that no bones of children were found. Their bones being smaller, and containing a less proportion of earthy matter, would be entirely consumed."

"At the Santa Rosa mound the method of burial was different. Here I found the skeletons complete, and obtained nine well-preserved skulls.... The bodies were not apparently deposited upon any regular system, and I found no objects of interest associated with the remains. It may be that this was due to the fact that the skeletons found were those of warriors who had fallen in battle in which they had sustained a defeat. This view is supported by the fact that they were all males, and that two of the skulls bore marks of ante-mortem injuries which must have been of a fatal character."

Modern Burial Statistics

Each year, 22,500 cemeteries across the United States bury approximately:

30 million board feet (70,000 m³) of hardwoods (caskets)
90,272 tons of steel (caskets)
14,000 tons of steel (vaults)
2,700 tons of copper and bronze (caskets)
1,636,000 tons of reinforced concrete (vaults)
827,060 US gallons (3,130 m³) of embalming fluid, which most commonly includes formaldehyde. However it is worth noting that embalming fluid chemically changes in the act of preserving the body and is not largely present as a fluid and this figure refers to embalming fluid before it is introduced to the body.

(Compiled from statistics by Casket and Funeral Association of America, Cremation Association of North America, Doric Inc., The Rainforest Action Network, and Mary Woodsen, Pre-Posthumous Society)

While a thorough exposure to burial practices is helpful in expanding the knowledge of the SAR dog handler, it does not in itself create a "better handler". However, it does lay a groundwork for attention to detail and expanding the skills of observation while searching for a body. With that in mind, one continues the exploration of information which create a well-rounded HRD handler and reminds us that if the dog alerts and we do not actively "see" the human remains, it does not mean that there are not remains present or that some remnant of a past person does not mark this place.
Trust your dog and keep your eyes wide open for clues.

K9 Jess, Retired, Handler, Joe Gupton

K9 Emma Rose, Handler: Patti Gibson, Illinois-Wisconsin SAR Dogs

"Yes, dear, a bloodhound can do water recovery too!"

3
The Decomposition Process

Outline
Autolysis
Factors Affecting Decomposition
Mummification
Effects of Embalming Upon Decomposition
Peat Bog
Skeletonization
Forensics
Buzzards and Butterflies
Research Facilities

(Note: This is not a chapter for the light of heart...please be advised.)

Autolysis

Decomposition begins at the moment of death caused by autolysis (break down of tissue by the body's own internal chemicals and enzymes or self-digestion) and putrefaction (breakdown of tissue by bacteria). Autolysis begins about four minutes after death. This process releases bases that are the source of the odor of dead bodies. The next participant in decomp includes insects, typically fleshflies (Sarcophagidae) and blowflies (Calliphoridae). Larger scavengers such as coyotes, dogs, wolves, foxes, rats, and mice may also destroy and eat a body if given access. These are typically the animals which remove and scatter the bones.

Specifically, when the heart stops and the lungs no longer breathe the body cells no longer receive blood and oxygen. Blood drains from capillaries in the upper surfaces and collect in blood vessels in lower surfaces. Upper surfaces become pale and lower surfaces become dark. Cells cease aerobic respiration and muscles stiffen and remain stiff (rigor mortis) until they begin to decompose. Cells eventually die and the body loses its capacity to fight off bacteria. The cells' own enzymes and bacterial activity cause the body to decompose - muscles then lose their stiffness.

Brain cells die without oxygen in about three minutes. Muscle cells live for several more hours. Bone and skin cells live for seveal days. It takes about 12 hours for a body to cool to the touch and 24 hours to cool through the core. Rigor mortis commences after three hours and lasts until 36 hours after death. These clues help forensic scientists to estimate the time of death.

Factors Affecting Decomposition

A number of factors affect the decomposition process including temperature, availability of oxygen, prior embalming, cause of death, burial (depth), access by scavengers, trauma (including wounds), humidity or wetness, rainfall, body size and weight, clothing, the temperature surface where the body rests, and foods/objects inside the digestive tract. These factors, in addition to the season, affect the decomposition rate. A basic guide (Casper's Law) to determine how fast a body will skeletonize or mummify includes: "When there is free access of air a body decomposes twice as fast than if immersed in water and eight times faster than if buried in earth."

Insects, particularly flies in tropical areas, can reduce a body to bones in under two weeks. Acids in the soil can then reduce it to an unrecognizable mass. Under certain conditions where the body is under cool, damp soil, the body may develop a waxy substance called adipocere during the process called saponification. This is a result of the action of soil chemicals on the body's proteins and fats. The formation of adipocere slows decomp by inhibiting the bacteria that causes the putrefaction.

"Grave wax, or adipocere, is a crumbly white, waxy substance that accumulates on those parts of the body that contain fat - the cheeks, breasts, abdomen and buttocks. It is the product of a chemical reaction in which fats react with water and hydrogen in the presence of bacterial enzymes, breaking down into fatty acids and soaps. Adipocere is resistant to bacteria and can protect a corpse, slowing further decomposition. Adipocere starts to form within a month after death and has been recorded on bodies that have been exhumed after 100 years. If a body is readily accessible to insects, adipocere is unlikely to form." Australian Museum Online.

Mummification

Mummification occurs in extremely dry or cold conditions when decomp is halted by either lack of moisture or temperature which controls the bacterial and enzymatic action. Frozen bodies will restart the decomp process when thawed, while heat-produced mummies remain so unless exposed to moisture. Newborns who have not eaten food are an exception to the normal decomp process because they lack the internal microbes and flora that produce decomposition.

Mummified bodies may remain viewable decades after death. Such was the case of the murdered civil righs activist Medgar Evers, Vladimir Lenin (kept submerged in a special tank of fluid for decades, almost perfectly preserved), and Evita Peron, kept preserved for many years.

Effects of Embalming Upon Decomposition

Embalming chemicals repel insects and slow down putrefaction and actually kills bacteria which retards decomposition. The simplest form of embalming involves the removal of blood from the body and the addition of a preservative fluid, usually formaldehyde, or HCHO, which has been used since about 1888. Effective embalming involves the retardation of the decomposition process and keeps organisms from destroying the body. Even though we use embalming to delay decomposition, it still takes place, just at a much slower rate.

Peat Bog

Peat bog may naturally embalm a body by arresting decomposition and produce a preserved body known as a *bog body*. Bog bodies (found in Europe) retain their skin and internal organs due to the acidity of the water, lack of oxygen, and cold temperatures. This tans the skin very dark. The acid in the peat dissolves the calcium carbonate of bone and the skeleton dissolves. These bodies retain very intricate details such as the fingerprint or tattoos. Even facial features and stubble are preserved in some ancient specimens.

Skeletonization

Skeletonization refers to the complete decomposition of non-bony tissues of a body leading to a bare skeleton. It usually takes three months to several years for this to occur depending upon the climate and conditions. In the Andes Mountains or tundra, skeletonization will never occur if subzero temperatures exist. The rate of skeletonization and the present condition of the body determines the time of death.

After skeletonization, the skeleton of mid to large mammals such as humans takes about twenty years under optimal conditions to be completely dissolved by an *acidic soil* and leave no trace of the organism. In neutral pH soil or sand, the skeleton will still be present for several thousand years before it finally disintegrates. Under some conditions the skeleton will fossilize, leaving an impression of the bone that can last for millions of years.

Dr. William Bass, of the Tennessee body farm and Jon Jefferson, in their book Beyond the Body Farm, have developed a skeletonization formula to determine how long it takes a body to skeletonize. In their Accumulated-Degree-Days formula, one can tabulate the average daily temperature, add them together for a sum. Any sum above 1250 means the body has possibly totally skeletonized. This assumes that the daily temperatures are above freezing as decomposition ceases above about 38 degrees F.

To calculate skeletonization, multiply the average daily temperature (example 80 degrees) by the total number of days (for example 15 days) to find a total point span of 1200. Body is just before becoming totally skeletonized. This can be done more precisely by adding the average daily temperature for the time period to get a more probable calculation. For instance, 42 degree, 50 degrees, etc. for a total of three months to calculate the point span. and estimate the amount of expected skeletonization.

Forensics

The science of decomposition is referred to as "forensics" which determines the time and cause of death for legal purposes. Other common terminology in the study of death cases include:

Forensic pathology: studies the clues to the cause of death as a medical issue.
Forensic entomology: studies the insects and other vermin found on the body; the sequence in which they appear, kinds of insects, and their life cycle which might provide information on time of death, length of exposure to the elements and whether the body was moved.
Forensic anthropology: branch of physical anthropology that studies skeletons and human remains, to seek clues to race, identify and sex .

Buzzards and Butterflies

Griffon vulture

An Andean Condor soars in Peru

Now you had to know that the title of this book came from somewhere. Most seasoned handlers already know the correlation between HRD and buzzards. However, some may not realize the butterfly connection. Quite often, when the buzzard and butterfly is a resident of the area, they both may visit the deceased and unwittingly lead the handler or dog to the body. HRD handlers should be aware of the normal flora nd fauna and recognize when the natural processes begin to occur after death.

According to Wikipedia, in the Old World, buzzards are defined as:

- One of several medium-sized, wide-ranging raptors with a robust body and broad wings.
- In particular, those in the genus Buteo. In the Old World, members of this genus are named as "buzzards", but "hawk" is more common in North America.
- Specifically, in Europe, the Common Buzzard, Buteo buteo, where Buzzard is often used as a synonym.

- Any raptor which has the word buzzard as part of its name.

In the New World buzzards are defined as:

- A vulture, particularly the American Black Vulture and Turkey Vulture, or as a general term for vultures and condors.
- In parts of the United States where they are considered a pest, particularly in rural areas, a derogatory term for certain birds of prey, such as the Chickenhawk (a common colloquial name referring to both the Red-tailed Hawk and the Cooper's Hawk), or the Duck hawk (known elsewhere as the Peregrine Falcon). In the U.S., the term "buzzard" is *never* used to refer to birds of prey, like hawks, eagles, falcons, and owls, outside of this context.
- Rarely, a derogatory term for any large bird that happens to be a scavenger, such as a raven or albatross (in other words, any large bird that is neither predatory nor flightless).

(The Old World is defined as Europeans, Asians, and Africans in the 15th century, prior to Columbus' voyage. Afterwards, the New World included the America's and Australiasia.)

A particular characteristic of many vultures is the bald head devoid of feathers. Circling vultures overhead are called a *kettle* and a group of vultures a *venue*. They are scavengers feeding on carcasses. Common vultures or buzzards in North America include the Turkey Vulture/Buzzard, and the American Black Buzzard. The common buzzard that extends into Asia and most of Europe is also a carrion.

A California Condor.

California Condor Head.

Buzzards and Butterflies

HRD handlers should constantly scan the area for venues of buzzards. Their circling can easily provide a search area and is a common sight during regular HRD training. Develop a system of communication with your teammates to alert other crews of *kettles* (a group of buzzards circling above presumably near or over a target location). Remember it is wise to sometimes avoid the use of the terms buzzards and vultures out of respect for any family member who may be within earshot of a SAR radio.

Likewise certain butterflies are known to gather in the vicinity of a cadaver. Become familiar with the types of butterflies in your environment and watch for their visits during your regular training.

Butterflies feed primarily on nectar, but some also need pollen, tree sap, rotting fruit, dung, and minerals in wet sand or dirt. Several species need more sodium than is contained in their usual diet of nectar. They like the sodium in salt and sometimes land on people attracted by human sweat, blood and tears. Some also visit carcasses to obtain these minerals and nutrients. They gather at a carcass or cadaver in a behavior called *mud puddling* where they collect the nutrients. It is called this as it usually happens in damp or moist soil. It is usually restricted to male butterflies.

The carrion feeders (who visit deceased bodies) like the blue Lesser Purple Emperor, can smell a body from hundreds of meters away. Another yellow species is also known to lead you to the body. There are even some species of moths, like the Calyptra which is nicknamed the *vampire moth* because it sucks blood from sleeping humans. The HRD handler should be forever vigilant of the unusual activity of insects in the search area. More than one dog has followed the flies or butterflies (who now have scent of the deceased person on *their* insect bodies) straight to the body of the deceased person. Never assume your dog is just playing with the butterflies. Trust your dog.

Research Facilities

There are two known facilities which are conducting research on the factors affecting decomposition of the human body and related studies. The *Body Farm* at the University of Tennessee in Knoxville and the *Forrest* at Western Carolina University in Cullowhee, North Carolina, are both conducting research to aid law enforcement personnel and search and rescue personnnel to locate missing and unidentified persons. They have a number of bodies laid out in various situations in a fenced area near their research facilities. Both are attempting to determine how a human body decays in various situations in order to understand the decomposition process.

Several other areas of the country are contemplating and planning to open similar facilities. Sometimes these facilities are willing to allow cadaver dogs to visit as part of their research. However, handlers should plan for specific training activities and understand that the canine nasal cavity is only capable of so much cadaver scent before going into "overload" so to speak. Be sure to allow the dog to clear his respiratory system with regular breaks and have a planned (and pre-approved) training regime with specific training goals in mind prior to visiting any facility. Consult with other handlers who have visited similar facilities and ask for guidance from facility administrators. Sometimes special accomodations may be made to adapt to your training objectives.

K9 Kinder
Handler: Jim Ware, Brunswick SAR,, NC

K9 Storm working a Burn Pile, Jim Ware, Handler, Brunswick Search and Rescue, NC

4
Canine Behavior

Outline
Introduction to the HRD/Cadaver Dog
Selecting an HRD Dog

Introduction to Reading the Dog
Behavior in Scent
How to Read the Search Dog: Natural Communication
Canine Ethogram with Interpretation for Search Dogs
by Julie Hartell- Denardo and Susan Martinez

The HRD Mind: Emotions and Reactions to Death
K9 Reactions to Violent Death

Introduction to the Human Remains Detection / Cadaver Dog

The Scientific Working Group on Dog and Orthogonal Detector Guidelines are being developed by a group of 55 professionals representing numerous agencies such as the Federal Bureau of Investigation, veterinarians, law enforcement agencies and others knowledgeable about working dogs. They have identified what issues need to be researched and promote specific criteria for certifying various types of scent detector dogs. They have also established a collective vocabulary for scent detector dog handlers. Among the recommended terminology is: (for a complete listing of terminology, explanations, annotations and more detailed information, visit their web site.)

- ◆ Alert   A characteristic change in ongoing behavior in response to a trained odor, as interpreted by the handler.

- ◆ COB   Change of Behavior. The COB is a pattern of behavior that occurs when the dog detects a trained odor. May be unique to each dog.

- ◆ Interest   Any reaction to odor. Noticeable, readable, physical change in behavior when the dog is interested in the odor.

- ◆ Miss   When the dog fails to alert in the known presence of the target odor.

Buzzards and Butterflies

- Unconfirmed Alert   An alert with or without a final response for which the presence of a trained odor cannot be confirmed. May be residual or lingering odor that the dog can detect but which cannot be confirmed by technology or direct observation.

- Confirmed Alert   An alert with or without a final response for which the presence of a trained odor can be verified or corroborated.

- Final Response   A behavior that a dog has been trained to exhibit upon locating the source of a target odor. May be passive (sit, stare, down, point) or active (bark, scratch)

- Reliability   The extent to which a measure is repeatable and consistent and free from random errors; all measurements have random components because of imperfections in the measurement process, and the fact that when we measure something we usually change it a bit.

K9 Stryker
Locating source during HRD practice.
Handler: Kathy Lewis, Flathead County Search and Rescue.
Photographer: Jonah Libsack-Maynard.

Reliability refers to the sensitivity (low probability of missing targets when present), and specificity (high probability of finding targets when present).

Additional general guidelines recommended by the SWGDOG group include: (consult with the web site for a complete list and further descriptions.)

- The canine training shall use a curriculum with specific training and learning objectives.

- The handler shall be trained using a curriculum with specific training and learning objectives.

- Handlers shall keep regular maintenance training records.

- Double - Blind assessments are recommended. (Double blind refers to the fact that whomever places the training aids are not with the crew when the area is searched. In this way, no individual can consciously or unconsciously cue the handler as to the positive location of the training aid.

After the exercise or assessment is complete, the person placing the aids confirms the locations of the training aids.)

An informed dog handler will stay abreast of the latest recommendations, research, and trends in scent dog work. While there are many organizations undergoing similar interests, all stress the ethical behavior of the handler and documentation of training and related activities. Consult with your mentor to determine what is appropriate for you. Remember, at this time there is no 'law' on what is required for training, certification, or working a search and rescue human remains/cadaver dog. However, there are several 501 c (3) nonprofit organizations like SWGDOG (including your team, and your state standards and recommendations) that should be consulted, considered, and followed as appropriate for your mission and location. In other situations, your organization or agency will determine what standards, training, and certification procedures and documentation is required. In addition, industry standard (i.e. what most teams and organizations are requiring) may be the proof of reliability needed in a court of law.

Selecting an HRD Dog

Each trainer has a slightly different technique for selecting an appropriate dog for search and rescue. Some say temperament and "a nose" is the key. Others use nationally recognized puppy tests as a guide. Yet others think ball drive is the key to selecting a good puppy. In addition to these guides, handlers should develop problem-solving tests to see if the dog can solve varying complex tests. An example of the problem solving ability might be to get a treat out of a confined area, not easily accessed.

Some handlers look for excessive "ball drive", or "prey drive", or "hunt drive" or any other kind of drive you can create. A high tug drive simply indicates that the dog loves to bite and play tug-of-war. It is not a particularly positive characteristic but some look for it in an HRD dog. Sustained attention, attention to detail, and a sustained work ethic plays into every SAR dog description. Using a ball to determine "time-on-task" may be more important than the dogs' ability to respond to a "ball reward system."

Some handlers test for a high "hunt drive" by hiding food and determining how long a puppy will pursue the "hunt" for a jar of goodies. How do they respond to an aromatic food reward?

Candidates should also be exposed to cadaver material, both bone and tissue to determine if there is any aversive behavior. An aversive dog (shrinking back from the scent of HRD material) does not have the predetermination to seek out that scent. Others may roll in the scent, demonstrating wolf-like behaviors to mask themselves in the scent in order to "hide" and await their prey. Consider a scent test that offers the puppy several scents to choose from and document which the puppy selects when each is presented simultaneously in optimum scent conditions (i.e. each scent is offered in equal access). Sample scents might include a scented "live" shirt, food, and human remains. The HR should be the farthest from the puppy but equally available via scent conditions.

Is the dog eye, ear, or nose driven? What is the natural inclination of the senses? A nose driven dog is preferred.

The genetic draw of the deck influences many factors of the dog, including some known and unknown health issues. For this reason, it may be wise to select a dog from known stock to diminish the likelihood the handler and dog will have to deal with hip dysplasia, retinal atrophy or other genetic defects. This is not to say that a rescued dog from the pound does not turn into a great

SAR dog. It is to say that the time and effort put into training a SAR dog should demand a solid specimen likely to provide a long and healthy working career.

Another selection technique is to have the breeder place the puppy in an unfamiliar area away from the rest of the litter. Can you coax the puppy to you? Does he/she interact appropriately and boldly? A keen eye will select the optimum potential for SAR work.

There are those who will say that bloodhounds working as trailing dogs will be *ruined* if they are trained on HRD. Others have tried it and know it does not ruin a trailing dog. It is definitely an asset when disarticulated remains may be at the end of the trail. Handlers, some years ago, tried things they didn't know they weren't supposed to be able to do. New techniques and protocols emerged and teams across the nation began to diversify in their strategies and techniques. There is no one right way and no one wrong way to do anything. Variations on any theme often work. Try it. If it works, use it, and if it doesn't discard it. Others like Bill Tolhurst were just curious enough about everything in general to "just try it." We would do well to emulate him.

No particular breed is touted as "the SAR dog", however, structurally, the herding, sporting, gundogs, and working dogs tend to have a history of becoming effective working dogs. Select neither the most timid nor the most aggressive puppy (dominance factors.) Watch for a natural curiosity and confidence. Check for paw sensitivity. Will the puppy allow you to handle his feet and other parts of his body? Be aware of noise sensitivity. SAR canines often work around sirens and other construction noises. Look for one that embraces problem-solving situations. Place the puppy on a new surface...like wire or metal. What is the reaction? Select the structurally sound dog and once selected vow to provide the very best training, both consistently and effectively to become a "team." The dog I.Q. matters but the handler I.Q. matters more.

Introduction to Reading the Dog

Search and rescue dogs perform in a variety of disciplines. Live find search and rescue dogs can and are cross-trained to detect human remains as well. There are those who would recommend that a dog trained in only one discipline is more treasured, and would be easier to maintain (training). However, in many cases it is unknown whether the person is living or deceased. Which dog should be deployed when the condition of the missing person is unknown? Others tout the argument that in disaster situations a cross-trained dog could false alert causing undue energies to be spent recovering a deceased body while a live one is left to die without a timely rescue response. In addition, the handler needs to know if the dog will alert on live or deceased scent when both are present in the same search area.

Having hundreds or thousands of acres to search does justify the cross-trained dog for the lost, but there will still be a need for the HRD-only dog that can find that bone shard or tooth for the forensic anthropologist to identify the missing victim from years past. Some teams across the country require certification in another discipline prior to beginning cadaver or human remains detection training. They often begin canine training in a basic discipline such as air scent or trailing. The team dogs are duel certified and the handlers are quite successful with this approach. The decision rests with the team and handler. Regardless of the certification route all handlers need to be aware and become experts in "reading the dog".

Canines vary in their reactions in and around scent. No two dogs will react exactly the same around the scent of death or a body. Nor will any dog react exactly the same in subsequent missions where the situation may appear quite similar. Experience teaches the handler to recognize the subtle changes in a dog's behavior when he is entering scent or confused by scent. The following article aptly describes the characteristics of a dog that indicate a change in the scent conditions. The following *Ethogram*, written by Susan Martinez and Julie Hartell-DeNardo, is a concise and detailed outline of canine behavior traits that are readily observable. It interprets the dog behavior through keen observation by the handler. It is up to the handler to interpret "how" the scent conditions have changed and how that information will affect the search strategy or mission. The dogs' behavior simply provides the clues that the conditions "are" in fact changing or in some fashion different than a previous time and location.

Behavior in Scent

By Susan Martinez,
Greater Houston Search Dogs, Texas, and
Julie Hartell-DeNardo, Keeper II, Oakland Zoo
California

How to Read the Search Dog: Natural Communication

Body postures and vocalizations are the language forms an animal uses to communicate information regarding the state of mind of that particular animal and the scent it has located in the environment. A search dog handler uses this natural communication to decipher the body language of their partner in order to determine the location of a scent source they have been requested to find in a specific area. Each dog is an individual, therefore the human working with a particular animal must learn by close observation how that animal behaves when in the targeted scent and how the behavior changes with other scents in the environment. Behavioral data collection may help this process particularly in the early stages of training. The handler should document specific behavioral changes observed and note the frequency of those behaviors during training under a variety of conditions. Behavioral changes that indicate scent recognition will emerge and remain consistent with that particular canine each time it locates the target odor.

Scent is a potpourri of many smells which include not only the targeted scent we ask dogs to locate but also the scent of other animals both live and deceased in the search area and a mixture of vegetative smells common to that particular environment. Knowledge of scent propagation enables the handler to determine the location of the strongest scent. A scent source varies in strength according to the areas of obstruction that interfere with the wind movement and change in the airflow patterns. Examples of items causing obstruction are buildings, vegetation such as shrubs or brush and trees, large rocks, sand dunes, and cliffs. The movement of scent may be compared to water movement; therefore understanding how water flows around obstructions may enable a handler to understand scent "flow" in a given topography.

There are many fields of study in which a dog handler must gain a level of proficiency in order to execute their job efficiently and state the location of scent. The study of behavioral observation and documentation can be very useful in effective scent work. By working closely in the canine partnership throughout the working career of the dog, a handler has the opportunity to learn the individual animals' working behavioral patterns.

Buzzards and Butterflies

A detector dog is usually trained to give an indication when it arrives at the strongest scent. The dog may work very hard to find the strongest scent before giving the final communication to the handler. If the dog struggles due to scent propagation it may tire quickly. A handler who has studied their particular partner's behavior in scent will be able to help the dog by positioning it in areas where specific behavioral changes occurred. Scientists who quantitatively document the behaviors of animals will use an ethogram to define and distinguish behaviors.

Canine Ethogram with Interpretation for Search Dogs

An ethogram is a catalog of behaviors exhibited by a particular species or individual animal. Ethograms are used to observe, record, study and learn about animal behavior. They are used to standardize gathered data by ensuring that all observers use the same terms to describe displayed behavior. A behavior may be described by its motor patterns and have its frequency and intensity noted, or a behavior may be described by its function. An ethogram is not a complete listing of all behaviors exhibited by a species. Nor, is every behavior described in an ethogram going to be exhibited by all animals. Detailed descriptions and pictures are both useful components of a complete ethogram. Each relevant behavior must be clearly defined, including all qualifying criteria. Interpretations of particular behaviors can be derived from the data collected using an ethogram.

When working with ethograms it is important to remember that the behaviors and "meaning" or interpretation of the behaviors are different. Many dogs may exhibit the same behavior for different purposes. In fact the same dog may use what we perceive as the same behavior to communicate different things. It is possible to make generalizations about the purpose of different categories of behaviors but handlers must remember to be flexible in these generalizations as every animal is allowed to speak its own language. All animals are individuals and are affected by their environment. Breed, genetics, age, and physiological structure can limit the potential behaviors an animal will perform.

The purpose of the ethogram is to help one become more aware of the behaviors exhibited by a search dog and the situations in which those behaviors occur. Once there is a history of the factors under which specific behaviors occur then the handler will learn to understand what those behaviors may "mean" in a particular dog. This will be different for each individual dog and even different for dogs within the same breed.

The scent working canine ethogram that follows includes basic interpretations of some common canine behaviors. It is important to remember that these are open to variation and only included as a general guide. Different breeds and individuals have varying capabilities to perform behaviors. Physiological structure and medical history may limit the types of behaviors seen and the conditions under which they occur. With observations over time, a handler will learn which specific behaviors or categories of behaviors are relevant to a specific canine working scent.

A useful learning tool is to make a map of a specific search area and document behaviors that occur when each dog works that search area. It is important to include other relevant information such as wind direction, wind speed, precipitations, scent source and condition, and other pertinent details of the search. The information collected on the maps will enable the handler to identify behavioral changes in specific scenting conditions. Working dogs exhibit a great deal of information via behavioral patterns and by documenting this information; handlers will learn to interpret those behaviors concisely.

Categories of Behaviors
- Body Position
- Head Position
- Mouth/Nose
- Ear Position
- Tail Position
- Feet/Legs
- Marking Behaviors
- Vocalizations
- Movement
- Interaction with Handler

Behavioral Groups

Body Position
- Stand
- Lean in
- Lean out
- Crouch
- Sit
- Kneel
- Down
- Stretch Down
- Front Stretch

Head Position
- Up
- Down
- Straight
- Turned in
- Turned away

Mouth/Nose
- Sniffing (will be connected to head position and environmental landmarks)

Buzzards and Butterflies

- Panting
- Drooling
- Blow Out/Snort/Sneeze
- Biting at….
- Eating….
- Lick Intention
- Licking

Ear Position
- Turned forward
- Turned back

- Forward
- Back
- Cocked
- Close & High

Tail Position

- Straight
- Down X Degrees
- Between Legs
- Under Belly
- Up X Degrees
- Straight Up
- Over Back
- Wagging

Feet/legs
- Pointing
- Lifting
- Pawing
- Digging

Marking Behaviors
- Defecating
- Urinating
- Scent Scratching
- Scent Rolling

Vocalization
- Bark
- Air Bark
- Whine
- Whimper

- Howl
- Yip
- Yelp
- Growl

Movement
- Still
- Walk
- Jog/Trot
- Run
- Pounce
- Pacing
- Circle
- Quartering
- Observation Jump
- Shake Off

Focus at Handler
- Stare
- Nudge
- Jump
- Vocalize

Explanation of Behaviors

Body Position: **The overall position of the canine's body in relation to the extremities. A change in body position is typically related to a change in where a canine's weight is being supported. Body Position can indicate the canine's alertness or eagerness to become active or responsive. Passive Indicator behaviors (alerts) are often related to body position.**

The overall position of the body may indicate the canine's alertness or eagerness to become active or responsive. A change in body position is typically related to a change in which a canine shifts weight on all four paws which may be leaning in towards a scent or leaning away from the source. The dog may freeze in one position with the nose staring at the source upon initial acquisition of the recognized scent. A detection dog may also crouch to get closer to the scent or stretch if the source is buried in rubble and the dog is unable to access the source at the current position. If the scent is hanging, the dog must stretch in an upward position to isolate the scent with the nose pointing towards the odor.

A passive indication such as a sit or down trains the dog to relate a natural alert with a body position. The passive indication is often trained separate from the scent recognition work, then added into the behavior sequence and encouraged upon the dog's acknowledgement of the targeted scent odor. For example the scent recognition that is natural to the dog is an inquisitive nose that may go to the scent source. This behavior is reinforced repeatedly until the dog understands that when it goes to the scent it will receive reinforcement in the form of a toy or food treat. The scent recognition is then paired with the passive indication that the handler has determined works best for that dog and the specific odor. This may be a sit or down.

The dog may also include a posture that pinpoints the scent for the handler such as a stare with a nose pointed to the source or the dog may glance back at the handler and then reorient focus on the scent. This is the dog's natural communication to indicate it has found the scent. Following is an ethogram description of body position.

Stand: All four legs are straight and underneath the body of the dog. Weight of the canine is centered between all four extremities.

Lean-in: The front legs support a large percentage of dog's weight. The angle of the legs is leaning towards the anterior of the body. Head and neck are typically stretched out when lean-in occurs. This behavior is most often seen when navigating uneven terrain or when the dog is unsure of proceeding but intrigued by something ahead. Lean-in is used to investigate ahead without venturing ahead.

Lean-out: The rear legs support a large percentage of the dog's weight. The angle of the legs is leaning towards the posterior of the dog. Head and neck typically are pulled back when lean-out occurs. This behavior is most often seen when navigating uneven terrain or when the dog is reluctant to proceed due to some type of aversion. Sometimes this may be a reactive defensive behavior to a perceived threat. Usually considered an aversion behavior but this depends on the motivator of the behavior.

Crouch: Similar to stand but with more bend in all of the legs. Can be a moving or stationary body position. Frequently seen before a jump, during excited barking at target, and when going under low objects. Makes canine appear shorter or smaller – this may or may not be part of the intent.

Sit: Back legs are bent under hindquarters. Front legs are straight supporting the head and neck. A resting type behavior. Often trained as an indicator behavior.

Kneel:	Front legs are bent under with front feet tucked under canine. Forequarters near ground while hindquarters are up further from ground. Typically used when canine is trying to get close to something on the ground or below its level.

Down:	All four legs are bent down under the body. Body is touching or very near to the ground. This is often trained as an indicator behavior.

Stretch Down: This is the same as the down except the back legs are kicked out behind the body and the belly is in contact with the ground. This is typically a more relaxed behavior than down. Some dogs use this position to cool the underside of the body. This is a resting position.

Front Stretch: The front legs are stretched out in front of the dog. The back legs are straight and supporting rear. Head and neck are close to the ground while rump is in the air. This is frequently seen in playful puppy behavior and in testing large animals prior to the chase sequence in wolf behavior. This may also be an investigative behavior, as the canine smells a scent in a hidden area that it is unable to reach easily.

Head Position: Head position refers to the level of the head in relation to the canine's body. Position is an indicator of the direction of the dog's interest. Typically position indicates the angle and direction the dog is receiving sensory stimuli (visual, audible, olfactory, or tactile).

In the head up position, the angle between the shoulders and head ranges between zero and ninety degrees depending on the flexibility of the dog. The opposite angle occurs with the head down position in relation to the shoulders and the body and again dependent on the flexibility of the dog. In the straight position the head and shoulders are on the same horizontal plane and a line may be followed from the body of the dog to the head.

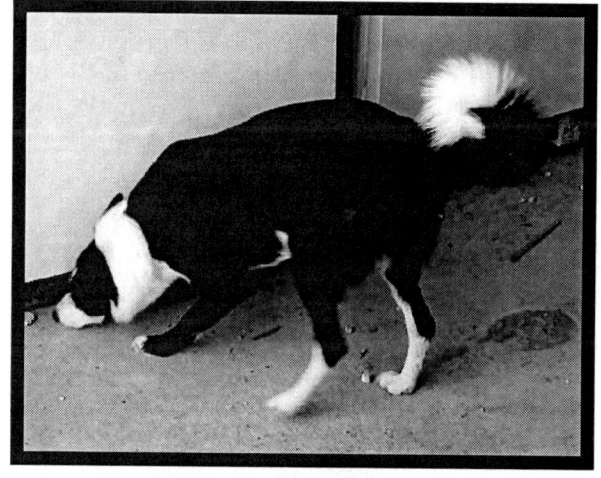

When the head is turned in towards something of interest, the eye contact is with the object or in the general direction of the object or scent. When the head is turned away from the body and something attracts the focus of the dog, the new sensory input slowly draws the eye towards the interest while the head is still in motion and prior to the head finishing its rotation. The dog may keep its eye on the interest even while turning to look back at the handler and listen for the movement of the handler towards the source. The dog is communicating a find to the handler and a rally of the pack to the find. In this situation, an active trained indication or bark would get the attention of the handler quickly while the dog stays in the find position to prevent the loss of the scent. If the dog was hunting game, then the stand and freeze position would not only locate the game but would also prevent it from running away.

During searching for a targeted scent source, the dog may do a quick head turn towards scent while in motion. The dog continues forward movement with the search pattern however the scent is not as strong at this stage. The head turn is ever so slight and goes almost unnoticed by observers if observational skills are weak or if one simply does not know to look for it. The head turn will indicate the direction the dog smells the source. A dog may work along a brush line and frequently turn towards the scent further away in the woods, however the big head turn and body realignment will happen when the dog narrows down the scent to a saturated area.

A freeze and stare is a stationary head position directed towards the scent source. The body posture is tense and the tail position is locked as the dog zeros in on the odor. It is difficult to break the focus of the dog at this time. This frequently happens in buildings, rubble, and vehicle searches.

If the scent is weak and on the periphery due to wind movement, the dog will follow the scent until it diminishes enough to determine it does not continue in that direction. When the dog turns and moves to another area it is said to give a "negative" indicating scent is not as strong in the previous direction of work. The head comes up and the dog turns to another direction to try to find the scent. The dog will begin to cast by moving in several directions and scenting the wind, vegetation, and ground in an attempt to locate a stronger source of scent.

Up: Head is higher in relation to the shoulders and body. The angle between shoulders and head ranges between 0 to 90+ degrees depending on the flexibility of the dog.

Down: Head is lower in relation to shoulders and body. The angle between the shoulders and the head ranges between 0 to 90+ degrees depending on flexibility of dog.

Straight: Head and shoulders are on the same horizontal plane. A line can be followed from body of dog to the head.

Turned in: Head is turned in towards something (object or scent). Eye contact is with object or in the general direction of the object or scent.

Turned away: Head is turned away from something (object or scent). Eye contact is usually slowly drawn away while or after head is turned.

Mouth/Nose: Olfactory senses obtain information via these routes. Canines receive more scent information when breathing is through a closed nose and mouth. This could possibly be an indicator of the dog's focus.

Sniffing: Breathing through nose that may be long deep sniffing or shorter and more shallow. Sniffing will be connected to head position and environmental landmarks. Note intensity and changes in intensity.

Panting: Heavy breathing through mouth. When a dog is hot and/or thirsty panting through mouth occurs. This is a physiological response to an environmental or physical stress. Panting can also be a response to a psychological stress. Panting is typically accompanied by some degree of drooling.

Drooling: Saliva drips from mouth. Drooling is common in many breeds as a physiological response to hunger, heat, and excitement. In some dogs panting can also be a physiological response to a psychological stress.

Blow Out/Snort: Clearing the nostrils by a forceful, sometimes noisy, double-barreled exhalation. This is seen frequently when working in dry, dusty environments or when the animal is over saturated with scents.

Biting: Canine uses teeth to contact something. Not a bite intended to harm but a bite to obtain scent/taste information. Biting may occur with foliage, air, and water when dog tastes scent. Note what the dog was biting.

Eating: Dog ingests something. Need to indicate what was eaten. Canine may or may not chew object first.

Lick Intention: An extension and flicking of the tongue between the lips or a licking motion performed at a distance too great to reach its intended target. This may manifest as a single small flick for several movements of almost the full length of the tongue. The nose is seen in the air as the tongue performs the licking motion.

Licking: Dog uses tongue to lick an object. This is done frequently at foliage, air, and water when the dog is in scent.

Ear Position: Refers to the direction a canine's ears are rotated in relation to the front of the canine's head and, when possible, the location of the structure of the ear in relation to the canine's head. This is an indicator of the direction of audible information. Ear position also indicates where the dog is expecting to hear audible information (i.e. feedback) from the handler. Position may indicate internal "mood" of the dog or a signal of behaviors to come. The potential for ear position is dependent on breed and physiological structure of K-9.

Turned Forward: Ears rotated to face the direction K-9 is facing. Structure of ear is still perk and

Buzzards and Butterflies

raised.

Turned Back: Ears are rotated away from the direction K9 is facing. Structure of ear is still perked and raised.

Forward: Ear structure is leaned forward. Typically ears are rotated forward.

Back: Ear structure is leaned back towards the top of the head. Typically ears are rotated forward. This is usually an indicator that the dog is uncomfortable and defensive aggression may follow.

Cocked: Ears are not facing or rotated in the same direction. This appears as an inquisitive look. It is frequently seen after the dog hears an unfamiliar sound or is unsure about the direction the sound came from.

Close and High: Ears facing forward, close together and positioned high on head. This is seen when the animal is nearing the "target" or when they have located a very saturated scent area.

Tail Position: Refers to the level of the tail in relation to the canine's body. The tail is an indicator of canine focus. Position may indicate internal "mood" or a signal of behaviors to come. The potential for and interpretation of tail position is dependent upon breed and physiological structure of the dog.

Straight: Tail and body are on the same horizontal plane. A line can be followed from the body to the tail.

Down X Degrees: The body is higher in relation to the tail. The angle between the tail and body ranges between 0 to 90 degrees.

Between Legs: The angle between the tail and body is positioned downward 90 degrees. Tail set just above or between the back hocks of the dog

Under Belly: The tail is tucked under the body between the rear legs and typically contacting belly. This may be a possible indicator that the dog is uneasy, stressed, or fearful of some environmental factor.

Up X degrees: Tail is higher in relation to body. Angle between tail and body ranges between 0 to 90 degrees.

Straight Up: Angle between tail and body is upward 90 degrees. Tail is erect and straight.

Over Back: Tail wrapped over body, typically contacting back.

Wagging: Description may elaborate on types, speed, and the intensity of the wagging.

Feet/legs: Refers to the position of the extremities in relation to the canine body. The position of feet and legs can indicate interest, injury, or other motivators.

Pointing: One front foot is lifted, back legs are staggered slightly, body slightly leaning forward, tail typically straight or slightly lowered. Frequently seen in setters, spaniels, retrievers, and other sporting breeds.

Lifting: Any of the feet is off of the ground. This behavior can be an indicator of injury, insecurity over unfamiliar surface, or general discomfort. Not the same as leg lifting for urination behavior; not accompanied by urination.

Pawing: Using front feet to contact an item or area with little pressure. The main point of contact is with bottom fleshy part of paw. Typically only one front foot is used. May be done to lift scent or unbury potential scents.

Digging: Using front feet to contact substrate with enough pressure to remove layers. The main point of contact is with nails and front area of paw. Typically both front feet are used. Some K9's even use back feet.

Marking Behaviors: Physiological relief behaviors can be controlled by a K9 and utilized to mark an area or object for many potential reasons. These behaviors are often used by animals to communicate with each other but can also be used to communicate back to themselves.

Defecating: Fecal material may indicate many things about the condition of an animal. The strong smell may be used as a marker.

Urinating: This behavior may be further broken down into squatting (all four feet on the ground) and leg lifting (one leg lifted and urine directed onto an object or area). Furthermore the quantity released when urinating may indicate the purpose of this behavior, smaller quantities indicate marking behavior while larger quantities indicate relief behavior. The specifics of this behavior also vary based on the sex of the K9.

Buzzards and Butterflies

Scent Scratching: Performed after urination and/or defecation. Canine uses feet to scratch/kick area next to urination or defecation. May be done to spread scent or to cover scent depending on direction of scratching in relation to scent.

Scent Rolling: A strong-smelling odor will elicit a scent roll where the dog bends at the knee, turns its shoulders and lowers its forequarters to the ground rubbing first its cheeks and then its neck on the odor. The dog may stand and repeat the process with the other cheek or it may lower itself to the flanks and on its back.

Vocalization: Different breeds of K9 have varying ranges of ability to make noise. Many animals use noise as a form of communication between individuals.

Bark: This vocalization comes in many volumes, tones, pitch, etc., depending upon the K9. Preferred indication bark is a crisp, clear, full bark. Mouth of canine moves during bark and each movement should emit a full complete sound.

Air Bark: Same as regular bark but not at full volume for duration of bark action. A more breathy air filled noise. Usually seen in early stages of training bark alert, or when dog is unsure what is desired from it. The teeth may click together as the dog makes the air bark. In wolves the "woof" is used as an alarm call to the other pack members that there is danger and they all leave the area quickly.

Whine: A long higher pitched noise accompanied by a sighing breath. Used to express frustration, desire for attention, or want for something.

Whimper: A lower pitched whine with breaks in continuation of noise. A bouncy whine-like noise.

Howl: A long drawn out tonal vocalization.

Yip: A quick high-pitched vocalization, not to be confused with yelp. Slightly faster, shorter and more monotone than the yelp. Occurs with some canines as they reach the fringes of the target scent source. May be a form of communication to the handler or other pack members, possibly acts as a rally call.

Yelp: A quick, typically high-pitched vocalization whose pitch tends to slide upwards in tone. Usually in response to a painful stimulus.

Growl: A low pitched, rumbling vocalization. Possibly accompanied by lip curl or bared teeth. Usually a signal the canine is upset with something or a fear response. A signal of canine boundaries.

Movement: **The stride, speed, and ground covered by a K9 will depend on the internal and external environment. Stride and speed can communicate an animals' excitement level, interest, health, focus and much more.**

Still: No movement. Similar to stand except legs may not be directly under body of K9.

K9 Handler Tom Hathcock
Greater Houston Search Dogs

Walk: Steady stride, slowest natural gait.

Jog/Trot: A slightly fast pace with a minimum of 2 feet on the ground at a time. A slightly bouncy movement.

Run: Front legs move in unison with each other and off beat of back legs that move in unison of each other. Fastest stride

Pounce: Leaping onto something with front feet out and a bouncy stride. Can end with a front stretch behavior. Tends to have a playful experience.

Pacing: Walking the same region of space in a repeated pattern. This is a form of repetitive stereotypic stress behavior. This behavior can indicate frustration, stress, decision-making, problem solving, boredom, or many other possible things depending on K9 and situation.

Circle: To walk around an object. The dog moves in a circle with a variable radius as it works an area where scent has collected or "pooled". The dog will work the edges of the scent pool first and define where the scent ends before working in closer to the strongest scent source. The dog will also circle when attempting to determine a location to defecate or lay down.

Buzzards and Butterflies

Quartering: To move back and forth in a "V" pattern narrowing toward the target scent source. This movement is referred to as a search pattern.

Observation Jump: A jump straight up with legs touching an object or forelegs folded. The body is perpendicular to the ground. This may be in an attempt to see over an object or to locate scent. Nose is usually at an angle in the air. This is seen when scent has collected on an object such as a tree, building, or even a street sign. The dog will jump up on several trees or obstacles in the area if the scent has collected on objects. The scent source may be upwind of the location of the observation jump. The jump is also noted when a dog is in thick vegetation and it attempts to jump up in a bouncy stride in the air to gather scent.

Shake Off: The body appears to oscillate vigorously on its longitudinal axis. It appears to start at the head and exits the tail. This is seen when the animal shakes off water. The dog will also demonstrate the shake off when it has lost scent or when the nose is over saturated with extraneous scent and not the target scent source. This is seen frequently in dry dusty environments in addition to a "blow-out".

Focus at Handler: the canine will perform many of the behaviors already described in an attempt to interact with the handler or get their attention. A behavior may have a different meaning when done in close proximity to the handler.

Stare: Dog will stare at the handler either at a distance or will return to the handler and gain eye contact then move off in the direction of the scent source. This behavior may be repeated several times as the dog attempts to gain the attention of the handler.

Nudge: The dog returns to the handler and gives a nose touch with pressure against the handler's body to gain attention. May be a component of the re-find indicator behavior.

Jump: The dog will jump on the handler with the paws making contact with the handler and the body position perpendicular to the ground. Typically contact is made, but this can depend on the canine. May be a component of the re-find indicator behavior.

Vocalize: The dog will give various vocalizations to gain attention from the handler. These may include air barks, strong barks, whine, whimper, or soft woof. The distance from the handler when vocalization occurs is variable and may be a trained indication for the particular dog. Can be a useful trained indication.

This comprehensive listing of canine behaviors offers the handler an insight into dog behavior through observable actions. It is the communication that creates the canine-handler bond that in turn forms the optimum dog team. A wise handler is in tune to the canine and all of his methods of communication, including these observable actions.

"Asymmetric tail-wagging responses by dogs to different emotive stimuli." "Current Biology" (Volume 17, Issue 6, 20 March 2007, Pages R199-R201). Giorgio Vallortigara, a neuroscientist at the University of Trieste in Italy, and two veterinarians, Angelo Quaranta and Marcello Siniscalchi, at the University of Bari, also in Italy.

The Dog Mind and Heart

One of the controversial topics in the search and rescue dog world is whether the dog can "think" and "feel". Does the dog respond to the handler in a rote manner simply for the reward? Can a dog think about what he is doing and make a conscious choice to do what the handler is asking him to do (for whatever reason)? Will the dog actually "think" and adapt his method of search for the conditions if need be? Does the SAR dog "feel" something when the victim is located? Is he happy? If the dog feels, is he likewise "sad" when the victim is deceased, hurt or injured in some way? Or is the dog reacting to the behaviors and feelings of the handler? Are the personal emotions of the handler affecting the dog? Does it truly travel down the leash?

Interestingly, most research papers on the topic do not study "whether" dogs have emotions but what effects, neurochemically or hormonally, these emotions have upon the working behavior. It is generally accepted that some veterinarians use psychotropic medications on some dogs with varying mental disorders such as extreme anxiety. These drugs seem to control those anxious behaviors. Although few research studies document canine emotions, the lack of a study does not discount their existence. In Darwin's *Decent of Man*, he demonstrated that although some may like to think that the lower animals do not have intellect, emotions, love, memory and other psychological features of man, they *are* present in the lower animals.

We know that dogs do not have a neocortex and therefore are not capable of higher language and mathematics skills. However, they do possess the rest of the brain structures that create emotions in humans. All vertebrates share these same brain functions. We know that dogs feel pain. The more we learn about animal behavior, the more there is to learn.

Dogs are very in tune to *our* body language. However, whether the dog is aversive or not to cadaver scent has nothing to do with our personal emotions or body language. There are some dogs that will immediately turn their heads away from the scent source or refuse to approach a scent source regardless of the encouragement of the handler. This dog is not a good choice for HRD work.

Most experienced handlers will acknowledge that SAR dogs can reason. They can make a decision based upon the environment and scenario. It is easy to observe in most training sessions. With observation we continue to learn more about a dogs capabilities and makeup. Expressions of interest, concern, fear, caution, happiness, aversiveness and many other "feelings" and "behaviors" are present in dogs.

HRD handlers who have worked known areas of mass destruction, with hundreds of bodies dying or dead, or where hundreds have laid for a period of time before burial, have observed behaviors in their dogs not seen in other conditions. One handler described working a known civil war battleground where over 600 men were documented to have been killed. The canine showed interest from several hundred feet away, heading to the central part of the killing field, thrashed her head back and forth akin to an elephant thrashing his trunk back and forth. The head went down, concrete alerts were observed, and the thrashing continued until the handler took the dog out of the area. Here in this location hundreds of men bled, possibly more than any other place in the United States. This dog acknowledged the blood soaked ground. Of course we realize the dog did not know the history of this location. The handler did not cue these behaviors. These behaviors were not learned or regurgitated for a reward. These were behaviors indicating a canine in stress that exhibited unusual behaviors, quite unlike any other HRD training to date. Regardless of the reason for the behaviors or what the dog was alerting *on*, the handler interpreted the behavior as the canine being extremely uncomfortable, in distress, and acting unlike anytime in the past. What did the canine sense? She can't tell us with her words. She showed us with her body language. Dogs respond in the moment to their physical surroundings, available resources, and social pressures and it is up to us to interpret what they are attempting to communicate.

We ask, "What *can* a dog learn to do?" We constantly raise the expectation of what we think they can do and discover that dogs are capable of learning a great deal more than originally thought. Dogs are capable of using that knowledge to interact with humans in helpful, meaningful ways. Only recently have animal behaviorists begun to explore dog intelligence and behaviors. Quite believably, dogs have intelligence. More and more studies are exploring both canine intellect and emotions. The near future will hold scientific answers to many of these age-old questions.

"Scientists, veterinarians, and dog-owners have long questioned the relationship between man and his best friend. Even philosophers have ventured opinions on the idea: Plato described dogs as "lovers of learning" and Voltaire refuted Descartes' theory that dogs were merely unintelligent machines. The idea that dogs feel emotions, specifically love, is debatable. Though older schools of scientific thought refuted the notion that dogs had human-like feelings, some researchers today believe the subject deserves more attention" such as Fred Metzger, Pennsylvania State University guest lecturer and veterinarian. He says, "All mammals, including dogs, have a "pleasure center" in their brains that is stimulated by dopamine, the chemical that regulates feelings of happiness. For example, when a dog is playing fetch, dopamine is released in the pleasure center and the dog is "happy." Since humans have similar brain chemistry, can we assume that dogs and humans are much more alike emotionally than previously thought?"

While heated debates continue to rage among dog lovers, time and research will find the answer to these questions. Research and interest in understanding the canine intellect and emotions will only enhance our search skills.

Reactions to Violent Death

Each dog is different. While some are adept at smaller quantities, when an entire body is present in a search scene, things change. Some dogs will continue to find and alert on larger quantities in the same manner they do with smaller quantities. However, many will react in totally different ways with a whole body or one that is in a more advanced stage of decomposition. Some will approach but not enter the *zone* of the hottest scent. They will not narrow down the source to the same degree that they do with disarticulated or smaller scent sources. Some will not get within 100 feet of a severely decomposed body but will *slap or touch* the paw at a skeleton. Each handler needs to experience varying degrees of decomposition in order to fully understand how their dog will react. With over 400 compounds formed during the decomposition process (as per Dr. William Bass of the Tennessee Body Farm), handlers can hardly prepare for each and every stage of decomposition. They can, however, expose the dog to as many of these varying stages as possible.

Do dogs react to danger? Border collies are known for their herding capabilities and many will not hesitate to apply those skills around young children should the small child attempt to enter a dangerous area. Handlers have experienced these heightened protective behaviors in various situations including other types of danger as well. Many have experienced the attention from a dog when the handler cries or is distraught. Their attentive behavior wanes when the depression or sadness subsides. Handlers observe dogs reasoning as they work through and solve scent problems.

Handlers have related extraordinary canine reactions to crime scenes involving a violent death. When a dog was brought to a murder scene within hours of the murder, the handler described a heightened anxiety where the canine hair stood on end like he had been "in a light socket." The dog began yelping. The handler interpreted this as specific to a violent death scene. The same behavior has since been repeated in additional violent death locations.

Scientifically, the body decomposes dependent upon the environment. Some are quite odorous and others not so much based upon heat and humidity. Some become mummified. All produce a chemical smell somewhat similar based upon intestinal bacteria, fat and proteins. When violent death occurs, the scent picture may be altered to add hormones and adrenalin, and other animal activity that may enter an open wound (such as gunshot or injury). Although a death such as a fall might be classified as natural, it would also produce the fear scent like a homicide. Moisture may also lead to the formation of adipocere as the fat decomposes. This produces a more intense and stronger scent picture.

Handlers have had experiences with canine reactions to violent death that are different from known natural death scenarios. It seems some canine's react differently to natural/suicide deaths than known homicide deaths. Heightened behaviors such as belly crawls, moans, elbow rocking and other behaviors demonstrate a stronger reaction to violent death scenes, with or without *the body* present. Sometimes this behavior will occur several years after the fact. Does fear scent remain? Does violence or evil have a scent of its own? Record your observations. Some dogs have been known to literally drag their owners away from the scene of a violent homicide. Later information confirms that the death had, in fact, occurred at the site. In one scene, a horrific crime occurred at that site involving dismembering a body. Scent lingers. Violent death scent lingers. Observe the dog. Record the data. Continue to study the intense relationship between certain canine behaviors and violent death scenes.

Take careful note of the behavior of dogs in a human remains/cadaver crime scenes in wilderness areas as the reaction may instead be to a predator in the vicinity such as a bear or deer. Scat containing human remains can, at first glance, appear to be animal. Do not discount the action of your dog too quickly. A recent training demonstrated a similar scenario when a team dog alerted on an apparent location with nothing seemingly *there*. Upon closer inspection, a drop of blood was evident from a fellow team member who had scratched himself earlier. The behavior may be associated with the location or place where the death occurred, forensic evidence, or predator involvement. It is sometimes hard to determine at that precise moment but future information confirms or denies suspicions.

Another situation worth noting involves the canine coming face to face with certain people, particularly people who "have killed" or have extreme mental disorders. Do not discount the behavior or reaction of your dog. A seemingly calm and thoroughly tested and certified therapy dog may react totally different to teenagers diagnosed with conduct disorder or other illnesses. Observe and continue to document unusual and unexplained situations.

K9 Max in training, Handler, Wendy Long, BSAR, NC

5

Land Search

Outline
Introduction
Training Materials - Source Samples
Collecting Scent - Nancy Culberson
Concrete Samples
Storage of Scent Sources
Release Forms
General Guidelines in HRD Training
Training Scenarios - Jim Delbridge
Proofing - Laura Rathe
Search Strategies
Noninvasive Techniques to Locate Graves
Buried Searches
Avalanche Searches - Carol Sanner, Kim Gilmore
Avalanche Training-A Primer - Carol Sanner
Avalanche Search Strategies
Avalanche Dog Handlers Rescue Pack
Mountain Searches - Kim Gilmore
Disaster Searches
Building Searches
NIMs Compliant Human Remains Detection Training Criteria
Flankers Guide

Introduction

Case law requires that testimony by a search and rescue dog handler be based upon the fact that the dog is trained, certified and reliable. These three guiding factors define what the industry standard shall be in terms of documentation of training activities. All handlers should keep a written record of SAR training. At a minimum, the records should include a description of the types of training activities and frequency of training. Various formats of documentation have been designed by individuals including written and computer models. Some examples of appropriate forms are included in the appendix. (Bound Log Books are also available from this author at www.lulu.com/spaniels).

Buzzards and Butterflies

Training Records must document information on training, certification and reliability of the dog. All three are crucial to assessing the dogs' reliability. The initial training and maintenance should be included in the records. Law enforcement training recommends about 200-400 hours of initial training and about 4 hours a week of maintenance training.

Training logs should contain date and total training time, the training scenario, length, age, depth of find, etc. It should also document the success of the training session and goals of future training sessions. No dog is perfect; therefore remedial activities are also documented in addition to the successful training activities.

Certification tests of the dog/handler team should be documented. Each certification should be associated with a standard and the evaluator's training and experience. Reliability should be documented including both training and mission experience.

Training Materials - Source Samples

HRD handlers should check local, state and federal statutes that may apply to storage and training activities involving human remains. Your local law enforcement agency, coroner, or district attorney is a good source of information and can guide a handler in the proper procurement, storage and use of training materials. Laws vary in each area and country. The handler is responsible for following local, state and federal regulations. Some countries do not allow the use of human remains for search and rescue dog training purposes. Become knowledgeable about what is required or allowed in your area. More specifics on the law are included in the chapter on HRD and the Law.

For those countries and area that DO allow the possession of human remains for training purposes, a wide variety of sources provide the handler with scent source samples. Among those are blood (team members are great sources), bone (www.boneroom.com), teeth (your local dentist), placenta, fluid soaked towels and dressings (local EMS, hospitals, coroners, etc.), and dirt (where a body has laid for a period of time).

Pseudo scent sources can be purchased which chemically mimic the decomposition process. There are also "drowning" pseudo scents that provide the scent picture of a drowning (www.sigmaaldrich.com). The drowned victim scent provides a reliable scent source for 30-45 minutes, in still or running water at depths of 1-12 feet. Additional pseudo scents include products that provide scent pictures for early detection or below 0 degrees centigrade to post-putrification detection. These pseudo scents are rated from an irritant to toxic hazardous materials and should be handled safely, as with all HRD source samples.

Some formulas of pseudo scents describe their safety and risk factors as: toxic if swallowed, irritating to the skin, danger of very serious irreversible effects, limited evidence of carcinogenic effect, risk of serious damage to eyes, may cause sensitization by skin contact, risk of explosion if heated under confinement, and may cause cancer. Handlers should take extra care to ensure that dogs do not come in contact with or ingest any pseudo scent product.

Collecting Scent

Handlers may collect scent using standard and accepted practices. When embarking on a search, there are many cases when the handler or command staff is uncertain of the condition of the missing person. Those handlers that have scent specific (live find) dogs will need to collect a scent article. There are protocols that help to ensure a relatively "clean" scent article. In all cases, handlers should use personal protective devices such as rubber gloves and if needed, face masks and goggles. With the risk of communicable disease, personal safety practices are necessary. The same holds true of handling cadaver-training aids. Person protective devices (gloves) are always required and all samples should be labeled appropriately.

In addition, HRD handlers are often placed in a situation where they need to collect samples or scent to be used in training at a later time. The same basic scent collection techniques can apply to preserving human remains. Examples of scent collection items which might be used for HRD training at a later time include dirt which was underneath the body of a deceased person for some period of time, towels or other clothing known to have been in contact with a deceased person, or gauze and other medical supplies.

Nancy Culberson, of the North Carolina Search and Rescue Dogs Association, has written a helpful description of scent collection techniques that allow for a relatively pure scent collection in the field.

Scent Article Collection Method

By Nancy Culberson
NC Search and Rescue Dogs Association
K9 Tasha

The "Scent Article Collection Bag" contains the items a handler may need to collect or make a scent article. It contains freezer bags, gauze pads, gloves, and a marker to record information *about the collection* of the scent article.

The label on a 2-gallon freezer bag describes the materials contained inside:

> **Scent Article Collection Bag**
> Contains:
> 2 Pairs latex gloves
> 5 Gauze pads
> 5 Pint size freezer bags
> 2 Quart size freezer bags
> 1 Gallon size freezer bag
> 1 permanent marker

The following label is placed on the pint size bag to identify the collected scent article.

```
Subject: _____
    Date: _____   Time: _____
    Collector: _____

Known contaminates:

Article used for scent:

Where article was obtained:
```

How to Use the Collection Bag

1. Open the collection bag and remove the glove bag (which is taped near top of bag to help reduce contamination).
2. Put on gloves. (Use the bag they came out of for trash).
3. Remove gallon size freezer bag.
4. Take out a quart size bag containing the gauze pads.
5. Place gauze pads on/in subject's scent article.
6. While gauze pads are absorbing scent, take out quart size bag of pint size freezer bags.
7. From the gallon bag, take out the permanent marker.
8. Using the marker, complete the label on the pint size bags.
9. After filling out labels, place the gauze scent articles inside the pint bags.
10. Place the pint bags inside the gallon bag to give to the search commander.

If one prefers to take the original scent article to the search commander (in case more scent articles need to be created), place it in the 2-gallon Scent Article Collection bag. Document on the outside of the bag all the information that was written on the pint size bags.

Reminders and Suggestions Related to Scent Articles

- To reduce contamination, only one person (with gloves on) should be reaching into the bag that contains scent article bags. It's preferable if the person is command staff and not going into the field on the search. This minimizes some problems with scent contamination.

- The K9 handler should consider re-bagging the article (if they were not the original collector). This helps to reduce scent transfer from the collector and the person distributing the scent article bags.

- NEVER handle a subjects article with your bare hands. Always wear clean gloves and when possible use a coat hanger/tongs/tweezers to pick up the article.

- NEVER use green, black, or white garbage bags to collect or store scent articles, they are usually chemically treated to kill/control odors. Use clean, clear freezer bags when possible.

- If possible, the scent article should be used only once since the article will now have *minute* amounts of that "user" on the scent article, regardless of precautions used.

- Maintain the integrity of "clean bags" until they are used. Bags stored in the trunk of a police vehicle may have already been in contact with other evidence from previous cases or other evidence. That other evidence may be something that came in physical contact with the bags, or stored within proximity to "scent".

- Maintain the integrity of the scent article through chain of custody forms. Label the item with directions for proper handling (i.e. keep the bag sealed, do not touch the enclosed items, do not store in proximity to other evidence, etc.). Whether or not documentation of the chain is continued, it indirectly communicates the importance to do so. (Example: Rec'd by Lt. John Doe, Ace County Sheriff's Dept, IC @ Lake - - -, 1-12-08, 2 pm.)

- Think, think, think about possible cross-contaminations while collecting scent articles.
  - Clothes hampers usually contain multiple family members scent.
  - If collecting scent from a bed, ask if the subject was the only one to *ever* sleep there.
  - Dressers and clothes hung in closets– the clothes have usually been washed.
  - Socks could have been worn around the house, picking up other household members scent.
  - When collecting from a vehicle, consider whether the local authorities entered the vehicle? Sat down in the vehicle? What did they touch? Who else entered the vehicle? Sometimes it's a good idea to have anyone who entered the vehicle present for the handler and K9 so the dog can eliminate their scent from the scent picture.

Methods of Collecting Scent

1. *Direct* – Letting the K9 smell the subjects' article/source directly. Direct scenting poses the greatest risk of contaminating or destroying forensic evidence that may be needed later in the investigation.

2. *Swiping* – Wiping the surface of the article with a sterile gauze pad and transferring the human scent from the source to the pad. The pad is then placed in a bag and later used by the K9 handler to scent their K9. Unfortunately this method can remove or contaminate fingerprints, DNA, or trace evidence.

3. *Absorption/passive transfer* – Placing a sterile gauze pad on the surface or inside the article/source (something that was directly next to the subject skin is best). The pad is left in place for 10 to 20 minutes. Some handlers use the collection baggie to make a mock tent

over the article to help condense/trap the scent. The pad is then placed inside a freezer bag for later use. This method is more time consuming.

Regardless of the safety and care a handler takes, contamination happens. It is sometimes impossible to avoid, but one can greatly reduce it by employing careful, practiced strategies.

Concrete Samples

Occasionally HRD missions include the possibility of burial in or under concrete. Handlers can prepare training samples of concrete by using paper cups with small samples imbedded in the cup of concrete. Another item that can be used is a concrete block, filling in the openings with the sample and additional concrete; however, these are heavy and cumbersome to transport. Smaller concrete samples are more convenient to hide and transport to various locations. A variety of source materials should be used to provide a wide array of sampling of mediums as well as mixtures of HRD samples.

Some handlers will use water, which has had an HR sample soaking in it, and then removed to mix the concrete. Rebar can be bent to create a handle and samples can be made in various size but need to be small enough for easy transport. Rebar handles also allow for ropes to secure them during water training.

When searching a potential burial under concrete, consider drilling holes into the concrete to allow scent to escape. The canines can search the area before the drilling and again afterwards. This is similar to probing the ground in historic burials. All concrete is porous. However, the pores are different sizes and different shapes, thereby having different permeability properties and allowing scent to escape at varying rates. Additives like latex will also alter the properties. Since there is a point when the concrete may become water-proof or vapor-proof at some level, it is also important to know that although it may be deemed water-proof, there is no information available to determine whether it is "scent proof" and if the dog can detect odor or not. Try it and simply record the reactions of the canine.

Storage of Scent Sources

Scent tubes, such as the PVC tube pictured above work well for preparing sources for training. Holes drilled into the PVC pipe allow scent to escape. A small rope handle allows easy tossing into the brush. Multicolored tags, allow an identification system for "types" of scent samples. In addition, black PVC blends into the environment very well reducing the cueing of the handler who spots the source. When using any type of container, the handler must "proof" off of the material itself. Reserve several tubes with no source in them and store away from sample sources to avoid cross contamination.

Other types of containers include canning jars, which allow for double lids...one with holes punched in them and one to store. A variety of containers are recommended, including small cages like cricket cages, to avoid the unintentional training on type of containers. While some handlers use glass exclusively, others use a wide variety of containers. Empty spice bottles work well as do containers such as empty shampoo bottles. Opening the container to release scent is convenient. Whatever type of container is used, proof off of similar or like containers to ensure that the dog is not alerting on the container instead of the content.

Cricket cages also work well for isolating the scent sample and helps to protect them from critters in the woods. This is especially true when samples are left out in the search area overnight or for extended periods of time. Be sure to anchor those cages. They have a way of disappearing into never-never land.

The ideal storage for scent sources is a freezer and refrigerator. (It is not recommended to store materials in appliances used for human consumption.) Freezing samples preserves the samples and allows for a longer training life. Small dorm sized freezers and refrigerators purchased strictly for this purpose work well. Relatively airtight containers such as ammo boxes work well to transport and store materials as do coolers and other types of containers. Whichever type of storage system or container is selected, mark them as hazardous materials and store safely.

Some handlers prefer to keep source samples separated and document training based upon type of sample. Other handlers realize that most cases involve a combination of scent sources and maintain samples in a common storage container, often only separating bone from other samples in order to maintain an "aged" scent source. Whichever method is employed, handlers should document type of source used in training records and NO source should be taken to a search scene without the full knowledge of the search commander in order to avoid misconceptions or temptations to alter the crime scenes in any form or fashion. Under NO conditions should a handler take a scent source into the field. If the handler deems it necessary to provide the dog with a positive find for motivational purposes, care should be taken to inform appropriate command personnel and obtain permission to do so. However, it is recommended this be done back at base camp and not in the field where contamination may occur.

Scent Tube in the field.

Buzzards and Butterflies

Release Forms

When receiving scent sources from other agencies, persons or organizations, one should keep a log and documentation of the source and disposition of the source when no longer needed. Several forms are included in the appendix that may be used for these purposes.

General Guidelines in HRD Training

▶ **Vary the environment and soil conditions.** Vary the size of the search area. Remember, searches occur in all types of terrain.

Can you spot the working dog, Coyote? Marcia Koenig shared this photo showing what it is like searching for bones in the Pacific NW. When searching for bones that have been there for a long time, particularly if they have been scattered by animals, the dog needs to be right on top of them to detect scent. A detailed and methodical strategy is warranted. (Hint, look in the center of the picture, the head is not visible. It is hidden behind stumps.)

▶ **Vary the time of day** of training. Select training days with a variety of **weather conditions** and humidity levels. Scent behaves in different ways under different conditions. In extreme temperatures, search in the early morning or in the evening or nighttime. Wind tends to pick up in the evening many times, so the air scent dogs can work the problems. Trailing dogs tend to work best in early morning hours when the dew is still on the ground. Listen carefully when the wind dies down as you may actually hear the cries of that little three year old. Just ask Greater Houston Search Dogs team (Texas). He was almost two miles away hiding under a bridge.

▶ **Vary the type of problems**. Buried 2 inches, 6 inches, 12 inches, 24 inches. Hanging - 4 feet above the ground, 6 feet above the ground, 12 feet above the ground. Birds have been known to take some remains into their nests. Just because you can't see it doesn't mean it isn't there.

▶ **Vary the age** and **quantity** of the source materials, **type of containers**, and **placement** of source materials: over, under, above, below, inside, behind, underneath, hidden, plain view, etc. Recognize that bodies or parts could be contained inside various types of containers or packaging. Train with varied packaging materials. (Plastic, tarps, boxes, plastic, wood, brick, cement, etc.)

▶ **Regularly work negative areas**. Vary the length of time and size of the area that negative problems are worked. Many handlers have a tendency to work negative areas at a faster pace and for shorter periods of time than actual search conditions. Remember that your training should reflect how you plan to work a real search mission. When is the last time you worked a search for six to eight hours with no results? When is the last time you trained in a negative area for six hours? Work a negative area for an hour or more before putting the dog back into the crate in the car with "a good boy, job well done."

▶ **Break regularly**. HRD work is very demanding on the dog. It takes sustained attention, and in some types of HRD missions, very detailed work to adequately cover the area. Take breaks regularly. In some cases, every twenty minutes is not too often to take a fifteen or twenty minute break.

▶ **Training is training and testing is testing**. Under most *beginner* conditions the handler should know the location of the source sample during a training exercise. This allows the handler to observe the dog and begin to understand the K9 behaviors under certain controlled scent conditions. The handler should also know when the dog has been into the scent source. If needed, station an individual near the scent source to radio back to the handler that the dog has approached and identified the scent source. However, once trained, handlers need to expand their comfort zones and work double blind problems.

▶ **Train as You Search**. Train as you search. Wear the gear that you would normally take into the field. Take along the water, food, and canine supplies that you would normally take into the field. Practice what you will do during a real search because you will likely "search" the same way you have "trained."

▶**Work Double Blind Problems**. Once you have a certified dog, *train as you search*. Work as many ***double-blind problems*** as you do *blind ones* or *known ones*. Double-blind problems involve having someone to hide the source samples without the knowledge of the flanker or the dog handler such that the handler works the problem totally blind. In addition, the flanker does not know the location either. The handler then returns to the base camp and reports what he / she has found or

Buzzards and Butterflies

not found and will get it confirmed or not from the person who has placed the source. Double-blind problems force the handler and flanker to "watch" the dog, not each other. They increase the level of difficulty for the handler, much like a real search. They tend to bring out the stress factor for the handler, create lots of hormones and pheromones, and compel the handler to make decisions about what their dog is doing or not doing. They grow in their confidence and skill and become a more valuable handler.
(Note: Some handlers resist doing double blind problems. For quite some time it was ingrained that "training is training" and "testing is testing." This *is* true for the beginning handler. However, with more experienced handlers, in order to continue to improve the dog and handler skills, it becomes necessary to move to a higher level of competence.)

In a ***blind problem*** the dog handler does not know the location of the sources, however, the flanker does. This set up allows the handler to reward the dog at the proper time rather than attempting to decide whether the dog has in fact located the source or not. This is the time when the handler learns to recognize the changes in behavior of the dog during the problem and becomes more confident in articulating what he/she has observed in the field. Caution: the handler and flanker need to be aware of unintentional cues being given to each other. The handler will have a tendency to watch the flanker to see if there is a reaction to what the dog is doing, whether the flanker continues to follow the handler when the dog is apparently not in scent, and whether the flanker nods his/her head affirmatively or negatively. Handlers should use this type of training problem when they need to learn to read their dog, build confidence, and ready themselves for a certification test. It is not a technique that needs to be used on a regular basis by the experienced dog or handler.

Roxye Marshall and K9 Mandy search the mountains of Virginia.

When used exclusively, it creates a crutch, not confidence.

In ***known problems***, both the handler and flanker know the location of the source samples. Beginning handlers use this type of training scenario when they are learning to read their dogs, learning scent theory and search strategies, and generally preparing themselves and their dogs for certification testing. With more advanced handlers and dogs, known problems are used for motivational exercises, if needed. It is not always necessary to work blind or double blind problems, but more experienced dog teams should limit the number of *known problems.*

▶When retrieving HRD samples after a training session, do not walk behind the last dog to run the scenario with the HRD container (like your ammo box) picking up the last sample as you continue to work the area and additional problems. All you will accomplish will be to totally contaminate the entire area with more HRD scent. This is definitely *not* a best practice.

▶When working buried problems, be sure to **probe suspected negative areas first** (those areas which do not have planted samples contained in them) before you probe positive areas (those areas where you have buried samples). If your dog alerts on the probe....you have been given information. Do not discount that alert.

▶Observe the dog to determine **what his nose zone is**...in other words, a dog will leave the potential search area in order to get into a clean air zone to clear his scent receptors and then return to the area where HRD scent is located. This is a natural behavior for the dog and one in which you can observe how widespread the scent picture actually exists.

Training Scenarios

As Jim Delbridge said in a training article he wrote, "make it fun or the dog will invent his own games." The variety of training or crime scene scenarios is only limited by the creativity of the handler and trainer. You get what you train for. Train for as many scenarios as possible and vary them in some small manner each time you train.

1. Single Tooth Surface Search

Place each tooth in 3-4 inches of dead grass and totally invisible to the handler. Set up flags on each corner of the search area to provide the handler with boundaries. Place flags first regardless of the scent conditions that may occur in the search area. Be aware of possible "critters" that may move about your teeth. When the dog says the tooth is about two or three feet from where it was first placed, do not discount a gopher to have tunneled into the area and relocated the sample.

Jim Delbridge described a *Single Tooth Surface Training* with his dog Murphy. "When I worked Murphy on the last six teeth it was a miserable day (for me), strong north wind, cold, overcast. I'd forgotten my game face and went out to work Murphy very businesslike. I did all the right motions, but didn't put myself in the head of a 20-week old puppy. Murphy quickly set me straight. As Tempe did this to me from time to time, it didn't floor me, but it was a good reality check."

"Murphy didn't like the idea that I wanted to "SEE the TOOTH". He wanted the party NOW. So, twice he got his point across by picking the tooth up in his mouth and spitting it at me. There's something about an Airedale going Ptuhhh at you with a tooth flying that just cracks me up. I quickly became more the huckster at the Medicine Show and rewarded the young fellow with entertainment for his hard work."

"With the two boogers, I confirmed the problem was hard and even I was pretty sure why the problems were difficult, topography, air flows, and such...boring technical stuff. Murphy's solution to the really hard ones was to run back to the last one he'd found and re-find it quickly for another reward. Later on, he'll get told, "yea, yea, good job, we already found that one. Let's move on." At this time he gets rewarded for every find like that. My final solution to getting him to work the hard ones was to race back to those areas making a total fool of myself and acting like I'd lost something in the area. Murphy suddenly came to my aid and behold, he'd find a tooth."

Buzzards and Butterflies

"So, if your dog appears to be going through the motions rather than actively searching, you may not be so lucky to have an Airedale that likes to make its own entertainment. Instead your dog may choose to self-reward on cat poo, rabbit poo, deer skat, left over McDonalds Big Mac, ...you get the picture."

2. Indication Station

"Before I moved Murphy onto buried, we needed to solidify his indication routine without him choosing to bring me the scent source, spitting it at me, digging for it, etc. If he continues on this path and finds sources he can't get to, then he'll be tempted to dig. That could destroy evidence or ruin it if his teeth marks on a bone hide a knife cut. So, Murphy gets to do some rounds of *indication stations*. These are structures created to allow scent to travel out where Murphy can pick up on it, but hinder getting to the source itself. This style of training also forces me to begin introducing blanks to young Murphy. Six brick structures were created using some surplus bricks I had on hand. These bricks have mortar cuts on three sides, so that can also be useful for scent travel. Two of the brick structures have a suet cage in the base with human bones in them. One structure has a blank suet cage in the base. One structure will have teeth and a phalange in the groove, placed such that scent can puff out the groove on two sides. Two structures are totally blank. Near each structure are two flags (crossed for one with scent in it and one flag straight up for a blank.) As concrete material is porous and tends to absorb scent, I'll have to keep track of the bricks I've had sources in for use on future rounds."

Indication Station Set-up:

Remember that "used" concrete bricks are always considered "hot" from that point on. It may be helpful to mark them in some fashion as hot bricks. Clean, unused bricks should be placed in any type of training scenario using "hot" bricks to proof off of the bricks themselves. Placement of bricks can be any configuration...circle, square, lines, random, etc.

3. Up

Remember to train "up". Place materials four feet, six feet, nine feet, etc. up in trees and on top of roofs to determine what the dog will find. Remember that scent pools may be drifting down, or towering up leaving literally no scent down below. Practice with samples placed on top of small storage sheds or hunting tree stands. Teach the dog to look up by rewarding high and close to the source.

K9 Bailey alerts on HRD in tree.

4. Cans, Boxes, Bins

K9 Gypsy alerts on a circle of cans.

Initial imprinting and short exercises can be done with large cans arranged in a circle or other configuration. Place sample sources in two of ten cans with other types of containers in the remainder of the cans, leaving those *clean*. Dogs can be started anywhere within the circle of cans so that it is not always the 3rd or 7th can with the source sample. Vary the type of training aid used. Other similar tracks can be arranged with concrete blocks, wooden containers, plastic bins, etc. Always store the 'hot' containers separate from the 'clean' containers to avoid cross contamination.

Buzzards and Butterflies

5. Proofing and Using Concrete Samples during Training

Proofing

By Laura Rathe
K9 Charlie

I will not take you thru a step-by-step process of how to train a dog. Hopefully, you have already trained your dog and are looking for new ways to proof your partner.

Lets first talk about working with buried human remains. In working with any kind of activity, it is important to set your dog up for success each and every time. This means to pay attention to wind direction and do *not* work your dog in the heat of the day if the temps are extreme. In the beginning you will *not* bury your sources in direct sunlight.

When I train on buried sources, I want to first make sure that my dog *knows* what we are looking for. I begin with above ground sources and work into buried. First, I would lay the source on the ground, then bury the source shallow, and work into deeper buries up to 12 to18 inches. When working buried sources, start with a "jackpot." Utilize many different sources together so that your dog gets a snout full of scent. Begin with the really *stinky stuff* rather than old bones.

Once you have worked a buried source, you need to move quickly to proofing. One thing I start with is false holes. Dig up a number of holes without ever having your source in or near. Work the dog thru this area using it as a "negative". Do not direct the dog in any way, just give the dog whatever command you use for cadaver and let him begin. Use an area of about an acre…maybe five or six false holes dug throughout. This technique shows him that even though the ground is disturbed, it doesn't always mean that there is a reward that will be forthcoming. If your dog does start to dig or show interest, calmly redirect the dog and move on. Always use a clean shovel when making false disturbances; namely a shovel that was never used to remove a source. Many dogs will "hit" on grave dirt, and by utilizing a "dirty" shovel, you can inadvertently set your dog up for failure. No, your dog hasn't failed, you will believe that your dog is false alerting on fresh hole but this may not be the case at all.

Once you've worked the acre with the false holes/ground disturbances, move to another area that has two false holes as well as the source. Make sure that the source is far enough away and down wind from the false holes so the scent doesn't "drift" into your negative area. After your dog has found and alerted on the source, make sure there is a *huge* party and let him know how wonderful he is. This exercise does not have to be done each and every time you train, but it would be wise to always have a false hole or two in your training area.

Collect road kill, and other non-human sources to lie in the training area for proofing purposes. Remember to ignore these proofing sources and just redirect the dog if he shows interest in the distracter. We have been known to bury baby pigs in our training area so that each time we train, we are working a negative source.

Map the area of negatives so that you are aware when or if your dog shows interest. Everything you do in training (or missions) must be logged including training on false holes, or buried pigs. Note the canine interest/no interest as demonstrated. If your dog does show interest in the negatives, be prepared to note what you've done to correct this issue such as moving on and redirection, voice correction etc.

One of the fun things we do for demos is make some concrete aids. These are also great for water training. I had surgery a few years ago and when I came home, I saved the fluids from the drains. I used these fluids, as well as human blood that I was able to obtain and made a one-gallon concrete aid. I used these body fluids in place of water to mix the concrete to the right consistency. I poured half of the mixture into the bucket. Then, if you do have another source, go ahead and put that in at that time, cover with the rest of the concrete, place an eyebolt in the middle, and let it set for a few days. While you have concrete available, go ahead and make two or three "negative" buckets. That is, buckets of concrete that are mixed simply with water. I cannot stress enough the importance of *not* cross contaminating your positive scent sources with your negatives. Do not use the same mixing implements for both.

Once all the buckets have set (a couple of days), remove the concrete from the buckets making certain that you mark on the BOTTOM of the source bucket a big X, positive, or whatever, using a permanent marking pen. You can also imprint a large X before the concrete dries for a more permanent designation of the "hot" block. Then, you must mark the negative buckets using an O, negative, or whatever. It is extremely important that these buckets not be stored together. It is also important that you mark each bucket because we don't want your dog to learn to alert on the bucket with the scent of the marking pen. Remember that when transporting these aids, the positive aid should be in an airtight container to prevent cross contamination. These are good training/demo aids. Remember that this should only be *part* of your collection.

When using these aids for demos place the buckets in a line up (making sure that you have at least 10 ft or more between buckets and the positive aid is downwind). Always set it up yourself so that you know which bucket is the positive. Do this at home a number of times prior to doing it in front of a crowd so that when you do your demo, you can be successful and *wow* the public. I am most always asked what is in the concrete. I reply that it is human body fluids, hair or teeth. Make sure that once the dog has alerted and been rewarded for the correct bucket and then turn the sources over and show the Xs and the Os. I can't stress enough that you *must* know which bucket is the positive. Remember; always set your dog up for success, especially in public.

The concrete source sample works well for your water training. That is the reason for the eyebolt. Clip a rope to the eyebolt and it creates a water training aid. You can sink these gallon aids to a depth of 50 + ft. The dogs do not have a problem locating this type of training aid. Have fun and experiment. (Hint: These make great gifts for your SAR friends).

Small concrete aids can be made using plastic type containers. Use these for training when you don't have time to lug around all your training aids. Again, be sure you keep the "hot" source separate from the negative source samples. If you use these concrete aids in wilderness training, you should also use the negative aids. Do this often enough so that dog does not learn to alert on concrete.

Buzzards and Butterflies

Do not use the negatives for water searching. Remember, that even if you don't touch something with your hands, your scent is going to collect on the aid. Your scent comes off your body, not just your hands.

Laura Rathe, K9 Charlie controlled exposure to whole body.

Search Strategies

▶ Buried Searches

Searches for buried subjects are often planned in advance. One technique is a tactic using "lanes." Depending upon the size of the search area, it may be helpful to create a six to ten-foot "lane" and work the dog in a very methodical manner to cover the search segment. Buried searches are more labor intensive and should be conducted in a more deliberate method.

Mickey Januszkiewicz and K9 Abby, assisted by Shelley Wood, search a colonial plantation cemetery.
South Carolina Search Dogs, Inc. and Brunswick Search and Rescue, NC.

Depending upon the size of the search area, probes can be used to allow the ground to breathe. One technique is to probe the ground directly in front of you, directly to your right, then to your left. Then take one tally step forward and repeat this process. If several individuals are lined up in a row and advance in the same direction, areas can be probed to ensure that no more than a six-foot area is left undisturbed. Have caution tape available to mark any areas that obviously contain a "void" when probing. The *prober* will know it is a void when the forestry probe enters the ground extremely easy and sinks into the ground, many times up to the handle with little or no effort. Mark these areas with caution or flagging tape. This allows the handler to be sure to cover that section thoroughly when working the dog. Allow the ground to breathe for at least 30 minutes. Most often, this is a good time to go get a sandwich.

Another *breathing* technique is to pound wooden stakes into the ground in a spacing that is no more than six feet apart. The stakes should NOT be painted or sealed in any manner. The raw wood will absorb any scent underground and channel it to the surface. It is helpful to put in the stakes the day prior to working the search area. Stakes should be put at least six inches into the ground. Deeper is better. Again, obvious voids should be marked with flagging or caution tape.

Now it is time for the dog to work the area. Some handlers prefer to work smaller lanes on lead. These handlers work lanes in a very orderly way to cover all areas thoroughly. Lanes remain no more than ten feet wide. Others work the dogs off lead and allow the dog to explore the entire search area often indicating on the strongest scent pools first. The handler needs to be in tune to what area has been searched and what areas has just been a "drive by." The handler can re-direct the dog to those drive-by areas at some point before completing the search area. Each time the dog alerts, a construction flag or other marking system is used to identify a possible burial site. At this time, there is no thought or process to identifying graves or sites. The handler is simply identifying what the dog has done and marking areas of interest or alert.

Buzzards and Butterflies

Jim Ware and K9 Storm identify another possible site for a slave burial.

It is helpful to work dogs in short rotations when working ancient or very old burials. Burials require very intense "smelling" by the dog and it can quickly become overpowering to the canine olfactory system. Canine rotations are dependent upon the working time of each dog. Some dogs will need to be rotated out after 15 to 20 minutes. Others can work a bit longer before being rotated out. With four dogs working the same small area, such as a colonial cemetery, a 15 minutes rotation allows each dog to work 15 minutes and have a 45-minute break.

In addition to planned rotations, the dog may apprise the handler of his need for a break. Watch for the dog to voluntarily leave the search area and then return to the search area. During this time, he has cleared out his nose and might do "a re-start." A re-start is when the dog shakes his entire body, shaking off the old and starting anew. This is one way the dog can clear out the old scent (which may be overpowering or extremely dense). HRD dogs should have plenty of water breaks, to moisten the nasal passages. This is one tool they use to help them work multiple burial sites. Note that there is a difference between strategies used for "one" burial versus a cemetery or multiple burials. Those planning to work historical sites or multiple burials should seek out someone experienced in this discipline, as it requires a keen observation of the dog's behavior. As always, the success of the canine team is dependent upon the soil composition and environmental conditions, not necessarily the age of the buried victim. (Age: amount of time buried.) There has been documentation of burial sites being located that are over 200 hundred years old and prehistoric Indian burial sites are still being discovered.

After the dogs have rotated through the area several times each, enter the search area and remove all negative stakes that do not seem to be associated with an alert of the dog. Then, have all dog handlers meet to determine which stakes are likely related to one potential site. In other words, if two or more flags (indicating an alert or hit by the dog) are in very close proximity, it may be determined that they indicate the same site and not two or more graves. Consolidate these. After consolidation, pound a wooden stake into each potential site and number them. Site 1, site 2, etc. Take a GPS coordinate for each site and record in your logs. Draw a sketch of the entire search area indicating approximate layout of each site. After drawing the sites, sometimes it becomes apparent that there are rows or some other orderly burial pattern. In other cases, there is no pattern and a random burial layout seems likely. Most slave cemeteries were random layouts.

Bonnie Laidlaw and K9 Aika work a Colonial Cemetery.
South Carolina Search Dogs, Inc.

After completion of the search area, indicate the outer limits of the search area by noting the GPS coordinates of the four corners of the search area. This helps to document the specific area that was searched in case it becomes necessary to return to the area to search a larger area. In addition, it is helpful to flag each of the four corners of the outer limits of the search area. Upon returning home, complete a search report identifying all the coordinates and findings.

Soil conditions in many areas of California make grave searching very challenging because of the adobe clay. In winter, this heavy clay soil becomes saturated with water trapping the fragile scent; and in summer, the clay soil becomes very hard creating different problems. Training the dogs is only part of the challenge of this work, the handler is also learning about different kinds of soils, historical cemeteries, history, growth rates of trees and plants to name a few.

Noninvasive Techniques to Locate Graves

The challenge of finding a grave using noninvasive methods - that is, to investigate without digging, using only geophysical, aerial photography and other remote sensing methods as they apply to the identification, evaluation, conservation, and protection of archaeological resources across this nation can also involve using dogs. In addition to ground penetrating radar, electromagnetic induction, DC electrical resistivity, aerial surveillance, laser imaging, and infrared imaging, the HRD canine rounds out the resource list. In more than one search the dog has confirmed alerts on areas very close to locations identified by magnetometer surveys and ground-penetrating radar.

Buzzards and Butterflies

Sometimes the area of alert by the dog is not exactly *on* the burial location. Even with multiple dogs alerting on a specific location, the body may be located 5- 10 feet or more away from the alert area. Various reasons account for this variation in alerts. The alert may be "downhill" from the spot of the murder or burial. Scent travels much like gasses or liquids and the decomposed human body scent travels downhill with rainwater or snow runoff. When the surface nearby slopes from the burial site, the strongest scent source may be somewhat away from the actual body. In one situation a murder occurred with the body recovered within 48 hours on dirt/grass. The method of death was violent leaving heavy pools of blood. Directly after the murder, it rained for eight days straight; very hard, pouring rain in moderate temperatures. Within ten feet of the body was a drainage ditch. The ninth day after the murder, the dogs worked the area. All dogs alerted down in the bottom of the ditch.

Carol Sanner, Hatchers Pass, Alaska, K9 Drew

Another reason the dogs may alert in an area not directly on the location of the burial is the "drip line theory." Once the dog alerts, look carefully at your terrain. If a large tree is near or "on" the alert area, note the length of the longest branches of the tree. Scent can be carried 1.5 times the length of the longest branch away from the actual source. Notably, the source may actually be that far from where the dog is alerting. Therefore, when working burials, handlers may want to indicate an *area of interest* by flagging off an entire area for further inspection using other dogs or other types of equipment. Remember, it is costly to dig. It is costly to excavate. Are you willing to say to the Sheriff that "yes, you should bring in several thousand dollars worth of equipment to dig this area?" Before that level of commitment, perhaps it is wise to have a second and third dog confirm the area of alert, take all dogs out of the search area, rest them, allow them to clear out their nasal passages, and return to the are to re-work it from multiple directions. When you have confirmed this is indeed a solid alert, make your report. When reporting, you are reporting what the dog has done, not what you "think" is occurring. Be specific, accurate in your description, and honest. Integrity in a dog handler is everything!! Consider the length of the drip line in your probably location. A similar situation occurred whereby five out of six dogs alerted in a very near proximity to each other on a cold case, eight years old. There was potentially a buried homicide victim in a fifteen-acre area. After working the area and reporting back to authorities, anthropologists were brought in to excavate. The murder weapon was located. A blanket potentially eight years old was located. A rope tied in a configuration likely to have been used in the homicide was located. A shovel handle was located, all within the flagged area by the handlers. Further information remains unknown, as the case is still an open case. A keen eye and well-trained dogs were able to assist law enforcement in identifying the probably location of the homicide.

A case in England brought to light a tragic case of child abuse in an orphanage type home. Forensic examiners and anthropologists recovered the remains of multiple children buried in cellars that were bricked up. Multiple cellars were opened, to the shock of townspeople, relatives, and previous residents. Dogs alerted on the areas being opened up. Their "extremely strong reactions" apparently indicated human remains beneath those sealed rooms. Additional evidence like shackles was recovered in this case also. Further information is not yet available on this most recent case (2008). Human Remains Detection dogs were critical in these burial/crypt-like graves.

Sometimes only very subtle changes in the dog alerts the handler to the evidence of scent. Sometimes it is only a quick whiff and then it is gone. Sometimes the situation is so bizarre we could not even imagine it. The handler must be astute enough to recognize these very minute changes of behavior in the dog. Recovery of the victim may depend upon it. We assume such horrors would not happen in this day and age. They do.

Avalanche Search Preparations

As one handler so aptly put it "Our job as a SAR dog handler/trainer is to refine the technique, show the dog examples of scent problems, and teach them that in order to play the game they must include their moronic handler in on the find."

K9 Drew, 1995-2008
Handler - Carol Sanner
Alaska Avalanche K9

▶ *Avalanche Searches*

Kim Gilmore and Carol Sanner

Avalanche searches pose a completely different set of challenges for a dog handler. The survival rate for victims of an avalanche varies depending upon the depth of burial and trauma incurred to the avalanche victim. At 30 minutes, chances of a live recovery are around 50%. At 45 minutes, below 25%.

Buzzards and Butterflies

Working avalanche conditions poses an element of risk for the handler. The handler should remain calm and collected, have planned, and trained for these specific conditions. This is not an area of rescue that can be done without intense preparation and skill. An avalanche dog handler should have a strong command of using arm signals with their dog. This is critical to direct the dog to suspect areas without endangering the life of the handler on the unstable snow.

Ski patrols, backcountry skiers and snowmobilers are typically those that are the victims of avalanches, which are referred to as "white death." Imagine ten feet of snow coming at you at 200 to 250 miles per hour. If the person could survive this impact, the resulting trauma from being sifted through trees and debris and the limited amount of air provided once the slide sets up provides about a fifteen-minute lifespan. Beyond wearing an avalanche beacon and having your party have a visual on a part of you that you have managed to get out of the snow before it freezes, an immediate canine response becomes the best chance for survival for the victim.

A working knowledge of avalanches and proper preparations is crucial to safely responding with an avalanche dog. Although the chances of survival for the victim are limited, finding and recovering the body give the family and friends a sense of closure.

Avi dog handlers will also need specialized equipment over and beyond what is normally carried by dog handlers. Some of those items might include: goggles, snow shoes, skis, ski poles, avalanche rescue shovel, probe pole, avalanche beacon, marking flags, body insulating clothing (for handlers and dogs) and other survival gear for this specific type of weather and terrain. The dogs must be used to arriving on the avalanche scene by riding a snowmobile (either between driver and handler or in front of the handler, by short haul helicopter insertion, from a ski lift or in the back of a rescue sled pulled by a snowmobile. They may have to navigate through deep snow behind their handler to get to the scene that may be up to a mile in some cases from where snowmobiles can safely access. Both handler and dog must be physically fit to work long shifts on steep terrain.

Some avalanche certification tests require the handler and dog to locate one to two victims and possible articles buried in snow in a search area of approximately one acre within a 20 minute time period.

Search strategy is very important. Introduce dogs that will be working the area at the same time. It is important to communicate with on-site command to determine safe zones in the event there is a threat of additional slides and to know what the signals for evacuation will be. Handlers should carry marking flags, identified with their dogs name and organization, to mark areas of interest by the dog. Always probe the area of K9 interest before calling for shovelers. Probing allows deeper burials to vent scent and will help the handler determine if the dog is indicating on a buried victim or is interested in residual scent from other searchers. Dogs should be exposed to the distractions they will encounter such as snow machines, the sounds associated with avalanche mitigation (mortars and artillery) and working around dozens of people in the search area at the same time. Share your concerns with command if there are distractions that prevent you and your dog from performing most effectively. Report immediately and accurately.

Operational and technical proficiency in personal survival in mountainous terrain, and, snow and ice environments, is required of any avalanche dog handler. Handlers should be proficient in winter camping, ice climbing, recognition of avalanche hazards and the use of SAR dogs in these environments. They also need a basic understanding of mountain weather, the ability to walk in mountainous terrain and be able to backpack their personal equipment for at least four miles in an elevation gain of 2000 feet. This is not a job to be taken lightly. Your personal safety and the safety of your dog depend upon your knowledge, training and experience. Be prepared.

Carol Sanner and K9 Meg contemplate the possibility of an avalanche as they scan possible locations for a mishap in Alaska. 2007.

Avalanche Training-A Primer

By Carol Sanner

K9 Meg, Search and Rescue, Alaska Avalanche Search in Alaska

Understanding the Scent Picture

Training for avalanche rescue is no great mystery for a multi-modal dog that has trained in disaster (collapsed buildings) or even water. While the environment differs in complexity, the behavior of scent in the medium is similar from the dog's point of view: scent diffuses from the source (an area of higher concentration) through the snow via pore spaces until it can be detected at the surface by the dog.

Buzzards and Butterflies

This does not mean the dog will alert directly over the target. On the contrary, just as in a collapsed structure, in avalanche debris, scent will flow through the path of least resistance (air spaces) that might be laterally until it emerges where it can be detected by a dogs nose.

In avalanches, snow layers or "slabs", flow down a mountain and are deposited along its contours, often deeper deposits where it collects near natural obstacles such as topographic benches, rocks or stands of trees. Though we will discuss search strategies across a debris field, later, these are also likely sites where victims may become lodged.

Alaska

K9 team works avalanche debris above probe lines on Turnagain Pass, Alaska, 1999. Note: there were 6 snowmobilers buried. Five were found at 6 to 8 feet deep, each below their machines. They saw the slide triggered by the 6th rider above them and tried to out run it but were overtaken. Oddly enough, their exit route ended up being near the toe, where you see the probers. It also became the staging area for searchers, so the area was compacted and heavily contaminated, not to mention full of people and distractions. Probers found five victims here within 4 days of the slide, but we worked dogs behind the probe line to confirm body strikes as human remains. Family and friends searching high above the others found the 6th rider later in the spring. This avalanche was incredibly daunting from a searchers perspective it measured at least ¼ mile wide and was almost a mile long.

Time is the enemy of successful detection and a rapid victim recovery. Once the snow has been disturbed in its travel down a slope it becomes denser as it consolidates under gravity, crushing air spaces, and reducing a dog's ability to detect a scent close to its source. It is urgent to begin a search as soon as it is safe for searchers to set foot on the slide debris.

Training Methods

The basics of training are similar to wilderness, cadaver or disaster training. The dog is habituated to the target scent in controlled, repetitive exercises until the desired alert becomes automatic. For snow work, the goal is to gradually increase the time and distance that the dog is started relative to the target source. Most handlers begin with live subjects because most dogs seem to have a stronger drive to find a live subject. There is a more enjoyable game for all concerned. First the person runs away over a snow berm and lays on the surface. The next time the helper jumps into a trench, then she pulls a tarp over her, and so on, until the dog understands it is looking for a person hidden beneath the surface. Eventually, your search subjects are hidden in pre-dug snow caves in a snow berm (we use snow disposal sites in urban areas, or old avalanche debris on ski slopes).

Safety during snow burial exercises is paramount. Be sure your helper is equipped with at least a two-way radio in communication with another helper on the surface using established radio contact procedures. Another person may be standing nearby with a shovel in case of a collapse. Normally the maximum burial depth beneath the surface does not exceed 3 ft., which is commonly a certification test scenario. For training, we often pre-dig several caves over a 50-meter square area, leave them for a few days then return to the site for the exercises. Helpers need to be properly dressed for lying in the snow. We provide some comfort for the burial subject by letting them lie on a mat or blanket, and buttress the entrance to the cave with snowshoes or skis or plywood before carefully laying snow blocks. The entrance is covered with finer snow to conceal it. The advanced burial exercises should simulate that used in a certification test. Remember, if the dog has difficulty with drive, seems confused or does not work, go back to more basic problems, and simplify, simplify, simplify, until the dog works more happily. It is easy, in our desire for the dog to excel and progress rapidly in it's training, to move to more complex problems too quickly. Resist the temptation to move too quickly and always keep the interest of the dog at heart.

Alaska Avalanche

K9 Drew showed some interest in depositional areas along topographic benches about 1/3 the way down the slide. Deposition was approximately 30 feet deep there. Note: After the slide, it snowed another 4 feet in the days that followed. The search was suspended for 2 days after day 4 due to unstable conditions, unsafe for searchers. On day 4, Drew and I started at the PLS of rider 6, who had triggered the slide high on the slope. We were transported to the top via snowmobile and worked our way down a likely trajectory of the body and machine. However, the fresh snow made it very difficult going. Drew and I were exhausted after taking 3 hours plowing our way through fresh snow and heavy deposition to reach the bottom of our search area. It was a fruitless task, but he did have some interest areas. However, probing in the consolidated debris made it impossible to verify his scent hits.

Just this year (2008) there was one slide just on the other side of this same slope that killed 2 snowmobilers. Victim 2 was recovered several days after the slide due to bad weather and unstable conditions. A metal detector located him, though dogs were on scene. At the same time teams were recovering that body, another slide occurred on Turnagain Pass, trapping a skier. He was

Buzzards and Butterflies

recovered alive, amazingly by a Forest Service avalanche technician who just happened to be in the area at the time.   *Submitted by Carol Sanner, Girdwood, Alaska*

Dogs are also useful in avalanche searches to detect clues of the victim. A glove, helmet or ski found on the surface of a debris field may mean its owner is close below. To train for this, we use freshly scented clothing articles in successively deeper and longer burials. My friends and neighbors once thought my requests to borrow their socks and t-shirts were rather odd, but they are now accustomed to these requests and readily surrender their dirty laundry to me *for the cause*. Be sure to train so the dog does not *move* the clue, as it must be marked where found. It may be part of a debris pattern down the slide path that may help determine victim trajectory and likely define search areas.

Initially, you will have fresh scent near the burial site, as whomever buries the article of subject will leave fresh scent at the surface. Later, in more advanced exercises, it will be necessary to completely disturb the search area, so that the dog does not develop a habit of following a trail to the burial site.

Gradually introduce typical search activity distractions to your exercises, such as people talking, other dogs, packs or other gear dispersed over the exercise area. Implement training exercises with the dog wearing booties to get him accustomed to working while wearing them.

While the ideal outcome of our dogs finding a victim alive keeps us ever hopeful as rescuers, live recoveries are a rarity. Most avalanche victims or their companions trigger the slides. A victim's chance of survival diminishes after the first few minutes of burial. Furthermore, a large percentage of victims die of trauma injuries in the slide, rather than of suffocation. It is rare that a trained dog team is available within the statistically critical 15-minute period when victims have the highest probability of survival. Therefore, it is important to at least train your dog to recognize cadaver scent. Bodies, even under snow, will decompose to a certain stage before they freeze. Land cadaver scent tubes using recent decomposed scent material, artificial stress scent, or cadaver scents can be used in exercises designed just as with buried articles.

Carol Sanner and K9 Meg work the Alaska Mountains in August near a glacier

Avalanche sites are usually remote and logistics to get rescuers to the slide zone can be complicated. Training should include helicopter safety, riding in snowmobiles and attached sleds, or snowcats. If training at a ski area, it is important for dog safety to train them to follow the handler beneath a snowplow stance or behind to avoid other skiers. Chairlift or gondola riding should also be part of the training routine.

Avalanche Search Strategies

Dog Handlers intending to work avalanche search and rescue must become familiar with the incident command structure for your local SAR response. Training in avalanche and winter rescue is essential for safety and to understand strategies for locating and extricating victims. Many areas offer courses in avalanche training, Library and web resources are listed at the end of this article.

It is imperative for avalanche dog handlers to develop a good rapport with local avalanche rescue coordinators and rescue groups (e.g., mountain rescue, ski patrol). Educating them as to what can be expected of search dogs, as another tool in the recovery is *a must*. It is a disservice to the search dog community for handlers to misrepresent or present unrealistic expectations of search dogs as the magic bullet for successful recovery in every avalanche rescue scenario. Joint training exercises are a great way to familiarize rescue commanders with the value and appropriate deployment of dogs in a search.

The best search strategy is a collaborative one between the IC (incident commander) and dog handlers to determine if and where to deploy a dog team to the site. Dogs are not necessarily included in the initial hasty search. It may have been hours or days before dogs are called to the scene. Again, the time since the incident, the size of the debris field, current weather conditions, number of other searchers at the scene will factor into the best strategy for a dog team. Typically dogs will be directed to where the likely trajectory of the slide has carried the victim, where the deposition zones are, and to topographic features where victims or clues might have been carried by the slide. In a hasty search scene, one normally approaches from the toe of the run out zone and works the dog uphill. Multiple K9 teams can be distributed over the field accompanying hasty probers and beacon searchers looking for surface clues or victims. This approach helps to reserve the dogs' energy and to cover a large area in a short time.

At one scene where victims were buried an average of 6-8 feet in much consolidated debris, deploying the dog behind probe lines was useful. The probers penetrated the snow to depths of 12 - 20 feet, providing some aeration of the snow that actually assisted dogs in scenting. Probe lines indicated strikes of possible buried victims. The dogs were then able to confirm cadaver scent by sniffing at the probe holes.

Some have said that dogs have difficulty searching an avalanche debris field that has been contaminated by the live scent of other rescuers, equipment, snowmobiles, and other distractions found during rescue activities. However, if the dog has been properly trained and proofed on the target scents, distracting scents should not be a factor. Often, when called to a victim recovery (where no live rescue is anticipated), we take the dogs off site and run through a short cadaver exercise prior to releasing them into the search area. This provides a short "warm up" exercise and helps them focus on the search target scent. (In all cases when bringing any type of cadaver scent onto a search site, inform the incident commander or chief law enforcement officer and ask for permission to do so prior to arriving on site.)

To further broaden knowledge of working in avalanche rescue, handlers should be familiar with backcountry safety, the causes, evaluation of avalanches and rescue methods. Some suggested reading on avalanches for dog handlers:

Buzzards and Butterflies

The Avalanche Handbook 3rd Ed. by P.A. Schaerer. Mountaineers Books

ABC's of Avalanche Safety 3rd Ed. by Sue Ferguson and Ed La Chapelle. The Mountaineers. Books.

Backcountry Avalanche Awareness 7th Ed. by Bruce Jamieson Canadian Avalanche Assn.

Snow Sense: A guide to evaluating snow avalanche hazard by Jill Fedston and Doug Fesler, AK Mountain Safety Center, Inc.

The Snowy Torrents: a compendium of avalanche accidents in the U.S. from 1980- 1986 by Nick Logan and Dale Adkins. Colo. Geo. Survey.

Websites:
www.avalanche.org
http://www.1srg.org/
http://www.comdens.com/SAR

Dogs Handler's Avalanche Rescue Pack

Avalanche Beacon
Shovel
Probe
Headlamp, extra batteries
Radio, extra batteries
Wands for marking clues or dog alerts
Knife or multi-tool
Goggles
First aid kit
Notebook/pencil

Dog Vest and/or Bell collar
K9 First aid kit
Booties
Dog snacks/water
Mat or pad for dog to lie on
Light sticks
Overmitts
People snacks/water
Bivouac gear as necessary
Camera

Roxye Marshall and K9 Mandy approach a glacier during an HRD training session in Girdwood, Alaska.

▶ Mountain Searches

Edited by Kim Gilmore

Flathead Search and Rescue Team

Searching in mountains takes a physical stamina and acclimation to the elevation for both handler and dog that does not "live" in the same terrain. Do not assume that you are physically fit enough to perform for long periods of time in a mountainous terrain without having trained in a like environment. Many mountain searches have been known to occur where there is no vehicle access and searchers had to hike for six hours just to reach the search area when helicopter insertion is not available or reasonable due to weather or resources. This requires the true 48-hour pack, and in some cases a 72-hour pack, with all needed gear, equipment and supplies for the handler, the victim and the search dog. The searcher needs to be prepared to spend up to multiple nights in the search area and demonstrate necessary survival skills. A working knowledge of topographical maps, compass, GPS, making shelter and fire, in addition to being comfortable wearing a 40-60 pound pack while retaining the knowledge of how to utilize what is in said pack is but a basic requirement for deployment. Some civilian mountain searchers (not necessarily trained search teams but backcountry enthusiasts/hunters/sportsmen) have been know to "stash" equipment throughout common search areas, particularly areas where they frequent. Another strategy sometimes employed is to have air support to drop "cache's" of equipment and supplies into a target area. These can sustain both searchers and the lost victim. Mountain searches are difficult and take extreme skill and physical fitness. Do not become another victim.

Avalanche Search

Buzzards and Butterflies

▶ *Disaster Searches*

Disaster searches can be of three types: live or deceased persons or both. This type of searching is a specialty in itself and requires a dedication to intensive training to national standards to qualify for federal deployment. The FEMA (Federal Emergency Management Administration) dogs, are not trained to find deceased. They are trained to locate live victims only.

Jazzy, alerting in an urban, contaminated location in Louisiana where a body was recovered. Handler, Aki Yamaguchi. Greater Houston Search Dogs. Hurricane Katrina.

First responder dogs are usually those dogs on teams within a close vicinity of the disaster that arrive on scene very soon after the disaster, whether that is a bomb, tornado, hurricane, earthquake or other cause. First responder dogs may be live only, human remains only, or cross-trained/dual trained dogs. Regardless of the type of training, some common training objectives include: safety, agility, directional control (the handler being able to direct the movement of the dog from a distance), the ability of the dog to work independently, the dog ability to alert without the handler in near proximity, a strong leave-it command, and the dog ignoring other distractions such as noise, machinery, or food laying all over the place. The disaster scene cannot be predicted. What is predictable is the uncertainty of the scent, the danger and safety issues surrounding the scene, the hazardous materials at the scene, and the variety of agencies responding, the initial chaotic atmosphere, and the ability to sustain yourself and your dog for a period of time. Specialized equipment such as steel-toed boots and helmets are needed and should be required on scene at most disasters. Do not attempt to self-deploy (this holds true for all searches). You do not want to become part of the problem. Train the way you search.

Live/Rubble: Cooper searches rubble. Victim 15 yards from him, mouth open/close fast, tail straight and moves side-to-side fast when in scent. Handler, Aki Yamaguchi. Greater Houston Search Dogs. Texas.

K9 Bailey, Columbus County, NC Tornado, 2006. Handler Christy Judah, Brunswick Search and Rescue. Bailey searches with packs of frozen chicken scattered throughout the search area.

Hazardous Materials, Tornado Damage. K9 Bailey. Directional control from a distance was necessary for this search.

Buzzards and Butterflies

▶ *Building Searches*

An understanding of airflow is critical to any building searches. The handler should determine whether airflow systems are "on" and, if possible, the airflow system itself. Building airflow occurs when there is a difference between pressures. An area of high pressure flowing to one of low pressure will produce fast flow. The bigger the difference of pressure, the faster the airflow becomes. The negative and positive pressure controls the airflow in homes and buildings.

Building search. Source a foot from her. Tail high and wagging fast, twisting body with quick head turn.
K9 Jazzy, Handler: Aki Yamaguchi.
Greater Houston Search Dogs, Texas.

Ventilation is controlled airflow to replace stale air in buildings. It ensures acceptable indoor air quality. It also moves scent throughout the building. Therefore, if possible, all ventilation processes should be turned "off" prior to searching a building. The building should then be allowed to "rest" for a brief period of time prior to entering the building. This allows the scent to settle.

Infiltration occurs when air leaks into the building. This leak "could" also be a scent source. Therefore, dogs may have a challenge to identify the actual source of the scent when none is located inside the building. Scent sources may indeed be above, below or outside of the building. It takes a keen handler to understand the dogs' behavior and plan an effective search strategy that will allow the dog to identify the scent source as closely to the source as possible. If the ventilation sources are not turned "off", it only compounds the difficulty of the job. Exfiltration is when the scent source "leaks" to the outside of the building; again, a quirk in solving a scent source location.

Common air leaks can come from:

1. Orifice Air Flow: entry and exit point are linear such as a window frame opening.
2. Diffuse Air Flow: entry and exit point may be through porous materials such as fiberglass or uncoated concrete blocks.
3. Channel Air Flow: entry and exit points may be through openings in the building itself, not necessarily linear, forms moisture, and commonly occurs when two types of building materials meet such as between walls.

Two primary strategies are employed in building searches. Handlers may direct their dogs to enter a room unaccompanied. The dog is expected to survey the room to locate a human in the room. This is essentially necessary when the structure is not stable and it would endanger a handler to enter the area. A handler needs to assess the danger before sending in the dog. The dog is expected to enter the room, scan the area for a human, return to the handler and either alert or give behavioral indications that no scent is detected.

Another building strategy is to use a *detail method.* Detailing involves the handler entering a room with the dog and directing the dog to methodically "check" each section of the room, following the directional hand signals of the handler to scan all areas of the room indicating lower and higher areas. In some cases, the K9 is directed to crawl onto furniture or other structural items to gain a closer access to all areas of the room. Slowly, the handler works the room until the dog has been exposed to all areas of the room. This is especially helpful in cases where small amounts of remains are suspected. Handlers need to assess the areas to be searched, environmental conditions, and then select an appropriate search strategy to employ.

K9 Abby alerts on edge of trailer, possible burial underneath trailer.
Mickey Januszkiewicz, SC Search Dogs, Inc.

▶ *NIMs Compliant Human Remains Detection Training Criteria*

Although the National Information Management System has not yet finalized their recommended certifying criteria, there are items presently recommended for Human Remains Canine Search Technician, also known as a cadaver dog handler. Consult with the FEMA web site at www.fema.gov to determine those criteria as it evolves and is updated.

In addition, Human Remains Canine Search Managers (those supervising HRD dog handler teams) require additional coursework and certifications. Consult the Federal Emergency Management (FEMA) department for the National Emergency Responder Credentialing system that requires a national background check, specific incident command classes, a minimum of three years experience, and other coursework. There is also a designation as a Human Remains Canine Search Technical Specialist that may act as an advisor to staff.

Buzzards and Butterflies

Flanker Rules

The handler has many foci...the dog, interpreting the dog behavior, watching for clues, safety of self and the dog, environmental conditions, terrain, and search strategy. The one thing a handler does not need to worry about is the "flanker." A flanker is another crewmember that accompanies the dog handler into the field to complete a search assignment. It is expedient to train your flanker before entering the field.

1. The handler knows best how to work the search segment and what strategies work best for his/her dog.

2. All flankers need to stay "behind" the handler and dog. Do not get in front of or away from the handler/dog team. Straying too far away from the handler and dog creates a "second missing person" for the dog.

Wayne Rathe, K9 Emma Lee

3. Do not talk to the handler or dog unless absolutely necessary. Do not use the name of the dog in your general conversation. The dog may, albeit temporarily, be distracted by your use of his name. The handler is focused on the dog and the dogs' behavior and does not have the time or focus to become engaged in general chitchat. However, if the flanker observes a pertinent behavior of the dog, he/she should mention it to the handler. The handler will then interpret that behavior.

4. The handler will report back to the Incident Commander or Operations Chief when he/she feels that a relevant behavior has occurred during their mission. It is not up to the flankers or other crewmembers to ultimately interpret or report the dog/handler results.

5. Flankers should be self sufficient and adequately equipped. National organizations, individual teams, and search managers will provide a suggested equipment/supply list to take into the field. Do not look to your dog handler to take care of *you*.

6. Flankers should be clue aware and maintain the navigation, communications, distance tally, and appropriate search strategy (such as two critical spaces apart, etc.). The handler will instruct the crew on an appropriate strategy to employ based upon the type of mission, abilities of the dog, and conditions. (Example: Scent Specific Air Scent Dog, Trailing Dog, off or on lead, etc.) One team has recently adopted a "baseball theme" for communications when updates are needed and airways are not necessarily secure. A response of first base indicates the dog has some slight interest. Second base, more intense interest, third base - stand by for further, and homerun, victim has been located and is in VISUAL sight of the handler.

7. Flankers should act as a safety observer to detect any unsafe condition that may affect the crewmembers or dog. This includes not only the environment but also other individuals, other animals, or conditions (weather) that might affect the crewmembers. All equipment should be in working condition (flashlight batteries, radios, etc.), all crewmembers in a physically fit condition, and dog in an apparent healthy condition.

8. Flankers should NEVER leave a team member in the field. Not EVER.

9. Never criticize your team members while in the field. There will be time to debrief at a later time and place.

10. Flankers should never lose sight of your team members in the field. The dog handler will tell the flankers where they should place themselves and what they should be doing in the field during the mission. If you need a break or fall behind, be sure to let the handler know

Beyond these flanker rules, the handler will let the flanker know what additional guidelines are expected. If the handler does not volunteer this, ask prior to entering the field. The handler may be so focused on the task at hand they do not think about advising the flanker of any additional information such as "don't throw sticks around or into the water as my dog is a toy reward retriever." The time spent in a quick discussion can save much grief later in the mission.

K9 Jess, in training

Buzzards and Butterflies

6
Water Search

Outline
Introduction
Equipment and Supplies
Water Search Techniques
Spotters
Personal Floatation Devices
Scent Machines
Reaching Device
Side Scan Sonar
Boats and Boat Operators
Lakes and Quarries
Swift water
Hazardous Materials and Other Hazards

Family Interaction
Training Techniques
Thermoclines
Changing Conditions
Canine Floatation Devices
Marking Systems
Body Recovery Bag
Divers
Types of Water
Rivers and Creeks
Floods
Critical Incident Stress Debriefing

By Shelley Wood and Christy Judah

Introduction

When a missing person is thought to be in an aquatic environment, water search dogs may be called in to assist in finding the location. Most searches of this nature are the result of accidental drowning. However, this is not always the case. Some are the result of suicide or homicide.

A human body will typically sink and reach the bottom of the body of water regardless of the depth unless it encounters an obstruction. This sinking action of the body is affected by the body density, specific gravity, and Boyle's Law (the relationship between pressure and volume). As the body descends, the gases dissolve in the tissues and air in the lungs compresses decreasing buoyancy and adding to the rate of descent. The body becomes less buoyant the deeper it goes. A general rule of thumb is that the body will sink at a rate of 2 feet per second. The body usually lands

Buzzards and Butterflies

on the bottom in the general area of submergence. The exception is extremely shallow water or in the case of fast currents over 15 knots the victims body can travel a short distance in the current as it is sinking to the bottom. Also common is when the body remains suspended in the water, not fully reaching the bottom.

The position of the body is usually prone and somewhat relaxed. The arms and legs are slightly bent. This position is assumed due to the body's buoyant properties in the water. When the body begins to decay it produces gas increasing the buoyancy. In this case Boyle's Law works again but in reverse. Imagine being submerged on the bottom of a lake if you put a small amount of compressed air into a balloon then tied it and let it ascend to the surface, the air in the balloon will start to expand as the water pressure decreases on the ascent. It will rapidly rise and the balloon may even burst as it nears the surface. The same thing happens to a body. Even when heavy weights are attached to homicide victims they can return to the surface.

Many factors affect the time frame for the body to surface. Sometimes it may not surface for years. Some of the influencing factors include location, type of water, water temperature, current, victims height, weight, bone density, body fat, food consumption in the last six hours, alcohol consumption, clothing type, footwear, age, physical state of the body due to gunshot wounds, stabbing or other injury, thermoclines, obstructions and bottom conditions such as strainers, rocks, eddies and silt. The water temperature and time in water also affects the predicted time of surfacing. If the water temperature is 70° the body will usually surface in one day (less if the water temperature is higher), 65° - 2 days, 55° - 3 days, 45° - 4 to 5 days and below 38° not until the temperature increases. After the body returns to the surface it can be carried with the current, be moved by backflows, pushed into eddies or drift with the wind. When the body surfaces it is difficult to determine the exact location where it sank. Occasionally, a body can sink and surface again for a second time. The body first floats, the gases may escape and then the body will sink again. While on the bottom, it will continue to decompose and the gas rebuilds allowing the body to come to the surface for the second time. Bodies can travel a considerable distances in current after resurfacing. In some cases they may travel as much as forty miles or more.

It can be difficult to establishing the point that the victim was last seen, especially on large bodies of water. Distance estimates can be very deceiving and even if the accident has been witnessed, people don't usually look for landmarks

K9 Stryker locating scent in swift water context.
Handler: Kathy Lewis, Flathead Search and Rescue.
Photographer: Kim Gilmore.

or mark the location because they are traumatized themselves. If there is a witness it is important to take them to the exact location where they actually saw the accident occur. One of the biggest problems is verifying the accuracy of the point last seen, if there is one. Even command staff may disagree as to the exact PLS (Point Last Seen). A well-trained water search dog can be used to narrow down the location. When paired with other technologies, search dogs can increase recovery rates. The amount of time to locate the body can be greatly reduced and dive recovery teams can limit their bottom time as well as increase accuracy when cadaver dogs are used.

Water search is a recovery operation. However some searches start as a rescue and even though they are in recovery mode they still have a sense of urgency especially when a child is involved. As a water search dog handler, you may be part of an automatic call out whenever there is an incident involving a water related accident. You or your whole unit may be called as a resource to aid your county, a neighboring county or another state after recovery operations have begun. Searches come in all shapes and sizes. Some searches are very small with just law enforcement present, as in the case of some homicides or suicides. Cadaver dogs may be called in after the victim has not been located in several days or may be called in initially. Other searches become very large events, multi-agency and multi-jurisdictional with many people involved as in the case of water related disasters. Helicopters and planes may be used, scanning the water for a surface visual or shadows in the water. Thermal imaging infrared cameras or other heat sensing devices may be used by air support. There may also be a media presence at water searches.

The water environment is also extremely varied depending upon the area of the country. In water searches there may be single or multiple victims. The situation can vary from a car leaving the road in a storm and entering a swollen creek or river. It may be a boating accident, a swimming accident, flood event or airplane crash. The water feature may be man made or natural, a creek, large river, pond, lake, or swamp. Also, due to increased development and changing weather patterns, there may be a rise in flood-related disasters since the 1980s. The circumstances and locations are endless. There are hazards involved in the water search environment and one must be able to recognize and decline a search that is beyond the scope of your training and experience. If you are not qualified to do this type of search, don't go. Instead, help to find a resource that is qualified.

Family Interaction

A dog handler at a water or land search may have direct contact with the family of the missing person. The family is anxious to receive timely and accurate information from a reliable source. They are often waiting near the water or base of operations and in close proximity to where the dog handler is working. Be aware of the location of the family. Be sensitive to their location and your facial expressions that may be *read* from a distance. Sound can carry on the water. The SAR dog handler is being watched and the conduct observed. Some families are overwhelmed with grief and others are silent. Refer the family to the official public relations personnel on site. Remain vigilant and cognizant of their location, particularly as the missing person is brought to shore or returned to base camp. A respectful handler is long remembered.

Some teams or law enforcement personnel will assign a family liaison to assist the family members on scene. Check with the command staff before offering this type of service. Many Critical Incident Stress debriefers are trained chaplains and may be bi-lingual. Some agencies have recognized a need for this service and have protocols for an automatic call out. This enables the K-9, dive team and rescue personnel to concentrate on the job at hand. The liaison can also act as a buffer when important information is relayed from the incident commander, and protect family members from media intrusion.

Cultural needs vary. Some families may request that a floating candle be set at the point last seen. When a recovery operation is complex and prolonged and no remains are recovered, some families may request that the search and rescue personnel attend a memorial service. If and when the remains are recovered, the team may be invited to the funeral. Attending services is a personal choice.

K9 Carlos Riding in an Inflatable Boat

Equipment & Supplies

Searches are often in remote areas with poor access to the water. Be prepared to have whatever you think you will need for the entire day. If it is winter, items like hand warmers to keep you comfortable. If it is summer, there may not be any shade. Plan to create your own shade with tarps and screens. Have a plan to ventilate your vehicle. Water searches have the potential for the handler and dog to get wet and possibly muddy. The handler may not be able to access the boat from a boat ramp and have to wade out to load onto the boat. Bring towels and extra clothing appropriate for the conditions. For searches involving rivers and swift water a safety officer may require that you wear a helmet. Never attempt swift water searches without prior training and experience.

Clothing should be quick drying, such as nylon. Cotton is not quick drying. Zip-off pants are convenient in the warmer climates. In the colder months they can be paired with good quality long underwear. Layering is best. A large selection of lightweight, thin high performance clothing is available. Sometimes the search area is quite some distance from where the boat was launched. On the shore it may seem warm but out in the open water it can become cold, wet and windy. Weather can change rapidly, especially on large bodies of water. Depending on the bank access, various types of footwear can be worn. When the handler may get wet, have to navigate a steep bank or climb over rocks to get to the boat, a lace-up, hard sole, wet suit type boot works well. Always have a water rescue knife (with a blunt tip) to cut the straps and remove boots/shoes quickly in the event you end up in the water. Additional useful items include a hat, lip balm, water ski type gloves, sunscreen, polarized sunglasses, whistle, knife, compass, GPS, puff bottle and a towel. Take enough drinking water on the boat for yourself and the dog. A towel is handy when the boat surface is hot.

Wet towels also work well for the platform where the dog will work. Wetting the towel helps it to stick to the surface of metal boats.

Training Techniques

A water search dog should have a strong foundation in land HRD. This enables the handler to already have a solid working relationship with the dog and be able to read the dog's body language. The dog will be more restricted in a boat and may not be able to offer it's trained alert all the time. Puppies and young dogs can be exposed to the water environment by walking on docks, getting in and out of boats, riding in boats and socializing with divers rescue and recovery personnel.

Once your dog understands the fundamentals of water search, it is important to train yourself to be able to interpret your dog's performance in different situations. Safely train at all times of day and in all weather conditions. If you live in an area with numerous lakes, ponds and/or rivers, take the time to learn about the history of the area. A drowning tends to occur in the same locations over and over. Learn from the "old timers". Be aware of the release times of rivers or lakes that have dams. There may be unusual flow patterns. Train in as many different locations as possible.

Sometimes what is on the surface is not what is below the surface. Large rocks or even a whole town may be hiding below! Flooded bottomland created some lakes. Farms, roads, street signs and other features, even old forgotten graves, may be just below the surface. This was the case at Lake Marion in South Carolina in 2007. Dozens of graves were exposed as water in the lakebed dried up from a severe drought in the southeast. The graves appeared to be from a family plot that was flooded in the 1940s. Over 7,000 graves had been previously *relocated* from this same lake.

Become familiar with water intakes and sewage treatment facilities. Some people use bodies of water for garbage dumps. This is true especially around docks. Be aware of the hazards. Preplan with departments such as the water recovery team, rescue squad and fire department who may be responding to searches in your area. Build a working relationship. Document the locations of all boat accesses, both public and private. Invest in good waterproof maps of the larger lakes and rivers in your area. They can be found at most boating supply stores. Maps such as these will be helpful in showing an overall picture of the body of water and additional features that may affect your search.

▶ Use smoke bombs and plumbers dye to see what the scent is doing. When using dye it is much easier to see where scent may be and how it is traveling especially if your vantage point is higher than the water table.

▶ Using divers in water training helps the K9 to understand that a human being can be below the water. The monster (diver) from the deep has traumatized more than one dog. To avoid this, begin your training by introducing the dog to the diver dressed in only a wet suit. Then slowly add additional equipment while the diver plays with and treats the dog. Allow the diver to enter the water in full view of the dog. This sets up a scenario that humans can enter and disappear into the depths. Be aware of bubbles from air tanks and adjust them accordingly if you notice the dog is alerting on bubbles. Scent machines can be adjusted so that no bubbles break the surface of the water.

Buzzards and Butterflies

Water Search Techniques

Water search techniques vary dependent upon the type of water environment. There is no *one* "right" way to search an area. Search patterns and tactics will depend upon the environment, specific drowning situation, size of the water, resources available, and information available to the handler.

Turnagain Sound in Alaska which sometimes has visiting beluga whales. Imagine that type of distraction occurring on a search in those waters.

Marking the scent cone on water allows the handler to identify a smaller area for the location of the potential target (victim). Drop a marker (or buoy) when the dog first enters the scent cone (as indicated by the dog behavior...whether a bark, walking the gunnels, looking intensely or other behavior occurs indicating entry into the scent) and when the dog leaves the scent. This is sometimes observable when the dog turns around and faces the area where he first entered the cone. By approaching the area from different directions, the handler may be able to identify a more narrow dive area. Those areas marked by the canine handler will be the most probable dive area.

Empty water jugs or milk cartons can be quickly spray-painted in bright colors and attached to weights to mark corners and outside boundaries of the search segment. This helps the boat driver and handler to maintain a sense of direction and focus. It can be very difficult to maintain a sense of exactly where the dog alerted on the "last pass" when the lake is five miles wide and seven miles long. Trying to orient with buildings or other landmarks is difficult and they can become distorted the farther you are from shore (sort of like if your compass bearing is a couple of degrees off, the further you get from the starting point, the further *off* the line of direction you are). A water fence (made up of buoys or other markers) helps to charter strategic passes in methodical lanes.

In addition, mark each alert area with a GPS coordinate and compare coordinates where the body is eventually recovered to determine your effectiveness or possible movement of the body from the initial location.

If a handler is working closely with a diver, sometimes in adjoining boats and close proximity, maintain a safe distance from the diver to maximize *his* safety. Know what signals the diver will use should he/she get into trouble in the water. Be sure there is a backup diver in place and be prepared to assist if necessary.

Do not discount any behaviors of the dog during a water search. If the dog seems to be intensely interested in the bow of the boat, particularly compartments, note the direction of the wind and terrain. When on the water for an extended period of time, scent can accumulate in enclosed areas. Do not discount the fact that the victim "may" be very nearby the boat ramp and as the boat awaits your arrival, it has been absorbing scent.

Do not get "convinced" that the person drowned unless this aspect has been confirmed to a reasonable degree. Sometimes water cadaver dogs are brought in to "eliminate" an area. Even if your dog is "hitting" on an area in the water, be aware of the environment and possible sources of the primary scent. In one case in Texas, "the scent had collected on water in an old rock quarry. There were very high cliffs (due to digging) and searchers thought the victim might have drowned since the dogs all had hits near the water. Vegetation stopped the scent flow so it came over the treetops and dropped into the water. The missing person was eventually found with his trusty dog! He spent the night under a bridge and was recovered alive."

Notice buzzard activity in the area. Look not only nearby but also into the distance. Ground-pounders should have binoculars available as they scan the shores and skyline. Know the water temperatures, the depths of the water, movement of the water, thermoclines, and any other contributing factor to determine an appropriate search area. Swift water conditions and other moving waters greatly widen the potential search area. Topographical maps can help identify possible "catch areas" based upon terrain. In addition, local fishermen can help describe underwater conditions and suggest prime search areas.

K9 Pete, Ben Alexander, Cen-Tex Search & Rescue

Thermoclines

The thermocline (sometimes metalimnion) is a layer within a body of water or air where the temperature changes rapidly with depth. Wilkopedia describes thermoclines as: "Because water is not perfectly transparent, almost all sunlight is absorbed in the surface layer, which heats up. Wind and waves circulate the water in the surface layer, distributing heat within it somewhat, and the temperature may be quite uniform for the first few hundred feet. Below that is a mixed layer and the temperature may drop very quickly, as much as 20 degrees celsius with an addition 500 feet of depth. This area of rapid transition is the thermocline." In the ocean, 90% of the water is below the thermocline. This deep ocean may be as cold as 0 to 3 degrees celsius. It varies with latitude and season, is permanent in the tropics and variable in the temperate climates; and, weak to nonexistent in polar regions.

Deep lakes and quarries have cold bottom water. This slows down putrification and prevents a body from ever becoming buoyant. This is due to the extreme water pressure. Lakes with deeper water may have a thermocline. Most lakes have three layers. The top layer is the epilimnion, the middle layer is the metalimnion, and below that is the hypolimnion. The thermocline is the transition layer that separates the zones of widely different temperatures. Other lakes do not have a thermocline. Thermoclines can be affected by clarity. The clearer the water, the deeper the

Buzzards and Butterflies

thermocline will be. In water with more suspended sediment, the thermocline may be at 6 or 8 feet. In clear water it may be as deep as 30 feet.

In the spring and fall, the water in a lake usually mixes (turns over). Divers can see thermoclines and some depth finders can indicate them when the sensitivity setting is adjusted.

Thermoclines can hamper a water search. It may need to be broken up so that odor can penetrate the layers. One method to do this is to have a houseboat with an air compressor sink the air hose with a dive weight attached past the thermocline. The boat then runs a Z pattern releasing air to break up the thermocline and allow scent to come to the surface. The water search dog follows in a separate boat. A dive tank can be used for the same purpose, but the air supply is limited.

Spotters

A spotter can be extremely helpful because they have a better perspective of the whole search area. Determine pre-arranged hand signals to communicate with your spotter who remains on shore. This allows the spotter to tell you exactly (as nearly as can be determined) where you were the last time your dog showed interest or alerted. It also gives you a reference point on shore when other buildings or features are nonexistent.

Changing Conditions

Be aware of changing conditions on a real search. An example may be when a dam is releasing water with an island in the middle of the channel, bordered by large rocks. In these conditions the dog may alert on the opposite side of the island from where the scent is placed or indicate in a scent pool near the dam because of high walls. The rocks may cause the scent to swirl in an eddy or a secondary current may cause the scent to travel towards the bank. To prepare for these types of complex environments, train in various areas like coves with high banks, deep water, shorelines with undercuts in the bank and docks. Scent can cling to channel markers or other objects on the water. In lakes that are shallow and have little wind the accuracy of the dogs indication will usually be closer to the victim than in situations that are more complex or involve deep water.

Dams and varying water search conditions affect scent conditions.

(Note: Sometimes there are undercuts or dens dug underneath a bank or shoreline. These areas can be worked from the bank by the search dog. Studying the behavior of alligators, one finds that gators may drag a body to this type of den to save it for later use. Knowing this, handlers may choose to work dogs on lead and a safe distance from the actual edge of the shore.)

Personal Floatation Device

Safety is paramount. ALL individuals on every water vessel should be wearing a PFD, without exception. By the nature of the search, one person has already drowned. We do not want to make it two. ALWAYS wear a PFD, preferably rated III or higher. (If you are investing in the lighter weight canister type PFD's, be sure it is "armed" and ready to use. Read the instructions for how to arm it. It does no good to have a canister PFD unarmed.) Teams may wish to consider a swimming test for all canine handlers. In the very least, teams need to know who can and who cannot swim on their own team and make boat assignments accordingly.

Canine Floatation Device

While the choice of using a K9 PFD is a personal preference, remember that if safety for YOU is paramount and most basic, safety for the canine should be also. All HRD water dogs should be able to swim. This should be tested in a controlled situation before the canine is allowed to take a certification test. While many devices are available, selection of your preference depends upon the type of water you will most likely be searching. Water conditions vary, even on the same lake daily. Be aware of changing conditions and canine safety.

Scent Machines

Several plans for scent machines are available and readily shared by their creators. Each basically operates on the premise that a scent sample is place in a compartment, has air forced over the sample to a length of 200 feet of tubing which is placed into the water/pond/lake/stream. The forced air takes with it the scent of the source materials and provides a water training opportunity. Many scent machines also allow a regulator to control the amount of forced air, thus providing an opportunity to regulate the amount of scent forced through the tube, with or without bubbles. This is a safe method to introduce scent into the water without placing the scent source directly in the water. The tubing is weighed down with small weights so the scent drops to the bottom of the pond. Most electricians can easily build a custom model. Some are built onto a stage connected to a dolly for ease in transport to the training site.

Buzzards and Butterflies

Marking System

Each boat should contain a combination of various types of buoy marking systems, with extra floatation/weights, and brightly colored spray paint. More than once, handlers have found themselves in a situation where the marker is barely visible in the water conditions.

Marking buoys may be fishing bobbers with weights, milk jugs with weights, H-weights, or other hand-made or purchased buoy marker systems. It is helpful to have multiple types of markers on each boat for ease in use. Be sure to label your buoy in some fashion. One way to mark them is to identify your team (by initials) and symbol or letter of the dog's first name and a number. Example: BSAR (team), M (K9 Mandy), 3 (marker #3). This easily identifies where to return the buoy (if that is possible and occurs at some point in the future), which dog handler dropped that buoy, and which UTM the buoy correlates with. This is helpful when the body is recovered in determining the proximity of the dog alerts to the body location. Think ahead.

Reaching Device

Fishing Gaffs, or other reaching type devices have multiple uses such as safety, assisting a diver, snagging an item of clothing, or other evidence.

Body Recovery Bag

Although most canine handlers do not consider it their responsibility to actually "recover" and bring the body back to shore, there may be situation that requires your assistance in the actual body recovery. A body bag is a non-porous bag designed to contain a human body for storage and transport. Be proactive and think about whether you will be able to physically and emotionally handle this type of recovery. Talk about this with your teammates.

Side Scan Sonar

Side scan sonar technology involves the purchase of a special unit designed to allow a visual inspection of objects in the water and on the floor of the body of water. It uses medical ultrasound to increase the resolution of targets such as drowning victims. The actual sonar is dropped below the vessel and is towed several feet above the pond bottom. The reflected image is sent to a processor similar to an aerial photograph and viewed in real time. The side scan reaches paths of from about 60 feet to 160 feet wide although the range is dependent upon the size of the object sought, speed and water conditions. A wide variety of types range from simple fish finders costing a hundred or so dollars to thousands of dollars each. It takes great skill to understand and interpret the results of a sonar system. It requires dedicated practice to be able to accurately interpret the findings. Recent models offer real time "stop" photography, saving images on memory sticks, and documentation of temperature and depth conditions.

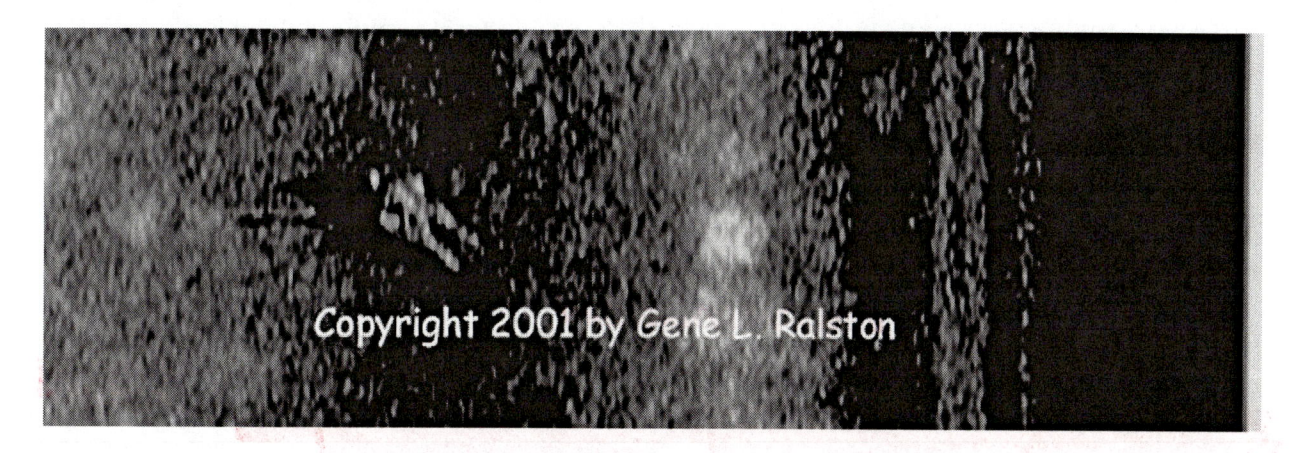

Image used with permission of Gene L. Ralston.

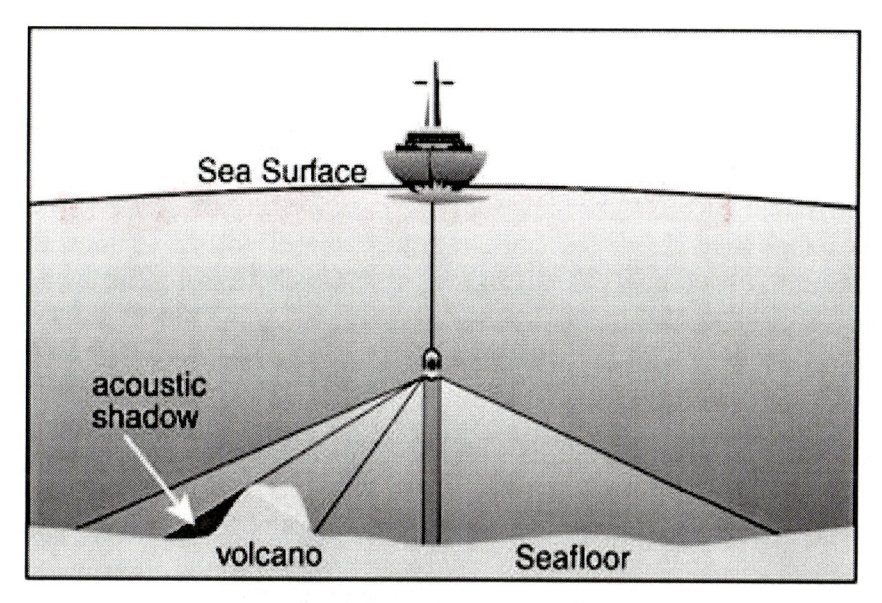

Illustration Side Scan Sonar

Divers

Divers search for and recover the victim. This specialty is not like recreational diving and specific equipment and training is used. Each dive team has set procedures and safety requirements. Most do not dive deeper than 60 feet. This gives them approximately 25 minutes of bottom time per dive. If they dive deeper, they do not have much bottom time to execute an effective search pattern. Divers use a number of search patterns to conduct a thorough search. The dive pattern depends on the circumstances such as shoreline, open water or currents. Random dives are not very effective. If

Buzzards and Butterflies

a location has been pinpointed using side scan sonar, a diver may dive deeper than 60 feet to do the recovery. There are some organizations that specialize in deep water recoveries.

The conditions below the surface may be very difficult. In some areas there is little or no visibility, there may be current and rocks or other dangerous obstructions below the surface. When there is no visibility, everything is done by touch. Dive operations are not usually done at night.

Boats and Boat Operators

A skilled and experienced boat operator is the most important asset to the dog team. At times you may work in a boat with an operator you have never met before. They will maneuver the boat in such a way that a search pattern is executed. Since the dog is not able to choose its path of travel the boat acts like the dogs legs. Following the nose is key. Positioning the dog so it can do its job is essential. This can be challenging at times when there are obstructions like large rocks in the water.

One search strategy is to record with a GPS (hand held global positioning system) the location that the dog comes into scent and where he goes out of scent, as well as the actual alert. When there is a strong alert on a location or cluster area, then a marker buoy is placed. An *out of scent* buoy may be placed as well.

When locations are marked with a GPS unit, the markers can be checked to ensure they remain in the correct location. Markers may also need to be moved when diver or dragging operations begin.

The choice of boats will vary with the situation and the location. Generally the boat should be relatively low to the water with a platform in the front. The boats may be operated from the rear or have a center console. Occasionally the boat will need to be carried to the shore when there is no access for a boat trailer. Lightweight aluminum boats work well in this situation.

Inflatable boats are may have a soft bottom or a rigid hull. Inflatable boats are more difficult to maneuver and do not turn sharply. They can also be more challenging for the dog and handler. In some parts of the southeast airboats are used. Electric trolling motors allow for slow maneuverability. Expose the dog to various conditions and types of boats to best prepare for water searching. You may not always have access to your team boat (if available).

Jazzy with source five feet to her right. Note Her nose up, tail high, ears back, quick head-turn. Handler: Aki Yamaguchi. Greater Houston Search Dogs.

Types of Water

Lakes and Quarries

Lakes can vary in size. Some lakes are shallow and less than 10 feet in depth. Lake Okeechobee in Florida has an average depth of 7 feet. Other lakes have a depth of over 1000 feet like Lake Tahoe on the California/Nevada border. This lake is 1640 feet at its deepest. Blocking streams and rivers to store water for electric power, irrigation and recreation artificially creates some lakes. Rivers feed some lakes and streams while others are fed by underground springs. Some lakes have inlets but no outlets such as the Great Salt Lake in Utah. Most lakes are fresh water.

Rivers and Creeks

A river is a large body of water that flows over land in a long channel. River water comes from a combination of rain, lakes, springs and melting snow and ice. The various streams that flow from the source to the river are called headwaters. At the end of the river, the mouth, the water empties to a larger body such as a lake or ocean.

Rivers vary in size and character. Some are swift, steep and narrow. Others are slow, wide and meandering. Some rivers are so small that they dry up in the hot months. Some are large and flow constantly, like the Rio Grande, Missouri and the Mississippi.

HR/Shore
Source was a foot ahead of her. Tail high, ears back, 'tasting water'. She indicated in the water few seconds later. K9 Jazzy, Handler: Aki Yamaguchi. Greater Houston Search Dogs.

Strainers

A characteristic of rivers and creeks is that they have strainers. These are created in waterways by downed trees and limbs. Objects floating in the current are pushed against the strainer with great force. Many victims are ultimately found in strainers. Some victims are found in eddies. Eddies are currents moving contrary to the main current often in a circular motion. They can be caused by obstructions in a waterway such as a large rock or other feature. Foot entrapments are also a cause of drowning in creeks and rivers.

Buzzards and Butterflies

A Strainer

Swift water

Swift water can be anything from flat water moving 2.5 mph to class VI rapids. They can be in any kind of environment, not just rivers and can be natural or man-made. In heavy downpours city streets can turn into raging rivers. This is a very dangerous environment. Victims of a swift water event usually die when they get pinned against obstacles or get trapped in submerged debris or vegetation.

Floods

A flood is a body of water that covers normally dry land. Most floods are harmful. Sudden and violent floods can bring huge losses of life and property. Rivers, lakes and seas can cause flooding. Floods can be created by storms and high winds. Seacoast floods are caused by tsunamis, hurricanes and powerful storms. Inland flooding is commonly caused by too much rain and sudden snowmelt. Heavy rains can cause flash flooding or the failure of artificial structures such as dams and levees. This type of water event usually involves swift water, various degrees of contamination and hazardous materials that may be in the water. Be aware of the risks and act accordingly.

Hazardous Materials and other Hazards

K9 Pete, Ben Alexander, Cen-Tex Search and Rescue, New Orleans

Be aware of pollution, algae blooms, chemicals, waste material, fuel and other things that may be in the water. Ask about the hazards before you search. Be prepared to decontaminate your dog and yourself if necessary. Submergence is not always the cause of contamination. Water in the bottom boat, spray from the wind, an airboat or water that splashes in the boat can cause contamination issues. Various areas may have different hazards. Be mindful of downed power lines and locations where the electricity may not be off. In some areas there are venomous snakes and alligators. Protect yourself and your dog.

Blue Green Algae Blooms

K9 Gypsy, Brunswick SAR

The warm days of summer may bring about searches in the local pond. Unknowingly, the handler may be placing the dog in grave danger if they allow that dip into a blue-green algae infected water source. Handlers should take special precautions to avoid allowing dogs to swim in freshwater ponds with blue-green algae blooms. The toxins borne by the blue-green algae can be fatal to dogs.

Blue-green algae flourish in lakes and ponds with poor water flow. If the water looks "cloudy", has a green or blue-green tint, be suspicious of an overgrowth of blue-green algae and do not allow dogs to drink from this water source. Freshwater ponds, lakes and streams are the most likely to contain the algae. Although the "bloom" normally occurs in early spring or late summer, deadly blooms occur throughout the season where growth only requires sunny days and shallow bodies of water.

Buzzards and Butterflies

Recent reports from the "dog fancy" confirm that several dogs have died from drinking contaminated water, first vomiting several times, and then becoming unable to stand. Immediate veterinary care may not help to save the dog. During this time the dog may maintain a normal temperature, have normal appearing gums (pink) and no apparent heatstroke symptoms. The dog, other pets, livestock and people who drink this algal infested water may not survive the deadly toxin. Handlers should provide extreme care to protect their animals.

This sudden growth of algae, called cyanobacteria, occurs in water environments year-round. At these times, blue-green algae suddenly "bloom" and produce the deadly toxin. These "blooms" appear as "foam, scum, or mats on the surface of the water", and often accumulate along the shoreline. They can appear blue, bright green, brown, or red (as in red-tide), although some blooms are not readily discernable by looking at the water. Although not all algal blooms are toxic, handlers should assume toxicity if algae is visually apparent. Toxic blooms can kill or seriously affect an animal as quickly as 15-20 minutes after ingestion. The amount of algal toxicity, size of animal, and amount of water ingested all influence the effects of the algae on the animal. The volume of infected water required to kill an animal ranges from a few ounces to a few gallons. Thirsty animals will not be affected by it's sometimes unpleasant smell and may ingest too much of the water when drinking from the pond or licking their paws and fur after swimming in the bloom.

Cyanobacteria blooms may exist for up to seven days, but the toxins may be apparent for up to three weeks. It may move up and down below the water surface and not always be apparent on the surface of the water. Surface winds sometimes push them towards the shoreline.

The Whole Dog Journal reports "An animal that has ingested toxins from an algae bloom can show a variety of symptoms, ranging from skin irritation, or vomiting to severe disorders involving the circulatory, nervous and digestive systems, and severe skin lesions. In the worst case, the animal may suffer convulsions and die. Toxic algae ingestion seldom seriously affects people because the unpleasant odor and appearance of water associated with blue-green algae blooms tend to make us avoid it. However, skin rashes, nasal irritation, or other health effects may result from skin contact with algal toxins. Swallowing or ingesting water with a blue-green algae bloom may cause symptoms such as vomiting, diarrhea, or nausea; headache, throat irritation, seizures, or muscle pain; and in severe cases paralysis or respiratory failure." Many of the affected animals had seizures within 5-10 minutes of leaving the water and were dead within 15 minutes.

The Center for Disease Control lists the following symptoms possible from exposure to blue-green algae or cyanobacterial blooms:

- Getting it on the skin may give people a rash, hives, or skin blisters (especially on the lips and under swimsuits).
- Inhaling water droplets from irrigation or water-related recreational activities can cause runny eyes and nose, a sore throat, asthma-like symptoms, or allergic reactions.
- Swallowing water that has cyanobacterial toxins in it can cause
    - Acute, severe gastroenteritis (including diarrhea and vomiting).
    - Liver toxicity (i.e., increased serum levels of liver enzymes). Symptoms of liver poisoning may takes hours or days to show up in people or animals. Symptoms include abdominal pain, diarrhea, and vomiting.
    - Kidney toxicity.

- Neurotoxicity. These symptoms can appear within 15 to 20 minutes after exposure. In dogs, the neurotoxins can cause salivation and other neurologic symptoms, including weakness, staggering, difficulty breathing, convulsions, and death. People may have numb lips, tingling fingers and toes, or they may feel dizzy.

Further, the Minnesota Department of Health recommends that humans not ingest, swim or wade in water with blue-green algae, or let children or pets enter it. "If contact does occur, the material should be washed off thoroughly, paying special attention to the swimsuit area. If your pet comes in contact with a bloom, wash off your pet's coat to prevent the pet from ingesting the algae while self-cleaning. If you suspect the animal is sick from the algae, call a veterinarian immediately."

To protect you from harm, searchers and handlers should:

1. Avoid boating, wading or swimming in water where algae blooms are visible or suspected or know to have been within the past month. Closely supervise young children and dogs.
2. Do not eat, drink or handle the algae or water associated with it.
3. Do not allow dogs to swim or drink from discolored or infested areas.
4. Swimmers and dogs should be rinsed in non-pond/lake water immediately after leaving suspected waters.
5. Don't irrigate lawns or golf courses with pond water that looks or smells bad.
6. Report any "bad" smells in drinking water or recreational areas.
7. Respect any water-body closures announced by local public health officials.

If you suspect exposure to these toxins, rinse with non-affected water and get medical treatment right away. In addition, request that your county or local health department test the waters in order to accurately understand the water conditions.

Note: Red tide toxins can make it uncomfortable and sometimes unsafe to be on the shoreline during a bloom; however, a red tide has been known to occur only once during the past 50 years along the North Carolina coast.

Critical Incident Stress Management

Most human remains searches are stressful. Responding to searches where there is a fatality can have an impact on the handler. It is important to take care of yourself so you can enjoy a long career in the search environment. Become educated about appropriate resources available to emergency services workers in your community. Critical Incident Stress Debriefing is a valuable tool to help the searcher handle an unusual situation in a normal and mentally healthy manner. Many a hero has asked for a CISD session or two. Many teams require Critical Incident Stress Debriefing after each search involving a death. Services are usually free to emergency services workers. Contact your mental health department or check with a chief of another emergency service, such as your local fire chief to determine what services are available in your area. Be sure that all team members are aware of the purposes of CISD and how to request services. Monitor your teammates for signs of stress following a search. More than one divorce and ex-team member did not get CISD after a particularly unfortunate search and suffered the consequences to his/her personal and search career.

Buzzards and Butterflies

K9 Nia, Handler: K. T. Irwin, Wyoming

7

HRD and the LAW

Outline

Introduction
Cadaver Dog Alert as Reasonable Suspicion, not Probably Cause
Possession of Contraband for K-9 Training Purposes
Crime Scene Preservation
Cross Trained or Not
Handler Protect Thyself
Videotaping Training Sessions and Searches
Handler Know Thy Place

Introduction

Simply by virtue that all missing person cases are potential crime scenes, the search and rescue (SAR) canine handler, particularly the HRD handler, must be aware of and responsive to the laws and case studies that affect each case. Understanding historical cases and protecting crime scenes, train us to provide services in a professional and industry-standard accepted manner. We must document all search activities to create a good working relationship with law enforcement officers. There is no room for the self-proclaimed, untrained, uncertified, or otherwise a simply well intentioned pet owner to perform the function of a SAR dog handler. Proper training and ethics are required to "help" and not "hinder" a SAR mission. A basic understanding of how the SAR dog team fits into the law enforcement and emergency service programs is necessary for all SAR dog handlers.

Initially, dogs were used by patrol officers to track criminals. As time progressed, dogs were used to detect drugs, bombs and other chemicals. Today, trained dogs are used by many agencies to track, trail and locate humans alive or deceased. Such evidence (what the dog has located) may be admissible in court or challenged in court. "If a person is able to demonstrate that he/she has specialized expertise in training, tracking or detection, and/or the operational performance of his/her dog, he/she is qualified as an expert to state an opinion as to the ability of the particular dog in question to perform the targeted task." (SWGDOG.) "Most dog handlers will qualify to testify as an expert as long as the handler can demonstrate sufficient training, education and experience in the targeted task." (SWGDOG.) As an expert witness, remember to dress in an appropriate manner for the court, respond briefly and concisely, and look at the attorney asking the question but respond to the jury when answering. In general, speak in a normal manner, avoid speaking too fast, and speak

Buzzards and Butterflies

in a natural, relaxed manner. Use voice modulation to emphasize important aspects of your testimony. Avoid specialized canine industry terminology that may not be understood by the jury. If referencing materials, be accurate. Have the factual aspects of the search at hand based upon your personal knowledge.

Terry Fleck, a retired law enforcement officer and canine handler, well respected throughout the nation, shares his observations, experience, and knowledge in the following article about a:

Cadaver Dog Alert as Reasonable Suspicion, not Probable Cause

By Terry Fleck

Under the federal and state court system, there are two different descriptions of police working dogs, the Human Scent Detector Dogs and Contraband Substance Detector Dogs.

Human Scent Detector Dogs: The police service dog, search and rescue dog, tracking dog, trailing dog, scent identification dog, etc.

The Federal and State case law states that when one of these types of dogs alerts to or locates human odor, that alert is only one reasonable suspicion indicator. Reasonable suspicion is defined as a "particularized and objective basis for suspected legal wrongdoing". In this case, the wrongdoing may be a suspect, a track or trail of a suspect or scent line up.

The dog alert is simply one indicator of wrongdoing. The peace officer in charge of the case must develop other reasonable suspicion indicators to develop probable cause. "Probable cause exists when under the totality of circumstances known to the arresting officer; a prudent person would have concluded that there was a fair probability that the defendant had committed a crime." Other reasonable suspicion indicators may be direct or circumstantial evidence. *The dog alert must be corroborated by additional evidence.*

Contraband Substance Detector Dogs are defined as narcotic detection dogs or explosive detection dogs.

The federal and state case law states that when one of these dogs alert or locate contraband, the dog's alert equals and gives the peace officer probable cause. Once the peace officer has the dog alert, which equals probable cause, he may apply for a search warrant, search without a warrant, based upon one of the exceptions to the search warrant requirement, or arrest. However, in order for the alert from a contraband dog to equal probable cause, the dog must be trained, certified and reliable.

Trained, Certified and Reliable

These three legality principles, trained, certified and reliable, apply to both types of dogs. If a case goes to court, the defense will attack these three concerns. SAR dogs have already been held accountable to these principles in recent court cases.

Cadaver Dogs

A question remains as to whether the cadaver or human remains dog is a human scent dog or a contraband substance dog. This question has not yet been answered in court. (As of this date, January 2008.) There is no federal or state case law, that I am aware of, that addresses an alert from a cadaver or human remains dog as probable cause to obtain a search warrant, search or arrest. Therefore, if the cadaver or human remains dog is placed in the contraband substance dog group, that alert would stand alone and meet the criteria for probable cause to search or arrest. If the cadaver or human remains dog were placed in the human scent dog group, that alert would have to be corroborated by other evidence. Based upon review of the case law below, an alert from a cadaver dog is *reasonable suspicion* and therefore other evidence must corroborate the dog alert.

Federal and State Appellate Case Law on Cadaver Dogs

FEDERAL Case Law:

Kerr v Lyford (171 F.3d 330 U.S. Court of Appeals Fifth Circuit, 1999)

The court found probable cause in this case, based upon these reasonable suspicion elements:

- Statements of the child witnesses implicating the Kerrs in their own sexual abuse and in Wilson's abduction, rape and murder;
- Medical examinations of the children that revealed scarring consistent with their tales of sexual molestation;
- Confessions and statements supplied by adult witnesses Geer, Martin, and Wanda Kerr, verified by polygraph, consistent with those of the children in implicating the Kerrs in the kidnapping, rape, and murder of Wilson;
- Corroborative physical evidence such as masks, knives, and other instrumentalities of restraint and torture that were referred to by the children;
- An infrared scanning device and a cadaver-sensing dog suggested the presence of human remains on the Kerr's property, and bones (albeit not conclusively human) were unearthed;
- The shed in the Kerrs' backyard--which had been identified by some of the children and the adults as the place where Wilson's body had been kept--was also alerted to by the dog and, suspiciously, showed signs of recent washing and repainting.

STATE Case Law:

Trejos v. State (2007 Tex. App. LEXIS 4045 Court of Appeals of Texas, First District, Houston 2007)

The dog scent evidence was admissible, due to the fact that the dog was trained, certified and reliable:

We apply the three factors to determine whether Missy and Chloe were qualified cadaver dogs.

Buzzards and Butterflies

The first factor is whether the type or breed of dog works well off lead. Missy is a mixed-breed dog, a Sharpei-shepherd mix. Chloe is a Rottweiler. Deputy Pikett testified that mixed-breed dogs and Rottweilers are capable of performing as cadaver dogs, and that cadaver dogs are dogs that work well off lead. Although his testimony does not directly show that these dogs work well off lead, his testimony reasonably supports the inference. Thus, the first factor weighs slightly in favor of the implied finding that Missy and Chloe were qualified and reliable.

The second factor concerns the training of the dog to distinguish between human cadaver scents and animal scents. Before the search in 2001, Bickel and her dog Missy had been to at least 10 different training seminars in addition to training several times a week. Deputy Pikett testified that he had trained extensively with Missy and she is a very good dog. In 2000, Missy was certified by two local organizations and two national organizations, including the North American Search Dog Network and the Lone Star Search and Rescue Dog Association.

Spurlock testified that she and Chloe, the confirmatory dog, had received training at various seminars from dog trainers and from law enforcement personnel and that Chloe exhibited a meticulous attitude towards cadaver work. In November 2001, Chloe had received extensive training for one and one-half years, was certified within the volunteer group of which she and Spurlock were a part, but was not certified by any national organization. An outside evaluator that utilized the same standards as the national organizations did the local certifications. Only dogs that meet the standards will be used for a cadaver search. The State's witnesses established that these cadaver dogs had received training and that they were certified and could be used in searches. The second factor weighs in favor of the implied finding that the dogs were qualified to conduct the cadaver search.

The third factor is whether the dog has been shown to be reliable in its prior experiences searching for cadavers. Bickel testified that as of November 9, 2001, Missy already had a good history of finding human remains. After receiving her certification, Bickel testified that she had never known Missy to indicate a false positive, such as alerting on animal remains. Spurlock testified that in Chloe's training she performed very well when distractions such as animal bones or fluids were put out in the field and was still able to find the human remains. Spurlock testified that she had tested Chloe using many different scenarios such as various fluid samples from the morgue and items buried as deep as five feet. Spurlock also testified that she and Chloe had conducted "numerous searches for remains" and that this case was the first time she had been called to court to testify about a cadaver search. Spurlock testified that during her training and searches, Chloe had never given an alert that was later proved false. Deputy Pikett similarly testified that based upon his training and dealing with Missy and Chloe, they were reliable each time he used them. The witnesses testified that a dog that could not consistently show its reliability in training was not used for actual searches. The witnesses' testimony established that Missy and Chloe had never falsely indicated human remains and that Missy and Chloe could consistently distinguish human remains from other scents. The third factor weighs in favor of the implied finding that the dogs were qualified.

The three factors, when applied to Missy and Chloe, support the trial court's implied finding that the dogs were qualified to search for cadavers. We conclude that the record supports the trial court's implied finding that the dogs were qualified to conduct the search for the cadaver.

People v King (04 Cal. App. Unpub. LEXIS 8280 Court of Appeal California, Fourth Appellate District, Division One, 2004)

The dog scent evidence was admissible, due to the fact that the dog was trained, certified and reliable:

- The dog's handler was qualified by training and experience to use the dog;
- The dog was adequately trained in distinguishing the odor of human cadaver scent;
- The dog has been found to be reliable in alerting on an area where a human cadaver scent has existed;
- The vehicle line-up wherein defendant's vehicle was placed and wherein the canine, Scout, and his handler participated was properly and fairly conducted;
- The defendant's vehicle and the scent within had not become stale or contaminated at the time of the line-up.

Clark v. State (140 Md. App. 540 Court of Special Appeals of Maryland 2001)

The dog scent evidence was admissible, due to the fact that the dog was trained, certified and reliable:

The New England State Police Association (NESPA) has certified Dan as a qualified cadaver dog once a year since 1991. The North American Police Work Dog Association has also certified him as a cadaver dog once every two years since 1991. Testing for certification takes one week. In order to be certified, blood, tissue, or other human remains are hidden and the canine must find the hiding place. During certification, Dan never failed to find what was hidden. Moreover, he never, in training, alerted on "false holes," which are dug in attempts to deceive the dogs.

It is true that Dr. Mires testified that the fact that a cadaver dog alerted at a certain spot was "not enough by itself" to prove the presence (or presence at some time in the past) of human remains to a reasonable degree of scientific certainty. But here, the alert by Dan at the spot in the Clark family graveyard did not stand-alone. Other circumstantial evidence pointed to the fact that there had been a clandestine burial at that spot:

- The fact that the Clark plot had been disturbed between October 14, 1992, and January 3, 1993;
- That appellant was present with his truck and shovel at the grave site on October 31, 1992;
- That a second cadaver dog alerted at the same spot two and one-half years after Dan's alert;
- And that the spot where the cadaver dogs alerted matched the spot, marked by an asterisk found on a map in appellant's truck on October 24, 1992.

Under all these circumstances we believe that there was adequate foundation for the admission of the testimony regarding the officers' interpretations of the actions of Dan and Panzer.

Sandra Anderson:

It should also be noted that there were several cases involving Sandra Anderson, a cadaver dog handler, who was convicted of planting evidence (human remains) at crime scenes:

- **Smith v Bobby** (2007 U.S. Dist. LEXIS 61361 United States District Court for the Northern District of Ohio, 2007)

- **State v. Kupaza** (2006 WI App 130 Court of Appeals of Wisconsin, District Four 2006)
- **People v Islam** (2005 Mich. App. LEXIS 3061 Court of Appeals of Michigan 2005)
- **State v. Smith** (2002 Ohio 4402 Court of Appeals of Ohio, Ninth Appellate District, Wayne County 2002)

Summary:

As the majority of the United States cadaver dog industry is civilian based, it is important to understand the impact of case law. The actions of civilian cadaver dogs affect the law enforcement cadaver dog industry and vice-versa.

An alert from a cadaver dog is *only reasonable suspicion*. In summary, the dog alert/indication must be corroborated by other evidence.

Possession of Contraband for K-9 Training Purposes

By Terry Fleck
K9 Tracker

Historically, the issue of a handler possessing contraband, such as narcotics, explosives, cadaver, etc, in order to train a police service dog, has been relatively ignored by our industry. Handlers routinely possess contraband for K-9 training purposes throughout the United States.

LETTER of the LAW:

In most states the letter of the law does not address this issue of possession of contraband for K-9 training purposes. Therefore, in these states, under letter of the law, it is illegal for a handler to possess contraband for K-9 training purposes. There are some states that do address this issue by letter of the law. As an example, here are the laws from the State of California:

Possession of Narcotics:

California Health & Safety Code Section 11367.5:
Controlled substances for substance abuse training; Immunity from prosecution; Custody and control

(a) Any sheriff, chief of police, the Chief of the Bureau of Narcotic Enforcement, or the Commissioner of the California Highway Patrol, or a designee thereof, may, in his or her discretion, provide controlled substances in his or her possession and control to any duly authorized peace officer or civilian drug detection canine trainer working under the direction of a law enforcement agency, provided the controlled substances are no longer needed as criminal evidence and provided the person receiving the controlled substances, if required by the Drug Enforcement Administration, possesses a current and valid Drug Enforcement Administration registration which specifically authorizes the recipient to possess controlled substances while providing substance abuse training to law enforcement or the community or while providing canine drug detection training.

(b) All duly authorized peace officers, while providing substance abuse training to law enforcement or the community or while providing canine drug detection training, in performance of their official duties, and any person working under their immediate direction, supervision, or instruction, are immune from prosecution under this division.

(c) (1) Any person receiving controlled substances pursuant to subdivision (a) shall maintain custody and control of the controlled substances and shall keep records regarding any loss of, or damage to, those controlled substances.

(2) All controlled substances shall be maintained in a secure location approved by the dispensing agency.

(3) Any loss shall be reported immediately to the dispensing agency.

(4) All controlled substances shall be returned to the dispensing agency upon the conclusion of the training or upon demand by the dispensing agency.

Possession of Explosives:

California Penal Code Section 12302:
Sale to, or purchase, possession, transportation, storage, or use of, by, law enforcement officers, military personnel, or firefighters:

Nothing in this chapter shall prohibit the sale to, purchase by, or possession, transportation, storage, or use of, destructive devices or explosives by:

(a) Any peace officer listed in Section 830.1 or 830.2, or any peace officer in the Department of Justice authorized by the Attorney General, while on duty and acting within the scope and course of his or her employment.

(b) Any member of the Army, Navy, Air Force, or Marine Corps of the United States, or the National Guard, while on duty and acting within the scope and course of his or her employment.

Nothing in this chapter prohibits the sale to, or the purchase, possession, transportation, storage, or use by any person who is a regularly employed and paid officer, employee, or member of a fire department or fire protection or firefighting agency of the federal government, the State of California, a city, county, city and county, district, or other public or municipal corporation or political subdivision of this state, while on duty and acting within the scope and course of his or her employment, of any equipment used by that department or agency in the course of fire suppression.

Possession of Cadaver:

California Government Code Section 27491.45:
Retention of tissues removed at autopsy; Removal of parts for transplant, or therapeutic, or scientific purposes:

(a) (1) The coroner shall have the right to retain parts of the body, as defined in subdivision (g) of Section 7150.1 of the Health and Safety Code, removed at the time of autopsy or acquired during a coroner's investigation as may, in the opinion of the coroner, be necessary or advisable for scientific investigation and training. The coroner may employ or use outside laboratories, hospitals, or research institutions in the conduct of the coroner's scientific investigation or training.

(2) Parts of the body retained pursuant to paragraph (1) may be released by the coroner to hospitals, medical educational research institutions, and law enforcement agencies for noncoroner training, educational, and research purposes, either upon consent of the decedent or other person, as specified in Section 7151 of the Health and Safety Code, or after a reasonable effort has been made to locate and inform persons listed in subdivision (a) of Section 7151 of the Health and Safety Code of their option to consent or object to the release, and the appropriate person consents or that effort has been unsuccessful. A reasonable effort shall be deemed to have been made when a search for the persons has been underway for at least 12 hours. The search shall include a check of local police missing persons records, examination of personal effects, and the questioning of any persons visiting the decedent before his or her death or in the hospital, accompanying the decedent's body, or reporting the death, in order to obtain information that might lead to the location of any persons listed in subdivision (a) of Section 7151 of the Health and Safety Code.

SPIRIT of the LAW:

As most states do not have law(s) allowing possession of contraband for K-9 training purposes, these states are operating under spirit of the law. When one obeys the spirit of the law but not the letter of the law, he is doing what the authors of the law intended, though not adhering to the literal wording. Historically, this is where the issue of a handler possessing contraband for K-9 training purposes under spirit of the law, has been relatively ignored. Although rare, there have been handlers that were confronted by their own agency, or another agency, regarding possession of contraband for K-9 training purposes. In fact, one State's

POST (Peace Officers Standards and Training), has verbally advised / warned their state's K-9 handlers regarding this issue.

LOSS of a CONTRABAND "TRAINING AID":

Unfortunately, numerous contraband training aids have been left behind at training locations, resulting in their loss. In order to prevent the loss of these aids, I recommend a primary and secondary custodian of all contraband training aids:

- There should be a "primary custodian" and a "secondary custodian" of the training aids. The primary would be the handler and the secondary would be the trainer or secondary person on-scene. <u>Both</u> custodians are tasked with training aid recovery and accountability.
- All training aids should be clearly marked "Training Aid; *Agency name*; If Found Call *Agency Phone Number*; Reward If Found".
- Lock boxes, built to nationally recognized standards, should be mounted in all K-9 vehicles to safely and securely transport training aids to prevent theft or loss.

COMPLIANCE with OTHER STATE LAWS or INDUSTRY BEST PRACTICE STANDARDS

With possession of contraband for K-9 training purposes, there are other laws or industry best practice standards considerations that should be addressed:

- **Narcotics**:
  Typically, there are no other issues in possession of narcotics for K-9 training purposes.

- **Explosives**:
  Due the safety concerns in the handling and transportation of explosives, there is a nationally recognized standard, ATFE (Bureau of Alcohol, Tobacco, Firearms and Explosives). I recommend that all agencies be in compliance with ATFE guidelines.

- **Cadaver**:
  There may be state law regarding the pathogen issues of cadaver handling and transportation. I recommend that all handlers / agencies be in compliance with their State Health Law(s).

SOURCES of CONTRABAND TRAINING AIDS:

- **Narcotics:**
  DEA (Drug Enforcement Administration):
  DEA will issue a law enforcement agency narcotics training aids. The aids consist of twenty-eight (28) grams of each substance. To apply, register at www.deadiversion.usdoj.gov. Register by filling out the DEA-225 form. There is a toll free phone number for assistance: 1-800-882-9539.

Agency Evidence / Property Section:
Once the Court has released narcotics, many agencies will dedicate the narcotics as K-9 training aids. If an agency does this, the narcotics should be tested in order to verify the type of narcotic and the percentage of the narcotic.

- **Explosives:**
Explosive Manufacturers:
There are several explosive manufacturers nationwide that sell explosives training aids specifically developed for K-9 teams. As an example, Alpha Explosives in Lincoln, California, sells these K-9 training aids.

- **Cadaver:**
Coroner:
As stated above, the Coroner is typically the person who releases cadaver-training aids.

POSSESSION SOLUTIONS:

Letter of the Law:
If you are from a state with no law exemption for possession of contraband for K-9 training purposes, I suggest addressing it by proposed law. You may simply copy an existing state's law(s) as a model and have a law enforcement friendly legislator sponsor it.

Spirit of the law:
If you are operating under spirit of the law, although rare, there have been a few issues as stated above.

Letter of the Law and Spirit of the Law:
Handlers and agencies should be aware of the issues stated above, loss of a contraband training aid, and compliance with other state laws or industry best practice standards. I suggest not only awareness, but compliance with these issues as well.

K9 Mandy alerts to handler just out of picture with a bark. Note K9 body position. Sample on bumper of car. Handler, Roxye Marshall, Brunswick Search and Rescue Team, NC.

Crime Scene Preservation

By Christy Judah

An important aspect of search and rescue is *the find.* With that find, the K9 handler is placed in a position to preserve and protect a potential crime scene. Any cadaver search (with a body recovery or not) has a high probability of being a crime scene. Until the scene is proven otherwise, all handlers should keep the scene uncontaminated until it can be recorded and evidence collected. The protection of the scene begins with the arrival of the first search team member on scene and continues until the scene is turned over to a law enforcement officer. This maintains a chain of custody of evidence.

All handlers are encouraged to attend a workshop or discussion on crime scene preservation. Among the most basic principals usually taught are:

1. When entering the scene, walk OUT the same way you walked IN. Approach the scene very methodically if practical. Take mental notes on the scene and surrounding area.

2. Do not touch anything. If you must touch the body to determine life or death, once that determination is made, immediately back away from the person being careful to maintain the scene as you discovered it.

3. Rope off the immediate area with flagging tape or rope to contain the primary scene. Rope off or flag three times the most probable sized area to ensure a large scene is protected.

4. Record the time entering the scene, time leaving the scene, personnel present, individual to whom you are releasing the scene, etc.). Record anything that may have been moved or changed from how it was found when you entered the scene. Note odors or damages to the area.

5. Do not discuss the scene with others except appropriate law enforcement personnel or team members during a team debriefing.

6. Report anyone that you observe who has altered or changed the scene in any form or fashion.

7. Team members not on the discovery crew should stay away from the scene unless a specific reason requires them to join the discovery team. Non-essential personnel should leave the scene and return to base camp.

K9 Mandy demonstrates a "touch" indication behavior.

8. Do not eat, drink or smoke in the crime scene area. The crime scene should be considered a restricted area.

9. In order to protect the handler or searcher, one person should never be left alone at the crime scene. For their safety, they should be accompanied by at least one other person. More than once a *suspect* has been in the nearby woods watching the scene.

10. Remember the cardinal PPE rules. Protect yourself with rubber gloves and provide only life-saving medical assistance when there are no other personnel available trained to do so.

Cross-Trained or Not

There are continual discussions on the merits of cross-training a search and rescue dog. Cross training (training the dog to alert on more than one basic type of scent) is a handler decision that may be based upon the need and availability of resources. What type of training is most often requested for the area of service? How many SAR dogs are available to respond to missing person incidents?

Some teams require the dog to be trained and certified in one area (either trailing, wilderness air scent, cave, etc.) prior to adding a Human Remains Detection training and certification. This premise addresses the needs to find a "live person" in addition to locating a deceased person. Human Remains detection dogs which are trained exclusively on human remains will not be needed in cases where it is unclear whether the person is alive or not. Exclusively trained HRD dogs may be quite valuable in determining the extent or location of the crime scene when no intact body is expected or located.

There *is* a major consideration for disaster dogs (those responding to a natural or man-made disasters) who are tasked with locating the living person that is trapped in rubble. A disaster dog cross-trained on human remains may become a liability when resources are limited. The available resources need to be targeted toward saving the living and not recovery of a body. In the interest of injury and "time", these scenarios require the dog to "pass" or ignore the dead in favor of the living. A cross-trained dog may revert to an alert on a cadaver scent regardless of the command given by the handler.

One might argue that wilderness air scent (off-lead) dogs may revert to a cadaver alert when given the live find command in a typical missing person scenario. There are differences in the mission of the searchers (finding the person vs. finding only the live persons) and a cross-trained dog seems to present no harm by locating a deceased person rather than a live one. When multiple victims are lost, or the physical condition of the lost person is unknown, the dog needs to alert on "any" human being in the vicinity, whether dead or alive. Therefore, the minimal amount of time lost in identifying the scent, as deceased does not adversely affect the outcome of the mission in most cases. Alerting on cadaver does not engage recovery resources to the extent that a cadaver alert might affect resources in a disaster situation. Since most missing persons case briefings are not able to definitively assess whether the person is alive or dead, the handler usually prefers the dog to revert to a cross-trained indication rather than by-pass the body.

There is also the unanswered question as to exactly when the human live scent *becomes* cadaver scent. At what point does the dog definitively delineate the scent as dead? And at what point do we expect our dogs to *think* for themselves rather than following the unknowing command of the two-footed searcher on the other end of the lead? Some trainers expect the dogs to do exactly as the handler has trained them. The only problem with this is that it is literally impossible to train for every scenario the handler may face throughout years of search missions. A medium must be met to a degree of control without breaking the bond of the handler and dog. Handlers should strive to reach the highest level of training within the boundaries of their abilities. Know your limitations and place in the hierarchy of search. Provide a service to assist law enforcement or emergency services and never supersede this role with a personal need for excitement, grandeur or publicity. Handlers work with LEO (law enforcement officers) to provide coordinated efforts to recover the missing person, maintain and protect evidence, and support the closure of the case which may or may not involve court proceeding, testifying, or search reports. Be an asset and not a liability.

Handler, Protect Thyself

Any role involved in a potential crime, whether protector or defender, creates a danger for all involved. SAR Dog handlers are no exception, especially Human Remains Detection dog handlers. In more than one aspect, handlers need to take precautions to protect themselves both psychologically and physically.

The most basic of all is to protect your identity. Do not list your home address on the team web page. Consider not listing last names on public brochures, web pages and letterheads. Remember that any HRD search is a potential crime scene which means there is a suspect / criminal involved. It only takes one personal letter received from a death row inmate who wants to provide information about a missing body to make a believer out of a handler. Teams should have addresses that do not place any individual at risk. Be proactive. Get a post office box.

Handler protect thyself against those who would do you harm. There are those who will set about to diminish what you have done through conscientious training and dedication. Know whom you are working with. Know whom you are training with. Know whom you are searching with. On more than one occasion, an individual who has attended the same search, but has never trained or worked with the handler has shown up in the courtroom to testify against the dog handler based upon hearsay or unfounded information. It would be disheartening to pay to attend a training seminar fully trusting the trainer and participants and later discover that trainer or participant sitting with the defense attorney. Highly paid ($10,000 to $15,000) defense expert witnesses are out there. Be aware of who you are associating with, training with, and searching with. Talk to other searchers. Pay attention. This is not a job to be taken lightly.

Handlers need to protect their psychological well being throughout any active search as well as afterwards. Remaining personally detached from the family is one strategy that protects the psyche. It is very distracting and can affect the clear thinking of a searcher/handler when the family is too involved in speaking with searchers and participating in a search. Handlers will usually operate with clearer thought processes when not involved directly with the family. Law enforcement and command staff is available to complete the necessary paperwork or documentation. A SAR dog handler needs to concentrate on their dog and the search mission, not the emotional state of the family. There will be time for that interaction, if at all, at a later date or time.

Buzzards and Butterflies

Handlers need to be in tune to the way they process the entire search scene, mission, and interaction with others during the search. Critical Incident Stress Debriefing is a valuable tool to help the handler process his/her feelings and thoughts regarding the search. A healthy dose of CISD can mean the difference between mental processing the search and all of its aspects in a healthy manner or a divorce. With the high probability of observing extremely unnatural scenes, an HRD handler *must be aware of the resources that allow them to work in this type of volunteer service.* This is not the job for everyone. More than one handler has completed precisely *one* HRD search because of the difficulty of dealing with the emotional aspect of death. Know how to request free CISD before you ever respond to your first HRD search. Searchers protect mental well being.

Videotaping Training Sessions and Searches

Unfortunately, it is not advisable to videotape training sessions or searches in progress. If you decide to videotape a training session to review your progress or critique yourself, it is advisable to erase that tape immediately after the training session. It is truly regrettable that there are those who will save those tapes for use many years down the road to discredit a hander-dog team. Do not be naive.

It is impossible to provide an accurate picture of the skills of a particular dog or handler without scientific documentation of the conditions of the search, whether a training situation or an actual search mission. Temperatures, wind conditions, scent conditions, humidity, number of hours into the training or search mission, travel time involved, health of the handler or dog, and many other factors play into what is being observed. Only the handler and those with many hours, days, weeks, months or years training with the dog handler team can possibly interpret what is being observed. However, there are those who would profess to evaluate a dog team with a five-minute tape and testify to the training, reliability, and certification of the dog.

In a similar vein, there are those who would testify about the skills of the dog from an observation six years ago at a seminar or the hearsay of others without first-hand knowledge of the abilities of the handler or dog. There is little that can be done other than to demand the highest of ethics in the canine handling arena seeking only to educate and improve the skills of all dog handlers, particularly civilian handlers assisting law enforcement. Only through LEO and civilian dog handler collaboration can the future of dog handlers continue to be a positive influence on missing person cases. You cannot control others. We must each lead by example with the highest of ethics, continual training, and professional behavior. The missing person demands it.

Handler - Know Thy Place

K9 handlers need to be in tune to "their place" within the law enforcement community. Civilian handlers are *not* LEO. K9 handlers and SAR teams are a resource to assist LEO and emergency management in missing persons cases...no more, no less. In this role, they must understand the working relationship with the law enforcement and emergency management (or other agency such as Parks Department, etc.)

There is no turf issue in a missing person case. The missing person is the issue, not the turf. There should be no hidden agendas or strange ulterior motives to work SAR cases. It is about the missing person. When a K9 handler misrepresents his or his dogs abilities, begs for media coverage, presents "self" instead of job, or otherwise promotes himself or his dog, it reflects badly upon all canine handlers, civilian and LEO alike. Do not lose sight of the real reason for the search - the missing person. Do not lose sight of the abilities needed to efficiently perform the job. Do not become a liability instead of an asset. Be sure you are covered by liability insurance for accidents to and from or in the field.

There are many who "want to be" a SAR dog handler. There are few who are willing and committed to doing the training, becoming informed in SAR matters, credential themselves and their dogs, document appropriately, and do *this* for the right reasons. If you are not sure, spend some time talking to a SAR dog handler with experience. You will know whether this is your calling after that conversation. May God Bless each who so unselfishly gives back to the community through search and rescue teams.

K9 Rascal, Handler Beckie Stanevich, USAR, West Virginia

Buzzards and Butterflies

K9 Maggie, Handler Laurie Babson, Brunswick SAR, NC

8
Searches

Outline
Search for Drowning Victim at Bear Lake, Utah
Search for Drowning victim at Lake Powell, Utah
The Search for Lacey Peterson
Plane Crash Recovery
Arvada Case in Wyoming
Some Days are Like That
Some Things I Wish I had been told
Special Victims
Small & Rural Streambed
Two Winters & One Summer
Oceanesque K9 Water Searches
Flash Floods
The Letter
Incidental Voids Become a Clue
Hurricane Katrina and the World Trade Center Dogs
Closure

Search for Drowning Victim at Bear Lake, Utah

Gene Ralston
September 2000

A 24-year old male drowned on August 13th, in Bear Lake, while swimming from a boat. He went down in 148 feet of water. The search efforts included a powerful underwater remote operated vehicle (ROV) from the National Park Service in Arizona, several local divers, search dogs from American Search Dogs, as well as a lot of other resources. We notified the SAR team and discussed our desire to help with the side scan unit. The official search had been called off, but they agreed to let us demonstrate the side scan unit.

We arrived at the Bear Lake State Park Marina in the afternoon of September 29th, set up and tested the equipment. (The) County Sheriff's Office, and side scan team member(s), came along to drive the boat while I operated the sonar equipment and Sandy assisted with the towfish cable management and general oversight. After briefing the following morning and boating across the lake to the scene, we began searching a 50 foot parallel line grid pattern I had set up using the best available estimation of a point last seen, in addition to search dog alert location information. By 2:55 p.m. we had found the subject. Additional images were made that afternoon and the next day to confirm that our target was indeed the drowned swimmer.

The next two days were spent working with local officials to establish a recovery plan. The water depth, combined with the 6000' elevation, made recovery using divers very risky. It was decided to request the National Park Service to return with the ROV for the recovery. A large

Buzzards and Butterflies

number of local SAR folks, sheriff's deputies from two counties, Idaho and Utah State Park rangers, assisted with the recovery.

The image below shows the victim. The towfish was at the right side of the image, so shadows are cast to the left. The bright "box" at the bottom of the image is a 4' cubicle acoustic target that we placed near the body to help guide the ROV. The ROV uses a sector scanning sonar, which produces a radar-like image, to locate the target and the body. The body was grasped with the manipulator arm and brought to the surface. Needless to say, the family was very relieved and appreciative since they had all but given up hope.

Side Scan Sonar

Search for Drowning Victim at Lake Powell, Utah

By Gene Ralston
October 2000

We had the grand opportunity to work with Glen Canyon National Recreation Area staff (GCNRA), while we were at Bear Lake. The National Park Service administers the GCNRA that encompasses Lake Powell. (They) had used a Deep Ocean Phantom 2+2, remote operated vehicle (ROV) to search for a drowning victim in Bear Lake several weeks earlier and had returned to conduct the recovery. (GCNRA staff) were impressed with the deep-water capability and the image quality of our custom made towfish.

On October 10th, a representative of the GCNRA called to ask if we would be interested in coming to Lake Powell to help search for another drowning victim. The victim, a 53 year old man, had been vacationing with friends on a houseboat and had fallen or jumped from the houseboat on October 7th. The houseboat was equipped with a GPS unit and it had been set to record the track of the houseboat as it entered Rock Creek Bay! An initial search was conducted using the GCNRA ROV, but they indicated they might want us to help with the search if they were unsuccessful.

The GCNRA search operations officer officially requested our assistance on October 13th. He indicated the water depth in the primary search area ranged from 200 to 250 feet and the bottom was very irregular with a 70-foot vertical wall running through the middle of the search area. A search dog had been deployed along the shoreline and had a very strong alert in an area downwind from the predicted PLS. Daily logs of the previous search activities as well as maps of the search area showing underwater contours were faxed to us for planning purposes.

Following completion of a mission to Casper, Wyoming, on October 19th, we traveled to the marina in Arizona to begin search efforts. We met with GCNRA search officials on October 21st to review past search efforts and to prepare for our part of the search effort.

A north/south search line pattern was established which appeared to parallel the underwater contours and coincidentally, nearly paralleled the track of the houseboat. The lines were extended well past the north and south boundaries of the previously searched area to allow for turns and repositioning. Search lines were programmed into the navigation computer. The incident commander (IC) requested that we start searching as near the eastern shore as possible and continue searching west towards the houseboat's recorded track.

The irregular terrain and large boulders on the bottom required imaging each "lane" in opposite directions to see into the shadow areas behind boulders and pinnacles. By the end of the first day we were near the houseboat's track line.

About thirty minutes into the second day's search, we imaged the body lying in 286 feet of water in a relatively smooth area of the bottom. The body was (located) in an area just outside of the area previously searched by the GCNRA ROV team. An acoustic target was placed nearby and the vessel with the ROV was brought into position and anchored. The ROV was deployed and the acoustic target was used to guide it to the victim.

Just as the ROV manipulator grasped the victim, a strong squall, with 30 to 45 mile per hour winds, swept into the bay. The ROV deployment vessel is 16 feet wide by 46 feet long and has a large cabin. Needless to say, the winds were sufficient to cause the large vessel to drag its two anchors and the ROV on a wild ride! When the storm had subsided, it was discovered that the ROV umbilical had been severely tangled with the anchor lines as well as with the acoustic target and the ROV had lost its cargo.

The next few hours were spent untangling the ROV from the anchor lines and clearing the area to begin the side scan search for the again missing person. We concentrated the search effort in the area of the original find and the two adjacent lanes. We found drag marks made by the ROV and the acoustic target during the storm, but could not clearly see the victim. We reviewed the images from several passes over the same area and tried to determine the most likely path of the ROV during the storm.

Upon closer examination and evaluation of the images, an object of the right size and shape appeared to be lying in the trench made by the ROV as it was dragged along the bottom (see image below). The slightly out of shape acoustic target was again deployed just as dusk fell. The IC then suspended the day's activities, since we had nearly a one hour trip back to the marina ahead of us, most of which was in the dark!

The following morning, the ROV mother ship was again anchored near the target and the ROV was maneuvered to the bottom. Since the object was in the trench with only a small portion above the "ditch banks" it was difficult to find. We guided the ROV operator along the trench to the object using a sector scanning sonar mounted on the ROV. The sector scanning sonar operates much like an aircraft radar screen. Visual confirmation was made only after the ROV had grasped the object and cleared the turbidity from the area using the ROV thrusters. The ROV and victim were then gently pulled by hand toward the surface. (Team members) donned scuba gear and dove to about 80 feet to escort the ROV and its cargo to the surface.

The National Park Service staff conducted this mission in a very professional manner. They prepared daily Task Assignment Forms for each team. In addition to our side scan team, they provided the ROV team and two to three "picket" boats to control other boat traffic in the area. Other staff handled press, mapping and documentation, logistics, safety, financial, family support, equipment repairs, and legal investigation. Missions began each day at 0500 and briefings were held at the end of each day. Safety officers placed medical oxygen onboard the sonar vessel for use in treating potential CO poisoning from the boat and generator exhaust. Frequent radio contact was maintained among all boats for status checks as well as safety matters. We were very impressed and look forward to working with them in the future.

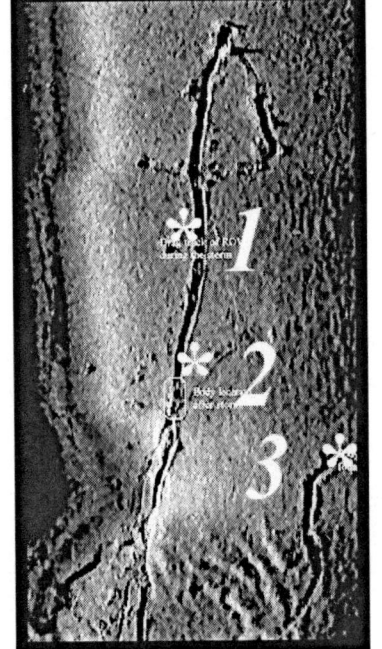

*1 Drag track of the ROV in 286 feet of water
*2 Body Location After the Storm
*3 Body Location before the Storm

The Search for Lacey Peterson

By Gene Ralston

(Information paraphrased with permission.)

The Laci Peterson case generated a tremendous amount of publicity. As a result of this case, Gene Ralston provided the following information in an interview describing his participation with the local law enforcement. These are the inside details of the evidence search for the remains of murdered Laci Peterson and her unborn son. In 2002, Gene and his crew had located four homicide victims for the FBI in 325 feet of water in a California reservoir in addition to many other searches. His crew spent more than 30 days on multiple trips to various locations searching for Laci.

As with most investigations, generally, little information is shared with the recovery crew initially. Essentially the crew needs to know the height and weight, with information regarding the type of packaging that may or may not have been used (was the victim bound or encased in another container). This type of information helps the observer through the sonar to identify the actual target shape.

Initially the target areas were beneath several bridges and later focused on San Francisco Bay. The bridges were challenging since they spanned deep channels, some up to 325 feet deep with steep rocky side slopes. Many had tall trees standing underwater which entangled the towfish. The largest challenge was the huge size of the search area, dealing with commercial ship traffic and the inquisitive boating public.

In homicide cases, it is imperative to have an idea of what you are looking for in terms of shape, otherwise every out of place object is a potential target of interest. Sometimes what appears as just a boulder or round shape is in fact the body.

The biggest factors in a body search include having accurate information and calm water conditions. Surface wave action from wind or passing boats can cause smearing of the sonar images. During the search, Gene and his crew were told to expect to find more than what they were looking for. And they did.

Specifically, the equipment used was a customized Marine Sonic Technology side scan sonar. The stainless steel tow body for the 600 kHz transducer was custom made. The towfish was six feet long and weighed about 130 pounds. The extra length makes it more stable and provides better images. The heavier weight allows it to work in deeper water. This system requires a powered hoist to deploy. Gene uses a variable speed electric motor with a remote control and is equipped with a slip clutch to prevent cable breakage if the towfish snags on anything under the water. An aluminum tow is used for shallow water.

Gene said, "We approach every search with compassion, determination, and the will to succeed. Horrific circumstances cannot be separated or ignored. Often those circumstances instill an even greater desire for success and drive us to work even harder to locate what we have been asked to find."

Plane Crash Recovery

By K. T. Irwin
Northwest K-9 Search & Recovery
Cody, Wyoming
K9 Nia

At the time I worked a plane crash recovery (Federal Express plane crash), my dog was cross-trained in trailing and cadaver. We worked the area two weeks after the crash and the dog alerted approximately 20 times during the grid. Each time she alerted, we found skull fragments and or brain matter on the ground or clinging to the brush. Her close grid work and alerts were amazing. I had trained her on small source beforehand as well as large source. I'd like to make the point that the dog adjusted to the search and level of scent very quickly. I have another cadaver dog that I seriously doubt could make this transition. The new dog can handle very large areas quite well but close search, because of her drive, is not possible and she will be a cadaver dog only (no HRD). It really depends on the dog and how well they focus their attention on their handler for direction or either the hunt drive, be it slow and methodical or fast and sure. Should I have a search with possibly scattered remains (very possible in our area), I would use both of my cadaver dogs to locate the remains but only the older dog to locate the scatter. I think handlers should really understand their dogs' attributes as well as their limitations and use the dog that fits the search.

Arvada Case

By K. T. Irwin
Northwest K-9 Search & Recovery
Cody, Wyoming
K9 Nia

Dates of Searches: November, 2004; June 2005; May 2006
Location: Arvada Area, Johnson County, Wyoming

K-9 TEAMS: K.T. Irwin, Certified Handler with Nia, a seven-year-old Chocolate Labrador Retriever, a Certified Man trailing/Cadaver/Evidence Dog. Indy, a four-year-old Bloodhound Certified in Man trailing and Cross-trained in Cadaver and Willa, a one-year-old Chocolate Labrador Retriever in Training for Cadaver and Man trailing.

Jenny Schneider, Handler in Training. Jenny is presently training a six-month-old Bloodhound pup in Man trailing and Cadaver.

Early in November of 2004, the subject's wife contacted me by telephone to search for her missing husband who had disappeared after being served divorce papers. I stated I could not respond unless requested by law enforcement. Approximately two weeks later, Captain Kevin Filbert contacted me requesting search dogs. The subject had not been seen since the first week in November of 2004.

Items left at the home such as car keys, paychecks, wallet and other personal items, and a pistol missing from the family gun collection that indicated the subject had possibly left to commit suicide. The subject's truck was parked at the ranch house while the family four-wheeler was found parked at the hunting cabin approximately two miles from the ranch house. The subject had been missing for approximately one month at this time.

Friends stated the subject had said he would never leave the ranch, which belonged to his wife before their marriage and which she would retain after the divorce. The approximate search area was the entire ranch, roughly 20,000 acres. During the past month, law enforcement and search and rescue personnel had searched the area with over 200 searchers including ground-pounders, airplanes, ATVs and equine teams with no clues found except that during a previous search (about two weeks after the subject went missing) a searcher on horseback had a bull elk charge past him while he was riding up a drainage. The searcher said he smelled cigarette smoke in the area and did not continue the ride up the drainage. Because of the smell of cigarettes, search managers thought it possible the subject was hiding out and eluding searchers.

I responded with two dogs; Nia, certified in human remains recovery and man trailing and Indy, certified in man trailing and cross-trained in cadaver. When we arrived, the temperature was between 0 and 25 degrees with three to four inches of snow on the ground. It was not certain whether the subject was alive or dead so I put K-9 Nia on the cadaver command and K-9 Indy on the tracking command after scenting him on the subject's clothing, and started at the PLS (place last seen: the cabin). We did not know if the subject had driven the 4-wheeler to the cabin but it was

Buzzards and Butterflies

assumed that he had. I informed law enforcement that, after a month, it was way too late to attempt to track the individual from the time he went missing but if he was alive and walking around and we happened to cross his fresh track, the dog would indicate and take the track.

The ranch house is northwest of the cabin. As you stand at the cabin, you are looking south with a very high ridge west and another ridge to the east. In between the two ridges are meadow areas and numerous drainages. There are also numerous drainages cutting down both ridges.

With such a huge area to cover by one dog-team, I decided to climb high and make the best use of the wind. Another dog team was due in later that day. We climbed to the top of the west ridge and proceeded south. Winds were coming from the southeast. Halfway down the ridgeline, K-9 Nia began to show great interest and proceeded south working the wind. She followed the ridgeline until it curved south-southeast and then slowed and stopped. I told her to continue forward but she would not go and when I tried to move forward, she positioned her body in front of me to block my way. At the time, I did not understand why the dog was behaving in this manner. When Nia finally obeyed my command (very dejectedly) to move forward, we continued south, east, and then north hiking a five-mile path around the area staying high on the ridges.

K9 Nia working drainage with K. T. Irwin in background.

I requested the second dog team to arrive at the search to check the area on the ridge where Nia had interest but that K-9 had no interest in the area. Later, after checking the map, the other team decided they had not made it all the way to the alert area. We covered areas north and east of the cabin for the rest of that day and the next day with no further interest from the dogs. During the drive out, we checked several drainages and caves but again no interest from the dogs or further clues.

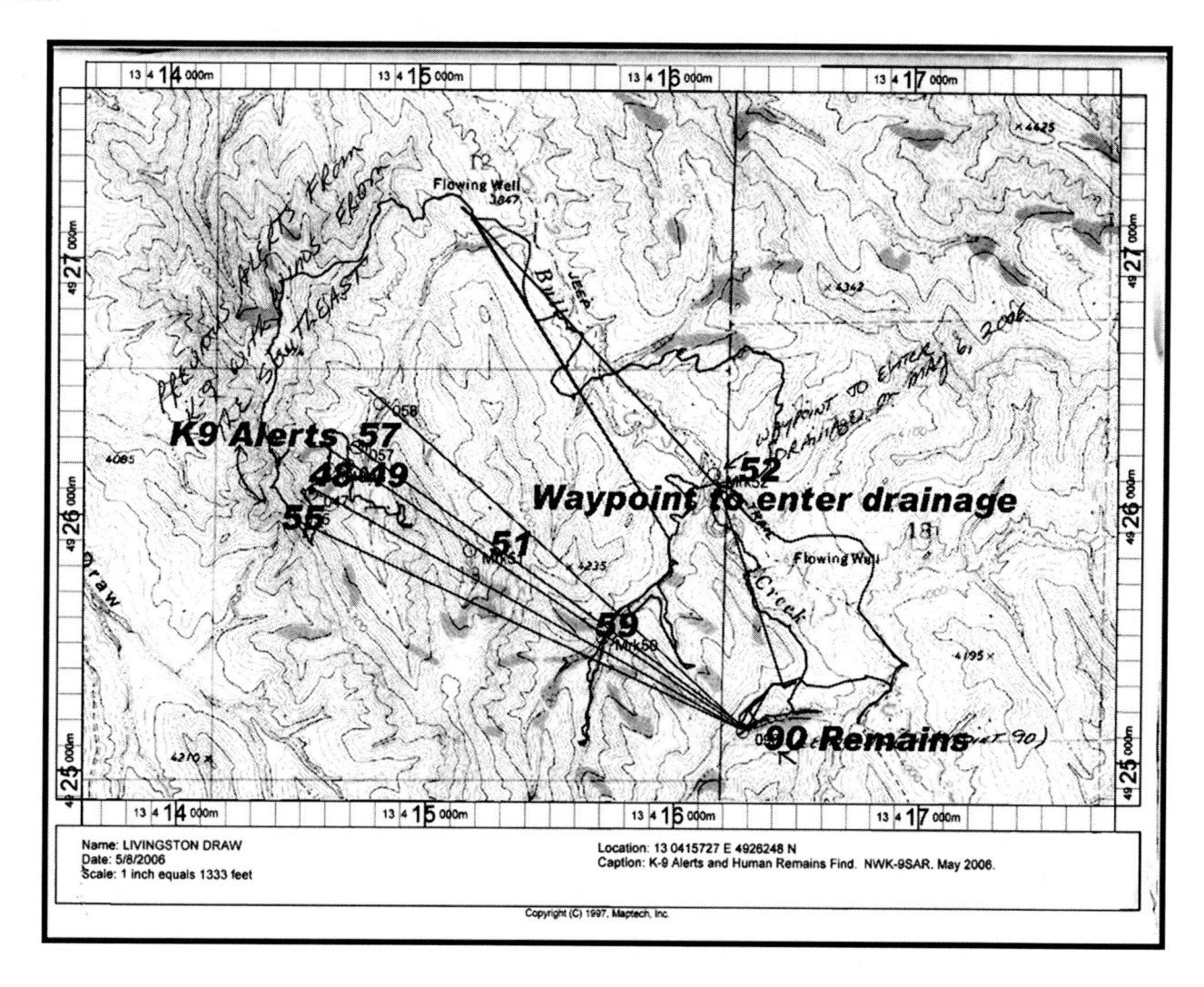

[Map: Livingston Draw, 5/8/2006, Scale: 1 inch equals 1333 feet. Caption: K-9 Alerts and Human Remains Find. NWK-9SAR. May 2006. Shows K9 Alerts 57, 48, 49, 55, Waypoint to enter drainage, and 90 Remains.]

By June of 2005, we were requested to continue the search again by Johnson County. Officials. Temperatures the first day were 103 degrees and sunny. Winds were from the west so I again walked the west ridge to clear a large area to the west. No response from the K-9s so I felt confidant the subject was not to the west. The next day, temperatures were 106 degrees and sunny. These conditions made it extremely difficult for the dogs and searchers. Winds had switched and were coming from the southeast so I climbed high to the west again and had very high interest from the Nia, who was on the cadaver command. Winds were only three to five miles an hour and intermittent but still coming from the southeast. Nia took off heading east off the ridgeline down to the meadow and began coning and working east crossing the meadow and heading southeast up the next ridgeline. This took approximately two hours with many rest and water stops. Because of the heat, the dog was nearing complete exhaustion so I had to stop and return to the staging area to mark the area on a GPS. (See waypoints 55, 47, 48, 49 and end of trail where the dog was too hot to continue working).

Buzzards and Butterflies

The next day the temperature broke and stayed in the 80s, however, there was no wind. We spent the morning gridding a large area south and east of the previous interest but there was no wind to bring the scent to the dogs. Later that day while working a drainage across from the west ridgeline, there was a puff of wind from the south-southeast and both dogs stopped and looked back with great interest. (Waypoint 58 on the map) Later that day we moved back toward the southeast but winds were coming from the north at 10 – 12 miles per hour and there was absolutely no interest from the dogs toward the north. This was the last day of the search. Because of the number of searchers, area covered and lack of interest from the other dog team, law enforcement decided that the subject was probably in Alaska alive and well and had just decided to leave the area.

At home in Cody, I downloaded my track logs and waypoints showing interest and mapped everywhere the dogs had traveled, wind directions, and alerts from the dogs. Because of the steady winds from the west and north during a few days of each search, and lack of interest from the dogs, I decided the subject was not north or west. However, because of Nia's extreme interest to the southeast while on the cadaver command and both dogs' head checks to the southeast, I decided that area needed further checking. I also thought about how my dog works during searches and trainings. She does not show interest unless she's in scent. All of the dogs are well proofed on animal (trained to *ignore* animal remains) and during these searches we encountered everything from dead coyotes to fresh elk placenta. The dogs would give the carcasses a sniff and continue searching. I could not let it go. Nia was getting scent "as the crow flies" and I knew it. I, rather apprehensively, called Captain Filbert and asked if he'd let us come out again, at our own expense. Captain Filbert called the subject's wife, received permission, and another search was scheduled for the weekend of May 5th, 2006.

K9 Indy, Handler: K. T. Irwin, Cody, Wyoming

Temperatures on Friday, May 5th were in the sixties and comfortable. We headed south from the cabin. Winds were switching from west to southwest. Based on the hits from the dogs, I decided to enter the drainage at Mark (waypoint) 52 and work it to Mark 50 where it split, work both of the drainages, then proceed to Mark 51 and work that drainage back up to the cabin (see map). We managed to cover most of the area that took over six hours. We had no interest.

The next day, we drove down the jeep trail a few miles, left the vehicles and hiked south. Jenny and I stayed high on the ridges for a while, and then dropped into a drainage south of the vehicles that split south and west. After checking the south end for a few minutes, we turned to the west to work the wind that was coming from that direction. The dogs immediately picked up speed and left us, showing interest above us, running trails to the top of the drainage and back down. It looked as if they were following scent to the top and then it was gone with the wind. Further west, they began to show extreme interest sniffing and digging at large rodent nests and about 20 feet further, Nia turned and headed into a thick, brushy area. Tucked into this area were human remains still inside a green sleeping bag. Less than a foot away was a flashlight, gun, water bottle and a lighter. Approximately 70 feet west was a camouflage hat and nearby a human skull. The time was 11:15 AM. The remains were well hidden behind a tree and brush and could easily have been passed by unless the dogs had not picked up the scent and turned into them. The subject had been dressed entirely in camouflage clothing.

Sleeping bag and remains of missing victim.

Buzzards and Butterflies

I climbed to the top of the drainage and radioed another searcher, giving the coordinates of the body. Johnson County law enforcement and the Johnson County Coroner arrived approximately four hours later and processed the scene.

K-9 Nia is an experienced and proven cadaver dog. She has been trained on human, blood, bone, teeth, tissue and organs. Because of her experience level and alerts on the ridge while on the cadaver command, I feel certain the victim was deceased at the time of the first K-9 search in November of 2004. I also believe the searcher on horseback was very close to the body and could still smell the cigarette smoke on the subject's clothing. The elk most probably spooked because it had walked up on human remains.

Clothing, Remains

Nia's effort to block me from continuing south down the ridge on that first day was, I think, her way of trying to tell me we had passed the scent cone. At the point where she first came into scent, we were still approximately one mile from and 370 feet above the remains with numerous valleys, drainages and hills between the body and us. However, the scent cone was almost ¼ of a mile wide and at our elevation, coming straight to the dog on the wind. We were very lucky to have winds from the southeast at the time we were gridding the ridge, lucky to have well-trained dogs with such obvious body language and doing their best to communicate, and lucky that during those moments, I remembered to trust my dogs.

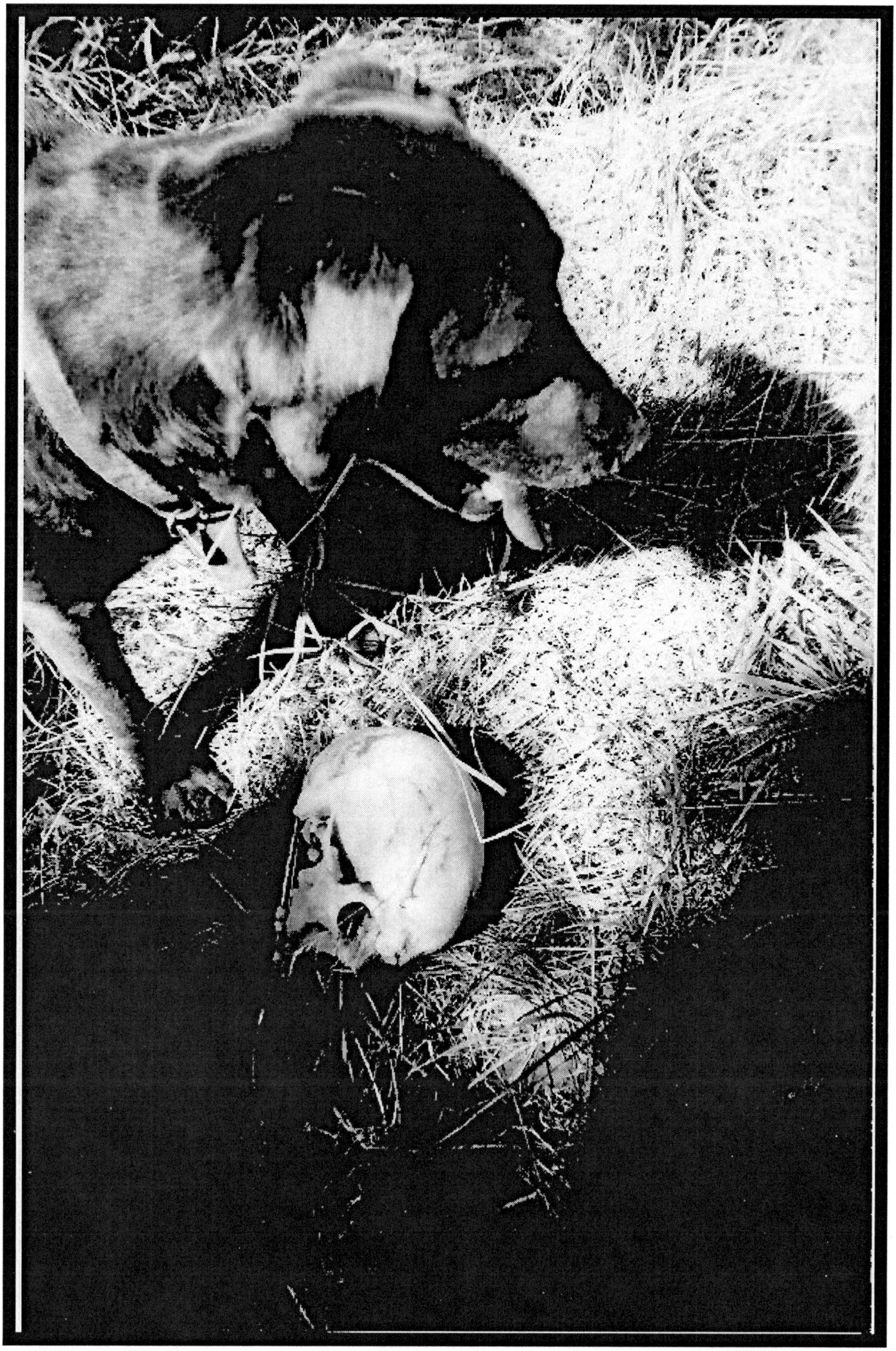

Buzzards and Butterflies

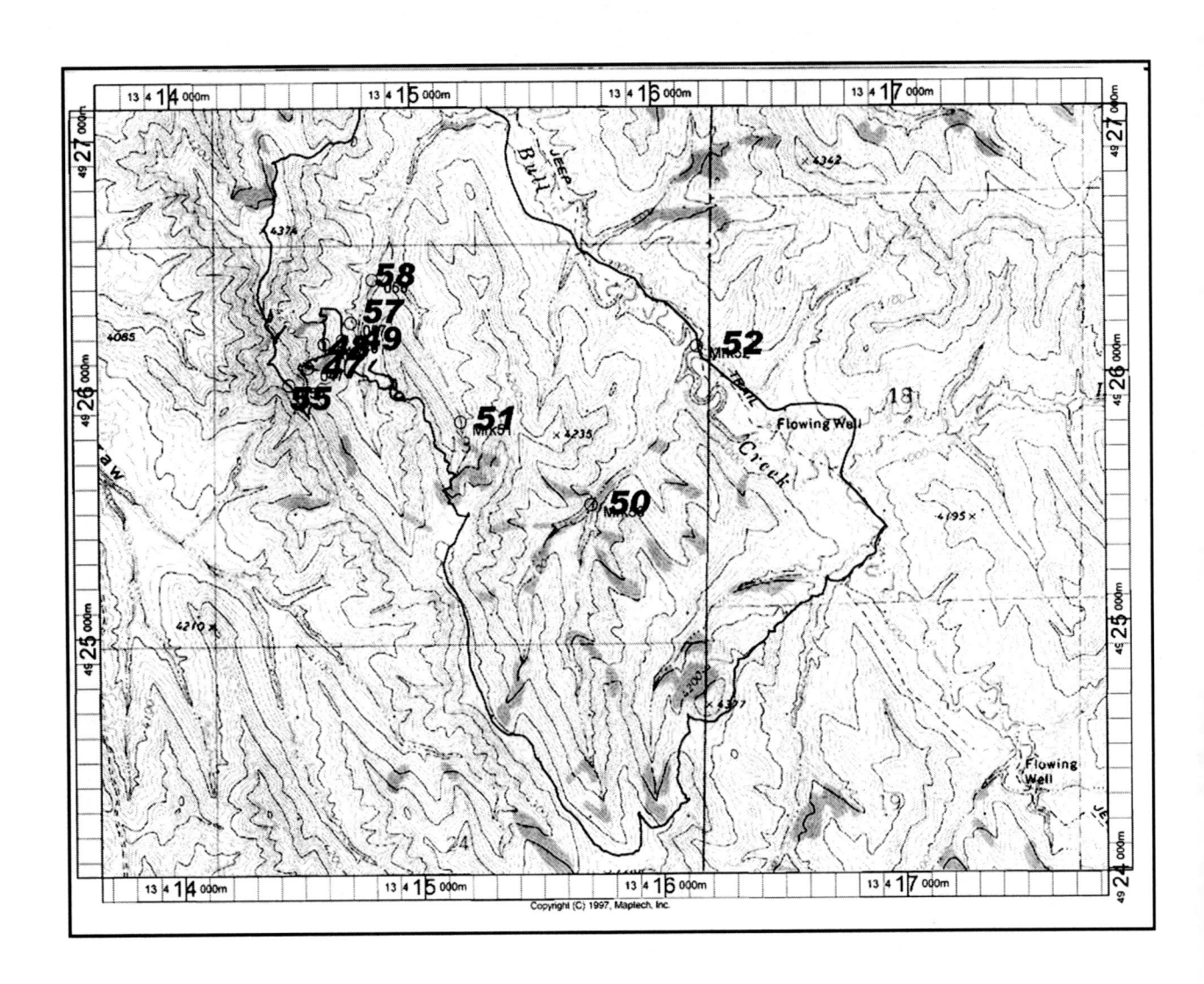

Some Days are Like That

By Sharolyn Sievert
K9 Ariel, Central Lakes SAR, MN
K9 Ariel

The call came in while I was at work; law enforcement needed a couple of cadaver-trained dogs to search a swamp area. At least the location was only an hour away, not the four hours I usually end up driving to searches. It seems they had an informant who claimed a body had been dumped and they needed to either find the body or dismiss the informant's story.

We arrived on scene and my field support joined us there. On route, we learned that the scene was overlooked by an apartment building, and in that building were the informant as well as the possible perpetrators of the crime. Thankfully after our arrival we learned they had been taken in for questioning and we had the place to ourselves.

Our LE officers outlined our area and when we asked about what searching had already been done, we were told none that it was swamp, and also asked if we brought waders. We quickly split the area in half, half being swamp, half unknown but apparently woods from what we could see. I pulled on my gaiters, unloaded my dog and had a deputy pull back and ask if my dog was bite trained. It seems he had a rather unpleasant encounter with a Rottweiler the day before. To his relief, my German shepherd didn't know anything about bite training.

We started into the swamp and found that it was totally dry, not a wet spot anywhere. In short order, we'd covered the area with no alerts from the dog. At about the same time we finished, our counterpart K-9 team finished the other half of the area. A quick briefing to let the other team know about hazards, we took off again.

The woods proved to be the best part of the search, but not for the reason one would have thought. Part way through the woods we came upon a huge leaf pile. Apparently every home in a multiple block area had found a place to dump their yard waste. It was a solid 10 to 12 feet across and 4 to 5 feet deep. My first thought was "good place to hide a body", so I called my dog over to check the pile.

He bounded up and I'm sure in his eyes, it looked like a small hill...so he bounded right into it and sunk straight down. He came floundering out and I couldn't help but laugh. He carefully shook and twisted and shook again. I finally realized that he had leaves where leaves didn't belong. I pulled leaves out from under his search vest and proceeded to finish searching the pile. I poked, prodded and walked into it and he learned to wade in and not drown in leaves.

Buzzards and Butterflies

We finished searching our area and didn't find anything. But on that search we had a lot of fun. We took a day off of work and played in a giant pile of leaves. Haven't done that in a very long time, and we enjoyed it, my field tech, my dog and myself.

On other days, there is "the find".

Some things I wish I had been told...

By Sharolyn Sievert
Central Lakes SAR, MN
K9 Ariel

When I look back at when I started training my first canine for Search and Rescue, I am glad I *wasn't* told some things right up front, such as that my dog would work off lead on air scent searches. Back then I would have envisioned my dog running off and never coming back. Now I know better. However, there are some things I wish I had known.

Did you know that cadaver searches aren't usually 2 or 3 acres? On our very first search only two canine teams were able to come the first day. Law Enforcement personnel rolled out the map and sectioned off 600 acres that needed to be searched. The other handler and I looked at each other across the map and knew it was going to be one of those kinds of days.

Training aids are always a touchy subject, whether you are talking about storage or obtaining them. The one storage plan I wish someone had told me is to keep the bones separate from your decomposition training aids, especially if you want to train for aged burials. I've heard many folks suggest putting the bones in with the other sources to refresh them, however bones will absorb the smell and no longer smell like bones; they will become decomposition-training aids. An aged burial no longer has a great deal of decomposition smell; it is the bones that the canines search for.

How does a person legally obtain training aids? In the beginning, I was given a couple of things from others who trained, but as they struggled to get them, I hated to ask for more. I finally learned of places like "The Bone Room" where you can order your own bones. Ask people to donate bandages or tissues from a bloody nose; when their child loses a tooth, ask the "Tooth Fairy" to donate them. I was 3 years into Search and Rescue before I had the courage to ask a pregnant co-worker to donate her placenta to our unit. Imagine my surprise when she agreed. And when I picked it up at the hospital, I learned the birth mom had told everyone what I was going to be using it for. Instead of being "grossed out", the staff were impressed that people were willing to train dogs to help find missing people. So I wish someone had told me "just ask".

I think the biggest thing I wish I had been told when I first started was about targeting source. The unit I joined had never mission-readied a K-9 cadaver team before and so I learned long distance from other handlers. I never learned how to teach my dog to not only locate the article, but also tag or target it if it should be "invisible" to me. He was quite good at doing it naturally, so we managed to get along without it. When I started my second dog, I learned what I missed with my first: to KNOW where the article actually is, not just where the scent is. As we progressed to aged burials, sometimes years old, I found that having my dog trained to tap the source with his nose or his paw is a huge benefit.

The *Phantom Search* is a description that I developed when I was extremely frustrated during a cadaver training that wasn't going well. I haven't heard another description that so aptly describes a cadaver search since. Sometimes you simply don't know if the search is over or not. You may never know. Do you trust your dog completely even when you can't see anything to prove they are right? "Trust your dog" sounds much easier than it is sometimes.

In HRD or cadaver searches, usually we aren't looking for a full body we can visually see. We are looking for something that may not be there, or if it is, it may be only the odor, with no physical proof. A body buried for years can permeate its scent over a very large area, leaving pools of scent in odd places not necessarily near the actual burial. Sometimes it is a few bones, bleached by sun and weather, looking remarkably like dead leaves.

How many times during a search or during training have you yourself said, or heard another K-9 handler say, "My dog alerted so there must be something there. Maybe someone cut themselves or something." We can all come up with interesting explanations for our dog's alerts and indications. Sometimes we are right; sometimes we are just blowing phantom smoke.

Consider this, which did happen to me. We entered our search area; my dog was still on leash and not under his search command yet. He pulled me hard toward a tree, sniffing all around the base. There was a delay before we were given the ok to search, but as soon as I released my dog, he went straight to the same tree and indicated (in Minnesota we call the final trained response an indication). He hadn't even really searched, but I duly looked around the base of the tree, I looked up the tree, I checked the ground around the tree – nothing. I encouraged my dog to work it out, to find the source. He searched around the area and indicated on the tree again. I trusted my dog, I really did. I kept asking myself where the scent could be coming from that it was ending up at the tree. So I expanded my search area, and again he took me back to the tree.

I'm sure there are those of you who are by now saying "I would have trusted my dog and rewarded him by then." There was nothing visual to prove the dog had located anything. What if I rewarded for something that wasn't there but actually 50 feet away and only drifting scent into the tree? Or looping into it from an even further distance away? Would I not be then rewarding my dog for locating scent pool instead of scent source?

Thankfully this scenario was a training exercise with another unit. The source of scent was fluids poured onto the base of the tree – invisible to the naked eye, but detectible by the dog's nose. The dog was rewarded for finding the phantom that day. On many days however, the phantom remains elusive and invisible, and those are the very frustrating days.

If you are planning to become an HRD, forensic, or cadaver dog handler, or maybe you already are, remember that there are *phantom searches*. Your dog may alert or indicate they have located source. You report it to the requesting agency, and your work is done. You leave the scene never knowing the final results.

Someone asked me when I first started in Search and Rescue if I would be able to handle finding a deceased person, even if it was disarticulated remains. I didn't know the answer then. My answer would now be that I'd rather find those remains in any condition than have my dog indicate a find but have no physical proof to show for it.

For me, phantom searches are the most difficult to work. Yet we respond each and every time we are requested. Every time, I pray for closure for the family and also for us, the K-9 teams who respond. *It is nice to find the phantom* but long live the handler who understands that an assist is as important as a find.

Special Victims

By Patti Gibson
Ill WIS SAR Dogs
K9 Josie Wales

A few yrs ago, we did a rape where the guy lived 4 houses away. He was already in custody. (The wife would have been more then happy to give us a scent article but we ran off his semen on the rug - i.e. used semen for the scent article). We went thru 18 backyards to get back to his house. Along the way, the bloodhound I was working indicated on a knife that he had shoved into someone's backyard woodpile.

The victims' shorts and underwear had been cut off of her with the knife and then he used them to clean her. These were located under another person's backyard deck. The perpetrator had thrown his own shorts up in the rafters of another neighborhood garage. My bloodhound was dancing on her hind legs at that find. Keep in mind that the forensic evidence is what usually helps to convict the criminal....and not the trail itself.

In another search some years back, on Mother's Day, my bloodhound found a hatchet in a stream with blood remaining on it. This was later confirmed by forensic tests. Yes, it was the murder weapon. Yes, it was important in the conviction of a killer.

In day and age of urban sprawl, we must prepare ourselves to work urban environments regardless of the discipline we choose. Training for scent specific trails and situations allows us to be more valuable and more specific in our job. This type of article search helps locate critical evidence including weapons. Human Remains detection dogs can also be used for this type of search and article search when human remains (such as blood) may be on the article sought. Although we do not usually participate in felony searches, this type of article search can be of value to law enforcement.

I would be remiss in not mentioning one of our recent searches....a 103-year-old woman with Alzheimer disease who had been missing since three am. Talking to the chief on the phone I was informed that she had "just" been located several blocks away. Our area got six inches of snow that night and the search location was one hour away. A hundred and three years old!!! I was loading my gear. This lady must have been a dog handler!

Small and Rural Streambed

By Bonnie Laidlaw
SC Search Dogs
K9 Aika

We received an emergency call to assist in a live search in a small, rural town in hot summer weather. A well-known and loved 83-year-old gentleman had been missing a day and a half. He suffered from dementia, diabetes, and was two weeks out of major surgery. None of that kept him down for long, but he was distressed after learning that he would soon have to leave his home of 45 years to be kept in an assisted living facility.

Hundreds of townspeople had been out searching, assisted by SAR groups, local and long distant. Air scent and trailing dogs had been working the areas where he had been seen walking. Two newly arrived air scent dogs (searching different, but adjacent, areas along a stream running through town) exhibited behavior confusing to their handlers. While working, the dogs kept returning to the water only to turn abruptly and seek their handlers. Unusual.... The terrain along the stream was low and thick with brush and briars – very slow going. The handlers finished their areas and returned to IC (Incident Command Center). After reporting in and comparing notes, it was agreed that since water holds scent, they needed to work the water. Shortly after a helicopter following the streambed found the subject lying in the stream in four to six inches of water. The coroner estimated he had been dead 24 hours.

The high banks of the stream and shallow, gently moving water produced a scent pool carried by wind and water all the way through town, but the cadaver dogs had not yet been called in, and it went unnoticed.

Observations:

1. I believe every live scent dog should be exposed to human remains as part of its training – exposed enough to allow the handler and other team members to be aware of the dog's behavior when it encounters scent from HR (Human Remains). The handler should be able to read that unusual behavior and search accordingly.

2. Looking back at the statistics – his age, his infirmities, the time that had elapsed -- instead of just flanking, I should have asked to work my cadaver dog, but it is challenging to do that without offending the community that wanted desperately to find him alive?

3. We were fortunate to have had an organized canine IC, no power struggles among the several different groups present in our areas, and no prima donnas for dog handlers.

4. Law enforcement and rescue volunteers were supportive and sharp – a textbook IC.

Two Winters and One Summer

By Kim Gilmore
Flathead County Search and Rescue, In.
Kalispell, MT
K9 Brenner

Three memorable searches come to mind...two were in the winter and one in summertime. Avalanches and cold-weather searches where the victim is deceased tend to significantly slow down the decomposition process. Avalanche dogs are trained on live people that provide the scent barely discernable between recent deceased and live.

Cold weather drowning, as well as avalanche burials, where the temperature is essentially a constant and somewhere near freezing, will preserve the body in a more natural state and significantly decrease the speed of decomposition. Snow is not necessarily a constant cold temperature, but is in fact very similar to water in that you can have layers and in each of those layers there is a different temperature. It may have up to a 5-8 degree difference between ground and surface snow. However, snow is still below 40 degrees, which for the most part preserves the body. Humidity is an "odd beast." In tropical climates it hastens the decay process. In arid climates it may mummify the body. During the winter 50-80% humidity would not be uncommon for our area with 20-40% maximum during the summer months.

One of our winter finds was a young man who drove out onto a beach area of the local river without knowing that it was dam controlled. The Corp of Engineers opened up the dam to let water out; his pick-up got caught in the rising water and started floating down stream. He bailed and instead of swimming back toward the shore he was closest to, opted to swim across (this is an approx. 300 yard wide river and this happened in February). He managed to get across, up the bank and froze solid in almost no time. Dogs came across him and were confused as to the type of indication to give (this is when I was trying to do a passive indication cadaver dog with bump refind on live)...not really dead/not really alive odor. There was a lot of conflict with the dogs for the body is capable of cooling to the ambient temperature around it.

On land we do refind/bump indications. On shoreline problems, dogs will tend to attempt to get as deep as they can before coming back to do a bump, then re-entering water where they arc hitting scent. On a boat, we tend to watch their body language, as it is hard for them to bump (obviously). My boy will turn and try to get near me for his toy immediately *over* scent Most of our dogs will run the length of boat then come back and bark. We don't encourage jump/plunge indications, as it would be deadly in our water (due to temperature and whitewater conditions).

Young dogs are trained on divers initially, then we train with source, sunken to various depths In this case the body was approximately 100' up the bank (he swam across, climbed up the bank and succumbed to hypothermia. Clothing froze solid and as he was wet, he too was a virtual iceman). My dog went up, acknowledged the find, came back as if he wanted to do a bump, and then sat halfway back as he recognized that the guy was not alive (lack of respiration?) and whined. He was my Type A, obsessive compulsive dog who HATED making a mistake and the conflict in his eyes was very evident and obvious as he didn't want to make a mistake on the indication but had no clue what indication to give. Since then, have went back to my KISS principle that the first three dogs were trained in and #5 has one indication across the board, live or dead. He does (on his own) triage and area search that may have both live and dead and has indicated on live first EVERY TIME before going back to indicate on dead.

The second search involved a young child. A two-year-old left the front door of his daycare headed for the vehicle while his dad went back inside to get another child. The father came out and the little guy was missing. Long story short, he was found at the bottom of a 16', filled to the top and within overflowing, septic tank. No indication by any of the dogs on the septic tank. Note that in a wilderness context, the dogs will show interest in an area where a person has stopped to urinate or defecate but will not indicate/alert on that area. They will indicate/alert on blood or other body fluids.

The crust which is typically on the surface of a septic tank was broken, but the "lid" (piece of board) was on top of the tank so there was no suspicion that is where the child ended up (opened the lid, fell in face first, plywood fell back over opening. Granted it was an unusual situation for the lid to return to the tank as it did.

This search involved assumed child abduction but the dogs kept giving negatives when trying to trail. Weather was in the single digits for the duration of the search, septic tank was inches from full and he was located jammed at the outflow at the bottom of the tank dressed in all his winter wear. This was a great learning experience as a) we don't train on human waste and b) the smell of human waste in addition to cold weather, chemicals in tank masked the odor of the completely clothed 25# child.

Firemen probed the septic tank initially (on day 1) and found nothing. My dog kept throwing negatives in every direction when trying to trail (only scent was in the immediate area where he had been playing that day. Finally on day 3 after extending the search way beyond the POD, command staff decided to pump the septic tank as it was almost overflowing (which was odd as the outflow that drains into the drain field should keep it much lower unless something blocking it). As soon as some of the pressure released, the body surfaced to the top. It was by chance and shrewd thinking on the septic tank owner's part that the tank was drained and the body recovered.

Oceanesque K9 Water Searches

By Amir Findling
Cayuga County Highland SAR
1st Special Response Group (1SRG)
K9 Stryder, K9 Radar

Oceanesque? Does it mean a K9 can search the entire Atlantic or Pacific Ocean? I would not even say that if I were jesting, but compared to traditional water searches, farm ponds, creeks, small lakes, the search area involved in the two searches I will share may as well have looked like an ocean as we began our search.

City Island, NY

The following is a transcript of the 911 call received at 9:58 P.M. on Friday, January 24th, 2003.

> Call begins (when the connection is made, the caller is already speaking)
> Caller: "taking on water"
> Operator: "Police operator number 10-"
> Caller: "Oh my God- Hello?"
> Operator:" Hello"
> Caller: "Hello - ah - we're - Listen - We're on the Long Island Sound, in a boat, off the coast of City Island - We're gonna die -"
> Call ends.

We were not called immediately after this call but much later, as the official search efforts had dwindled down and the parents of the four victims wanted more done to recover their children. I was privately contacted by one of the mothers, then I contacted the local PD to see whether they wanted us there or at least would tolerate our presence and when the latter was affirmed, as in "this is a free country", I decided to organize a search.

I didn't have any knowledge of the City Island, NY area, or at least not its waterways. I had good maps from Maptech, good aerial photography too, but no idea of prevailing winds or currents

Buzzards and Butterflies

etc. I decided not to really start planning from home but wait for more input from local people who might have the needed information.

I needed a second dog, as working such a large area with a single dog was unusual, let alone not having a second dog for confirmation. Christine Buff from Cayuga Highland SAR and her K9 Mittru came along. Mittru, like my dog Radar, are veterans from 9-11, having worked on the recovery efforts at the Fresh Kill site in Staten Island. Both are experienced and very dedicated dogs.

I talked to the parents and local people, mainly from the marina where the boys took the dinghy. Consulting with Chris, I came up with a plan to search an area of about 553 acres, illustrated by figure 1. Why that area? I felt that if the bodies were on the eastern side of Hart Island, it would be next to impossible to find them and the same logic guided me to the south, in the main channel of the Long Island Sound. One of the jobs of a search manager is to define an area he considers to be of prime importance and see that such an area is covered (searched) by the resources he has.

The next step was to make an actual search plan. Scanning the area, I decided, it would be easier to navigate between City Island and Hart Island following a given track on the GPS. This would also satisfy the prevailing winds expected the next day. Figure 2 shows the planned search track.

I drew the two tracks of Figure 1 and 2 using my laptop computer and the software program, Map Tech. I created them as tracks that I downloaded to our main navigation GPS. Our navigator's job was to keep the boat, as much as possible, on the planned track. The boat captain was responsible for the overall safety of the boat and crew, and free to steer clear of any dangers we did not know about, shallow waters, etc.

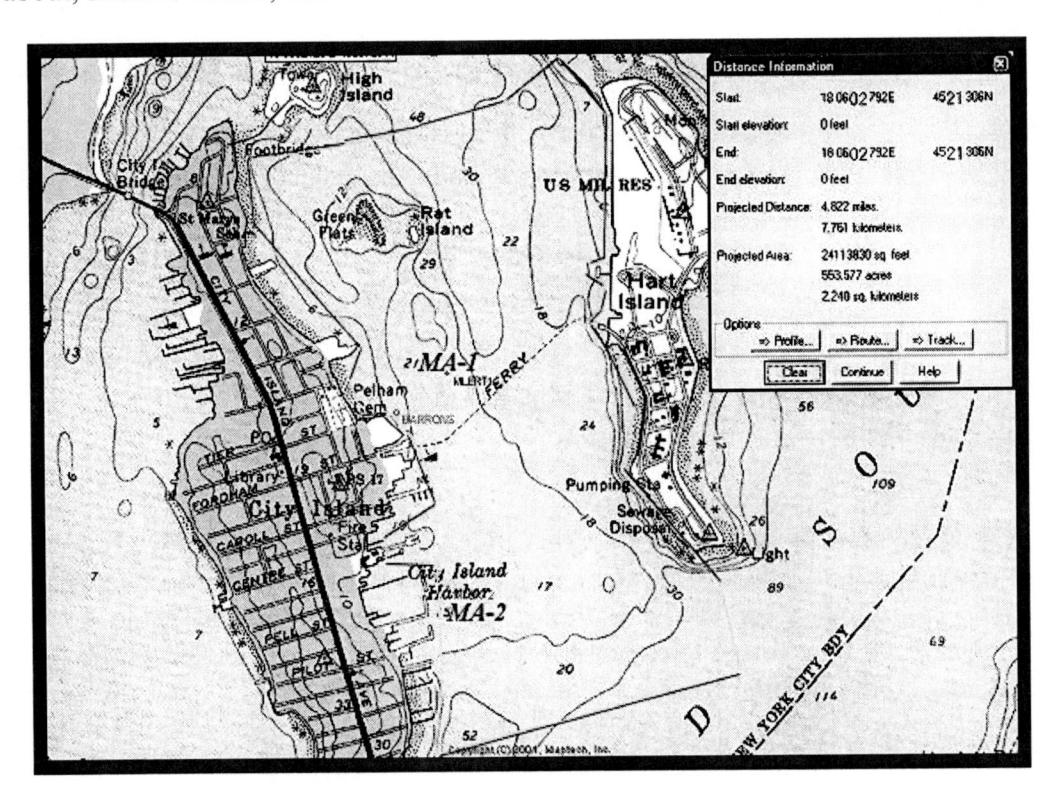

Figure 1

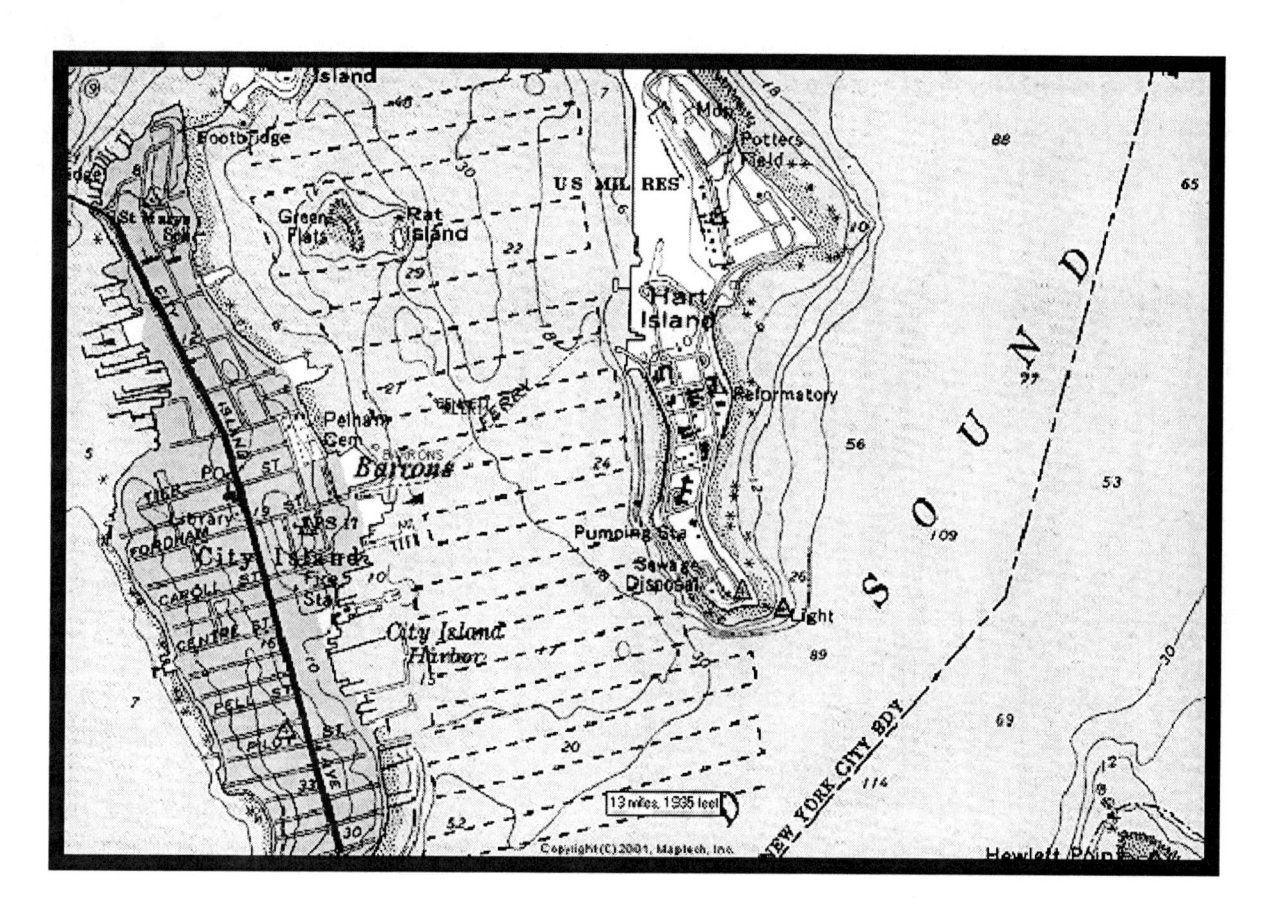

Figure 2

We kept the actual boat track on yet another GPS unit. This was done so as not to have such a cluttered screen. WE had plenty of GPS units, so this was not a problem. The same unit was used to mark points of K9 interest and alerts. This technique is one that I would repeat on any water search where I have the luxury to have my computer available and the time to draw a *search plan track* and download into a GPS unit. The drawbacks are that you can plan but the wind patterns may change which may change your plans. In this case, use the technique described later in the Lake Nipissing ON, search.

K9 Radar, Amir Findling

Notice in the photograph above that the boat is quite high above the water. However, we had a good breeze and it was a workable platform. I am sitting on a plastic equipment crate that allows the dogs to get on and off

153

Buzzards and Butterflies

the front of the boat. We also used a non-skid pad such as the ones put under throw rugs to provide a means for stable footing for the dogs. This gave the dogs a better footing on the boat's fiberglass structure.

K9 Mittru and Christine Buff, Cayuga Highland SAR

We decided that in order to save time, we would load both dogs on the boat and work one in front while resting the other in the back. Since both our dogs knew each other and had worked well in close quarters, we thought it would work for us. We realized too that each handler would of course know what the other's dog had done and where, but both handlers were experienced and we made sure not to cue the dogs to alert and just let them work. This method worked well for us. Handlers would need to determine whether this method would work for another set of dogs.

We noticed that the dog at rest in the back did show alert behaviors when the dog up front alerted. Whether it was due to the dog up front change in behavior or scent acquisition is open to conjecture. I can only relate that when it happened and Radar was in the back, resting, I noticed his nostrils flaring, prior to any other behavior. To me this meant scent acquisition. I later used this knowledge in the Nipissing Lake search. I realize that what have written could be considered anecdotal evidence with little scientific importance. I am not a scientist, but a mere K9 handler with, as of this writing, about 16 years experience. I work a very experienced dog, my second SAR K9. Chris noticed the same behavior with Mittru. Similar behavior was noticed in a subsequent major water search.

We worked this search in two operational periods. One track on Figure 3 represents the first operational period. We went to the northern end of the water to have wind advantage and worked towards the south in a grid pattern. As you can see, our actual pattern followed the plan.

Both dogs showed alert patterns in the penultimate pass during the morning operational period. It is located to the southwest center section just below the Hart Island name and adjacent to the *ferry* denotation on Figure 3. Knowing we had multiple victims, we continued and finished the pattern before breaking for lunch. During that time we downloaded tracks onto the computer and evaluated the effort up to that point.

Statistics: track length 7 miles and 3347 feet long, run between 0845am and 1039am. The water temperature was 41-42 degrees F and the wind SSW-SW at up to 12mph.

We then resumed our search, uneventfully till the City Island harbor where we had some very mild indications but saw some workers on a boat nearby and we decided that they had caused the dog's reactions. We cut our search pattern short of the stated goal as that area was in the middle of a channel used by very large barges. Not only did we give them right of way and a wide berth, we decided at that point to return to the mild alerts area we had by the harbor. During those passes, neither dog reproduced those alerts, yet we were definitely able to reproduce the alerts we had in the morning, which confirmed them.

Statistics: track length 9 miles and 1136 feet, run between 1206pm and 1510pm. Wind and water temperature showed no change. The total track length searched was 16 miles and 4456 feet for an area of 553.557 acres.

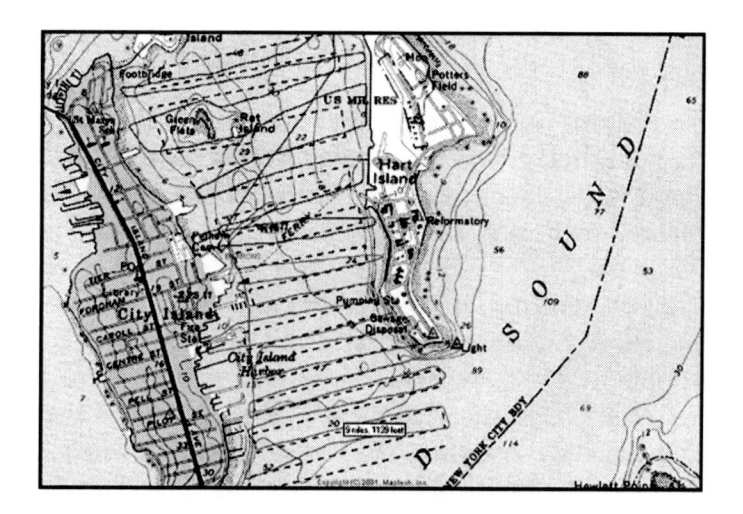

Figure 3

Barges in the Long Island Sound, south of our search area.

As I led the boat with the divers to the point of our alerts, not far from the Bennett Buoy, and while the divers were still all on board and suiting up, Radar went into a full-blown alert and was ready to jump into the water if I had allowed him. We definitely were in the right area and very close! Unfortunately the divers' effort did not produce the desired result.

Buzzards and Butterflies

Critique:

Wearing too many hats can lead to making mistakes and bad decisions, or not see the next obvious step. The latter was what happened. We did not pinpoint the location well enough. We should have re-worked the alert area the next morning to give the most accurate location possible with dogs. The handlers would have been fresh again and we could have finished the job.

Second Effort:

On April 25th, the body of one of the victims was found about 3500 feet from the Bennett Buoy. Two hours before the find, divers who dove near the Bennett marker had their search rope snag and had to pull hard to get them free. This probably freed the body too. We were asked to return to the location and returned on April 30th, 2003.

Since it was now almost confirmed that the bodies might still be *at or around* the Bennett buoy, we now had a small and manageable search area. So this time we worked one dog handler and one K9 at a time, the old-fashioned way, and shared information only when it came time to download the data to the computer. Both dogs indicated clearly on two different locations, quite close to each other. The difference in scent cone shape was due to the prevailing winds. Since we were able to see these alerts on an aerial picture we better understand what the dogs were telling us.

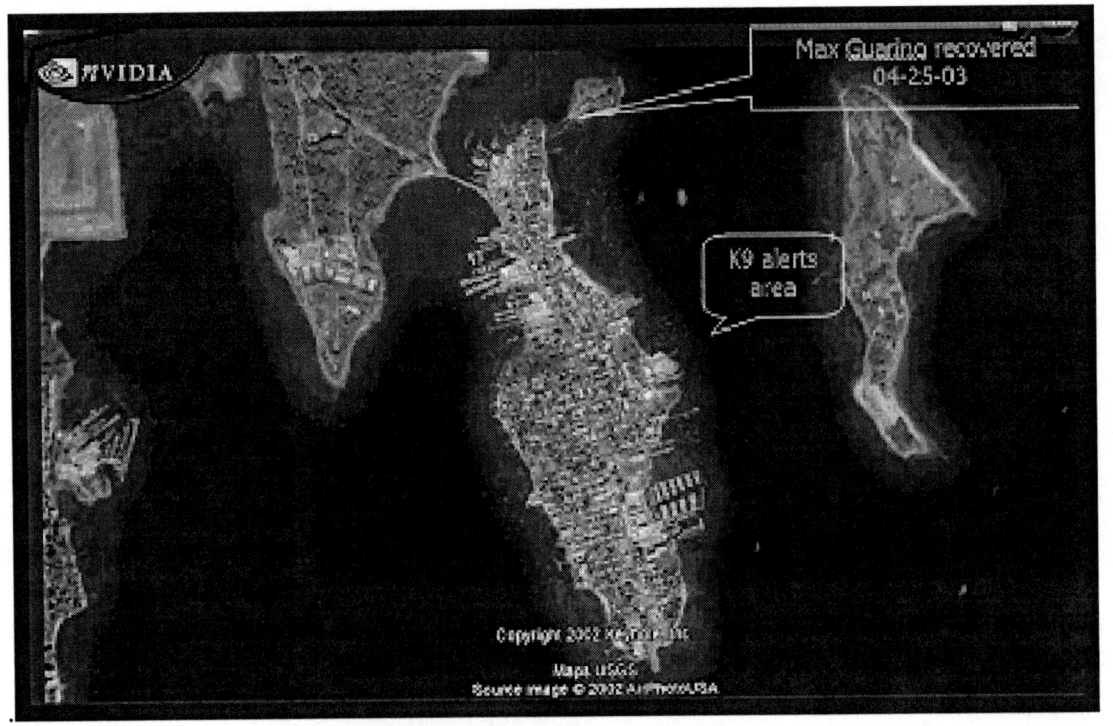

Figure 4 Topographical Map View

Figure 5:   #1 Area of Source of Scent
#2 99 feet
#3 Area of Source of Scent

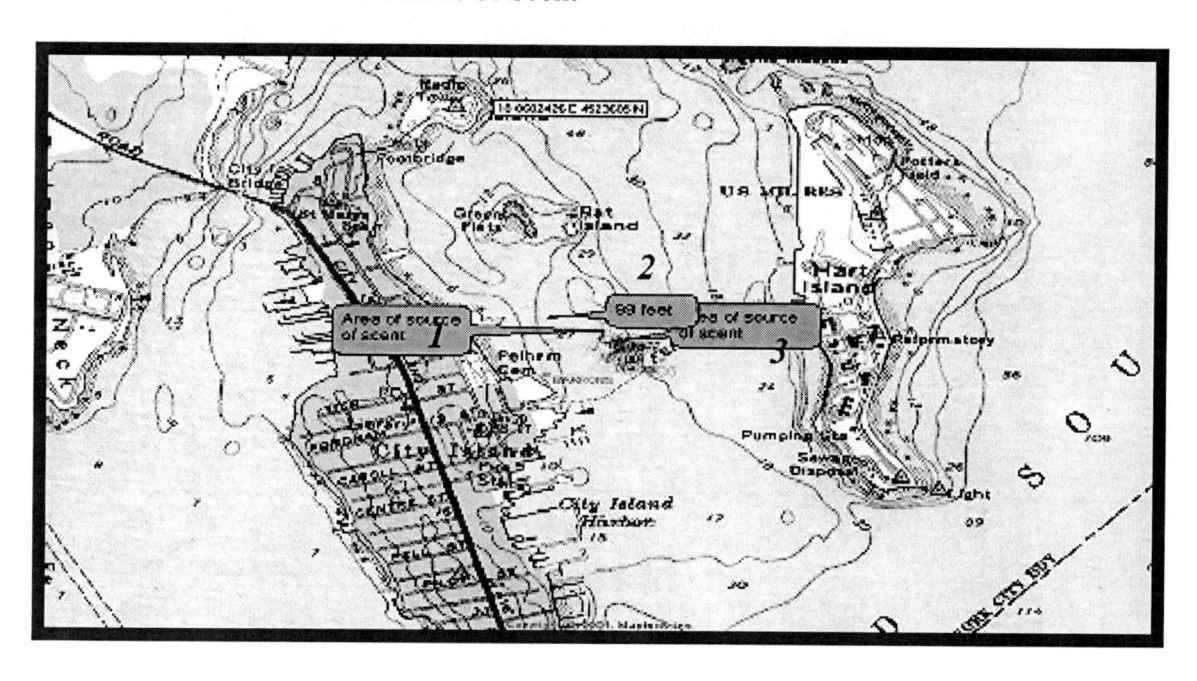

Figure 5

This is a somewhat better but not good enough, yet, result. Below is figure 6 where one can really see patterns, a scent cone, and the alerts of both dogs. Also noted is the location of the Bennet buoy and the original first alerts.

Mark each change in K9 behavior (mild alerts) till you get the maximum body language/trained alert. This works really well, and once on shore, blow it up to a scale where you can really see details makes the difference. Color-code each K9's alert behavior. This helps to be able to see whether the patters are similar and draw any conclusions. Remember to check the current and wind data on-site at that time and take those in account when interpreting data.

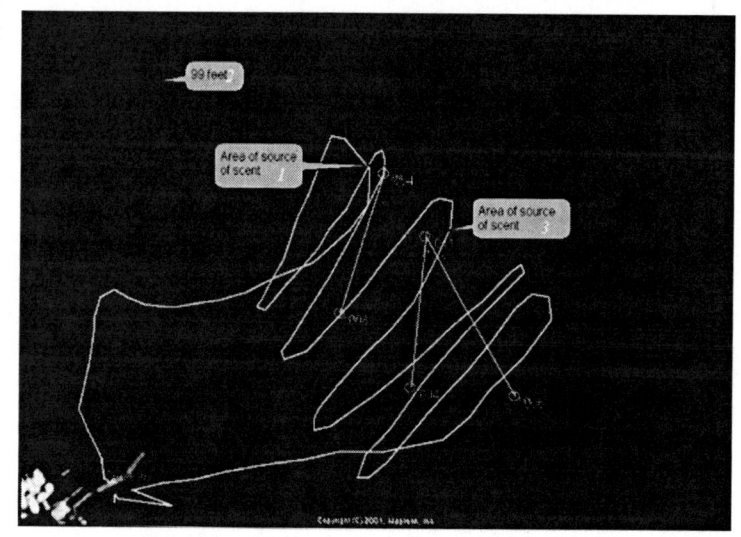

Figure 6

Buzzards and Butterflies

Unfortunately, despite our precision work and all, the divers did not recover the bodies of the three other victims. Figure 7 shows where the bodies were ultimately found.

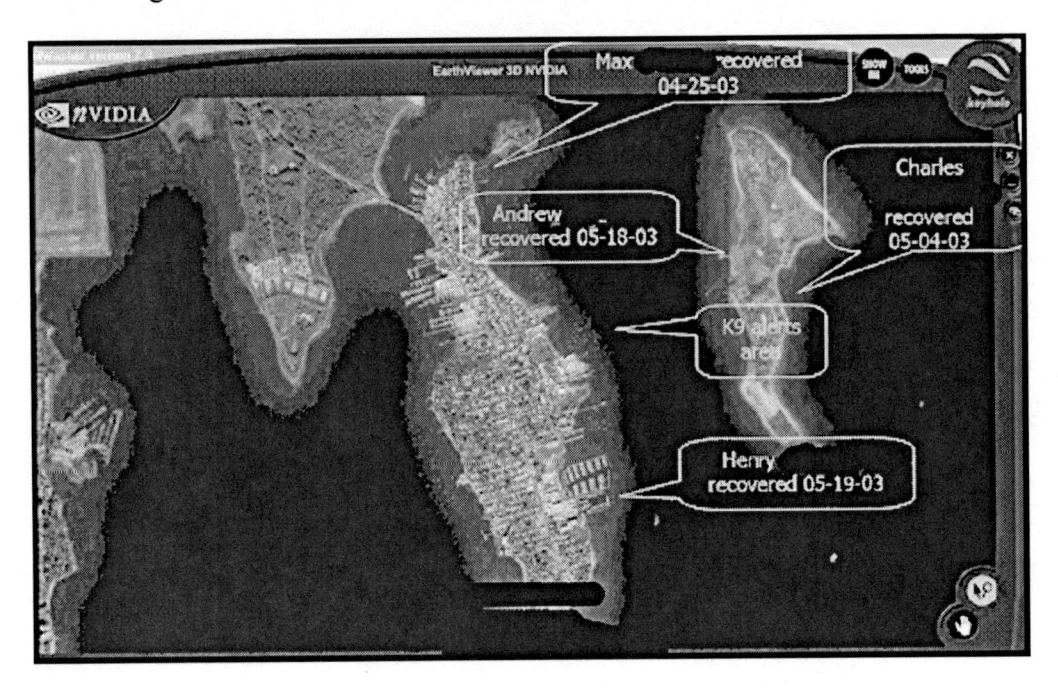

Figure 7

Looking at figure 7 the first question that comes to mind is whether the mild alerts we had in that area and dismissed as coming from boat maintenance crews, were actually due to Henry's body which may have been there all the time. At first we were not able to confirm the alerts on a subsequent pass. Consider the dates the bodies were found. When one takes into account body mass and conditions causing decomposition gasses to work, one can deduct that the bodies needed more time to rise to the surface of the water. Once they had risen to the surface of the water, pushed by currents and winds, they quickly arrived on the shore. The winds shift in the channel, sometimes being northerly, sometimes southerly. The body of Charles might have gone north with the winds and was then pushed to the east by the receding tide. With a shift in the wind, he was back on a southerly course when the returning tide washed into the shore on the east side of Hart Island. I believe currents and wind pushed Henri to the point where he was finally found. That occurred within 24 hours of him being located. A body does not linger in between stages, especially if it is snagged at the bottom. If it is snagged, it needs a certain amount of force to pull it up in order to break the snag. Once broken free (and no other external factor coming into play), it becomes very buoyant and will be on the surface until it reaches shore or until the decomposition gasses that kept him afloat escape from the body.

The death of the four teenagers, Henry, Max, Andrew and Charles have not been in vain. Their parents have worked to implement programs aimed at identifying a specific location of 9-1-1 calls by the 9-1-1 dispatch centers. We have learned many lessons, some that I have shared in this description, in hopes of helping other K9 handlers in water searches and training.

This experience helped to prepare me for another search that would make the City Island search look minute.. That was the search on Lake Nipissing Ontario, Canada.

Where in the World is Lake Nipissing?

The arrow on Figure 8 shows you the location.

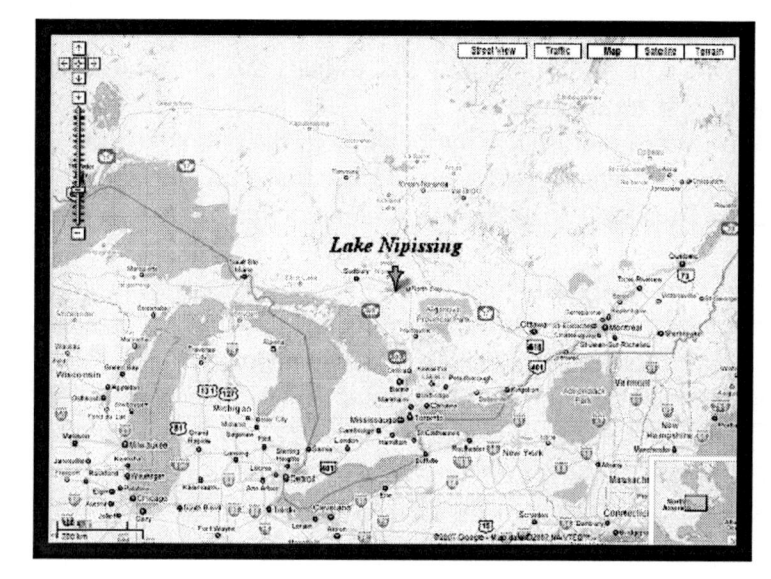

Figure 8

Lake Nipissing is located about 120 miles due north of Toronto, north west of the Algonquin Provincial Park. Road signs say, "Welcome to the Near North." It can be quite intimidating, but I was not there in winter. It does not compete in the same league as the Great Lakes, but it sure is in a league of its own. Lake Nipissing has 321+ sq. miles. In comparison, Seneca Lake and Cayuga Lake, the largest of the New York State Finger Lakes, each have 66.6 sq. miles.

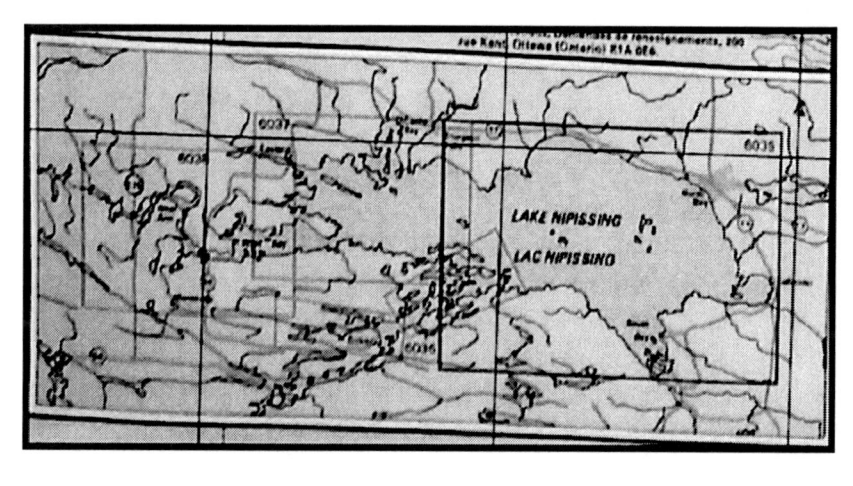

Figure 9

This call was a bit different from most other calls since the authorities, the Ontario Provincial Police, did not contact me. The person calling was Rabbi Isaac Leider whom I didn't know. I had not heard any reports about this search so I had to start from scratch, finding out where and what had happened and what is happening at the present. The only information I could locate was what the press had reported, blogs of individuals and/or organizations involved in one way or the other in the search; nothing precise or concrete.

Things were further complicated when I could not find a partner to go with me, nor a second K9 and handler. I had a decision to make. Could I work by myself? I know that not having a second K9 for confirmation certainly weakened my position, should K9 *Stryder* alert. I also knew it was difficult to be both the K9 handler and the search manager.

There was a victim in the water and not only his family but both the Toronto Jewish Orthodox community, as well as New York City's Jewish Orthodox communities were making an all out effort to try to recover Eli, the missing victim. Being Jewish myself, I understood the pressures on

Buzzards and Butterflies

the community to bring the victims body home for a traditional Jewish burial, and the importance it had for his widow etc. So I looked at my dog. I had total confidence in him and his ability to search and clearly indicate on water. Working with people of my own faith and having faith in my dog, I agreed to make the trip.

I could not promise anything but to make the best effort we could to locate Eli. I did not tell Isaac (the Rabbi) that my dog was the best in the world, I just told him we would work the area and hope for the best. I was not going on a wing and a prayer, but I knew that at least the latter would be well taken care off by Rabbi Leider and the congregation there.

Not having another K9 for confirmation bothered me. Radar, my black dog, the one who worked 9-11 at Staten Island and the City Island water search, was 11 years old at that time and close to retirement; but he had so much experience, I decided to take him and work him when Stryder needed a break.

It was a long ride from Syracuse, New York to North Bay, Ontario. The scenery was quite beautiful near the Algonquin Park and signs along the road announced: Near North! That was the farthest north I'd ever been in Canada. This was a four hundred and eighty mile trip.

Upon arrival, I first wanted to make sure that the Ontario Provincial police (OPP) who was running the search effort and allowing civilians to participate would not object to my dog searching the area. My presence did not cause any problem for them as long as we stayed away from their boats that were using sonar to scan for the victim. I examined their general search map and took a digital picture of it. I did not realize it at the time but that picture would be of utmost importance later on. It is actually the background of most of the maps presented in this description. I used a 6-mega pixel digital camera as a portable color copier, something that I continue to do.

Not having a map, other than the tiny picture on my small camera screen, I looked at the lake, saw how huge it appeared to me, and wondered where does one start? How can I keep track of the areas I will be searching? Figure 9 shows the enormity of this body of water. The shores were so far apart, as were the islands, and there were no good landmarks to take a bearing (compass reading/heading). Nothing. All I had was my trusty GPS, a Garmin 60CSx. I had a set of road map, no topographical maps. The 60CSx' screen was not much bigger than my camera's. It was quite difficult to really get a good grasp of the area as a picture.

I had been shown the area where the first body had been recovered and the area where the empty boat had been found, in opposite directions. The wind can blow in either direction and change quite suddenly on the lake.

I decided to search an area in the middle, closer to the Waltonian Resort as this was the PLS (place last scene.) The missing persons were thought to have been heading out from that point into the lake. As shown in the picture, the Manitou Islands on the horizon seemed to have been the only point where they may have steered.

Figure 10 shows the map of the eastern end of Lake Nipissing. I guided the boat west till we were close to some shallow islands and started a search pattern from that point, staying perpendicular to the prevalent wind. I had a good breeze working for me at about 10-15 mph. I decided to take both Stryder and Radar on the boat and try to work them one at a time from the front of the boat. Radar seemed very uncomfortable up in front so Stryder kept that position for the duration. I then decided that Radar would only be asked to do a confirmation, if needed.

We searched a track length of 19.2 miles. We were not working at a normal slow pace searching with K9s, nor were the passes as narrow as they would normally be. We had only one working dog and a huge area. That was the only way to give it any semblance of coverage. Stryder did not alert during that operational period. I also learned that he could not stand in place for that long. Sitting was not a good alternative either. I let him lie down but made sure he was awake and working. I carefully watched his eyes and his nose looking for twitching or other behaviors that might indicate he was detecting scent.

The following morning I searched another similarly sized sector, which was a little more to the north and east of the area, from the one I had worked the day prior. I had the previous day's track on my GPS screen and could related to it when I was close to it. It was not helpful when I was farther away. I loaned my spare GPS, a Garmin 60CX, to the boat driver. That helped him keep the boat on a straight line and relieved me from directing the boat once the first leg had been done. I could now concentrate on Stryder and only indicate to the driver when we approached the turns.

We searched a track that was 17.98 miles long. Conditions were not much different than the day before so we kept a similar speed and pattern. The map shows that the pattern is a little tighter and less hesitant, as both the boat handler and I became more familiar with each other, the task and the boat. It is called *on the job training* and helps one do the job more efficiently as handler and driver work together over extended periods of time.

In the afternoon, the plan was to extend the track to the west and I decided to give Stryder a break, so Radar was the working dog. Isaac Lieder was not with us at that time; another person replaced him. As we talked, this person noted that he had smelled something. He could not really describe it but said it smelled bad in an area of shallow islands he has been searching on foot earlier that morning. I asked him if he had reported the smell and he had not as he did not know how to describe it and what it was. A few more questions and I got very suspicious as to the possibility of it being decomposition scent. I decided to cut our search short and asked the person to direct the boat to the odor location. We disembarked and started searching from land towards the water. Indeed there was a decomposition scent. My nose is not good enough to tell me whether it was human or animal. Fortunately, Radar was there, and he never even flinched, telling me he was absolutely sure there was no human decomposition scent in that area. We never discovered the actual source, but it was probably under some part of a strainer, out of sight and certainly not large enough for a human body. In any case, I trusted my dog. That was Radars last search as on my way back home from North Bay, I decided that it was time for him to pass the baton to Stryder. I will share more about that decision later.

Monday, late in the afternoon, I finally got a marine map, the same one I had seen at the OPPs (operations) trailer. While I had taken my laptop computer, I had forgotten its power pack, so it was quite useless to me. I could not scan that map and geo-reference it using my GPS mapping software. At least I now had a better idea of where I had searched and could plot some of the major points on that map. This visual aid helped me to create a plan for the next day.

I noticed on my GPS that I had left a gap between the two areas I had searched. I also wanted to cover the area a little to the west of the track from Sunday. So I set up another track on Tuesday morning, starting at 0927 and ending past 1248, searching a track length of 18.54 miles.

Radar, Amir, Isaac Leider and our boat handler on Lake Nipissing in photograph above.

Buzzards and Butterflies

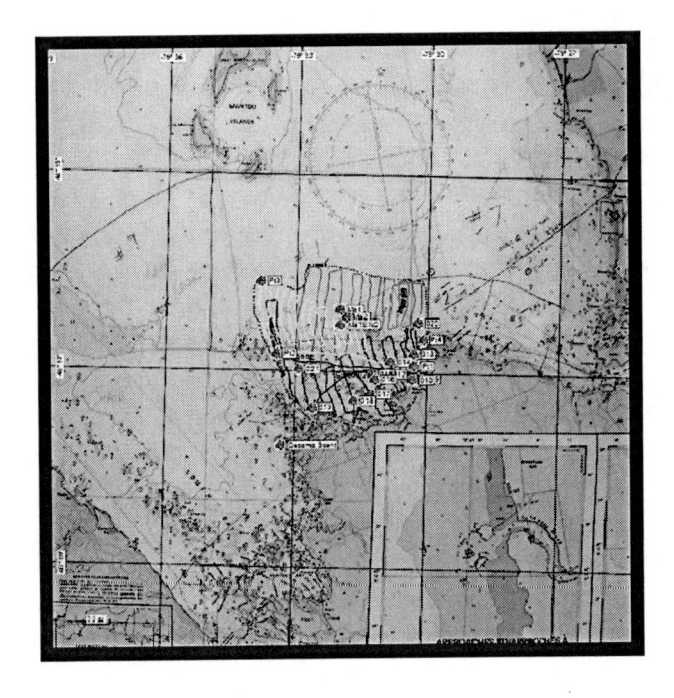

Figure 10 The East End of Lake Nipissing

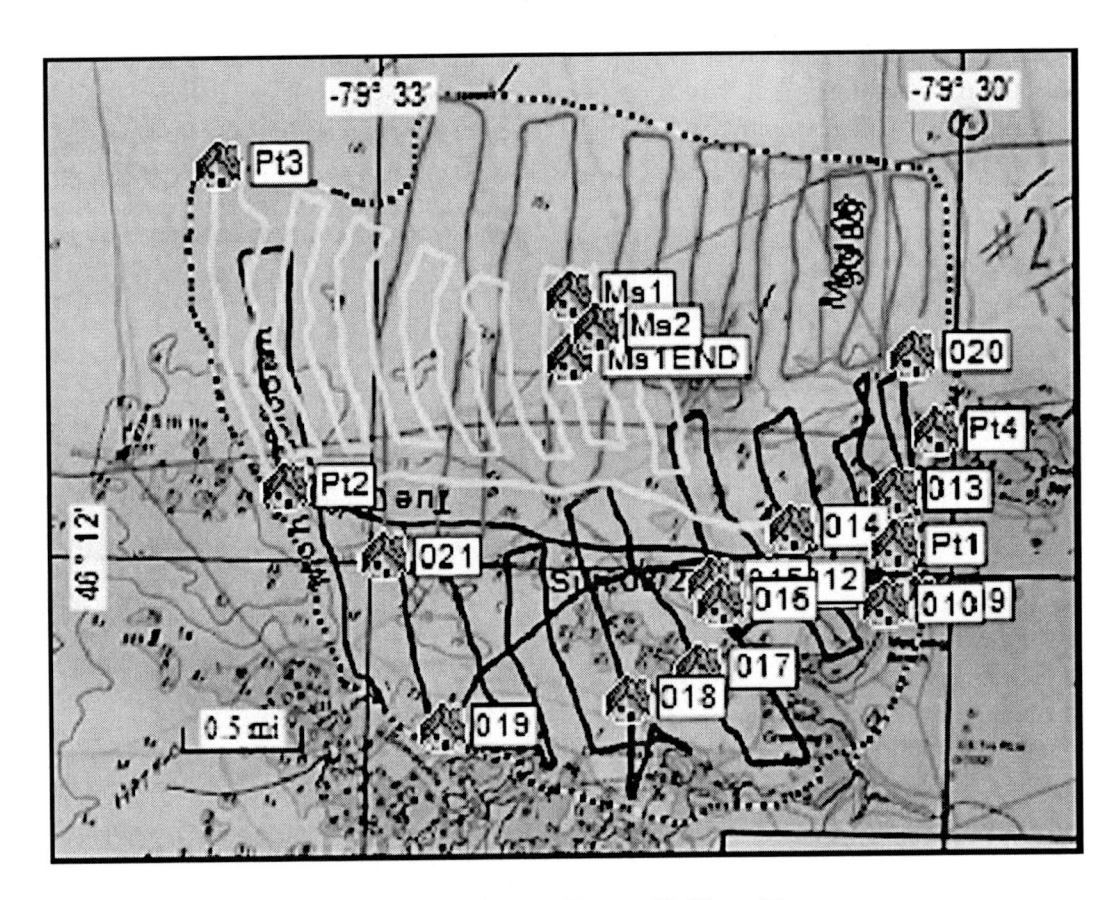

Figure 11 Showing Figure 10 Close Up

Shown on Figure 11, the blown up map, I had alerts towards the end of the track. Stryder had been lying on the front end of the boat, sometimes facing the bow, sometimes port or starboard, as he wished. All the pictures taken were not during actual searching. I was requested to dress the dogs in their search vests. I do not usually use them while searching. They usually wear a K9 floatation device during most water searches although not all as sometimes snagging can be a problem where the floatation device may become a hindrance. This is another tough handler decision to make. In Lake Nipissing, the floatation device is a safety must because of the distance to shore.

From a dog lying down, with nose and ears barely twitching every now and then, all of a sudden Stryder sat up, pointing his nose in the wind; then he stood up, stretching to reach into the scent cone. I observed additional behaviors like trying to bite at the water. (Stryder could not reach the water because of the boat configuration.) He was also pawing the bottom of the boat (again not at the water due to the physical constraints.) I marked the area where the behaviors were the strongest. Ma-1 marked the point where they stopped on that pass. I made another pass and got another alert, but not as strong, Ma-2, then nothing on the next two passes. I returned to the area of Ma-1 and had all of the original behaviors. I narrowed it down as much as possible. I cannot call it pinpointing on such an extensive body of water, but all things considered, the location I had marked as Ma-1 was the strongest alert, even the second time. It was about 37 foot deep at that location, according to our fish-finder.

We went to shore. I wondered if I should now take Radar and try to confirm what Stryder had done? Stryders' alert was clear as a bell. Even Isaac saw it and asked me what is the dog doing/telling? Point Ma-1 was about a mile and a half from shore. It would take quite some time to get there, work it and come back. I decided to trust Stryders alert and report its location to the OPPs (operations staff.) The OPPs accepted the report and acted upon it, and sent its divers to that location, almost immediately. It always takes some time for logistics to act upon a report, which is understandable. As the divers started working the area, the weather suddenly changed and the westerly winds became northerly at 20-25 miles, and gathering strength. The water became choppy and soon after all boating activities were put to an end, including the dive operations.

Waters remained choppy the next day. We loaded in a helicopter to do a visual shore search. There was a possibility that Stryder and I would work on land if necessary. The area is so remote and wooded that we could not find a place to land in order to reach the water relatively easily. Stryder settled down for a morning nap while Isaac and I strained our eyes. We searches mostly around the South Bay, just in case the body had resurfaced and was pushed in that direction by the northerly winds.

I decided to return home that afternoon. After all, Stryder had indicated, which was a miracle by itself, when one considers the time we spent searching, the length of the search track, and the size of the area.

We had spent 34.5 hours on-scene in four operational periods. Our search track was 61.1 miles long! The area we actually searched was 4391 acres or 6.86 sq. miles!

Could I ask anything more from Stryder? I did not think so. He did a magnificent job and it was now up to the divers to finish it. As I was pondering this search, while driving back home, it occurred to me that I had such a gem of a search dog that now, I could let Radar retire completely from his job. Stryder had taken the job and done so with flair and panache. It was icing on the cake.

On Sept 07, 2006 a Constable (K9 handler) with the Ontario Provincial Police, called me at home. He asked me for the exact coordinates of Stryders alert and when I gave him those, he stated that his dog had alerted on the same location Stryder alerted. The Constable confirmed Stryders alert, independently. The body was still not yet located.

This photograph shows how Stryder searched most of the time, lying down, as operational periods were very long.

In my opinion, considering the wind data, it is quite plausible that the body re-floated the night between June 2nd and 3rd, 2007 at or near point Ma-1 where Stryder had alerted almost a year before; and the westerly winds pushed it to the location it was found at the mouth of the Collander Bay.

I wish we had had a find by the divers at point Ma-1, but not having that, obtaining a second independent alert by a professional K9 handler and his dog, and seeing the location where the body was found and the prevailing atmospheric conditions at the time, I think the preponderance of evidence shows Stryder had a legitimate find at point Ma-1. It is a question of belief and I trust my well-trained SAR dog!

This report certifies what was done on this particular day using pertinent data at that time. Had I had use of my computer, I probably would have made some plans, drawn some areas, transferred these areas to my GPS and worked in a more organized way, as I had done in City Island, NY. This experience shows that large areas of water can be searched and searched well, with limited but well-trained resources. The secret lies in a well-trained dog, in a divide and conquers the area approach, and a systematic search pattern. The tool that made the systematic approach possible was my GPS. At the distance we worked from shore, details are too fuzzy to work with compass bearings and triangulation. I was lucky enough to have a superb and accurate GPS with mapping capability, so it gave me a picture of how the search pattern was being performed. I would never attempt such a search without a high quality GPS unit.

Flash Floods

By Ben Alexander
Cen-Tex Search and Rescue, K9 Pete

2007 brought extensive flash flooding and devastation to many areas of Texas. In return, volunteer search teams were called upon on many occasions to assist in the recovery of drowning victims. The following is a brief discussion of one such mission.

On May 24, 2007 a young man was swept away from a crossing on Barrons Creek in Fredericksburg, Texas. It was never determined if the young man was in or out of his vehicle when this occurred. His small S.U.V. however, was located ¾ of a mile from the crossing as the water receded in the days following the flash flood. The vehicle was found resting on a sandbar in a bend of the creek, and was badly damaged, with all windows shattered, and the front driver's side door standing open.

Local search crews from the region were deployed with canines immediately following the disappearance. Water levels were extremely high and treacherous. No indications of interest were shown by any of the canines. These teams searched from the alleged point of vehicle entry into the water at the low water bridge crossing to where Barrons Creek tied into the Perdenales River and then south from there towards the next major bridge crossing at Hwy 290. This was a distance of approximately 5-6 miles. These initial teams left, calling the area they had searched clear.

The rains subsided and the water continued to recede. On May 29th USHERO responded to a call from the Gillespie County Sheriffs office to continue the search for the young man. Cen-Tex Search & Rescue was deployed by USHERO as a mutual aid resource, to provide certified cadaver canine teams to assist in the search.

One canine team was put in to backtrack up the Perdenales towards Barrons Creek from the Highway 290 Bridge. Two other units were dispatched another 3 miles downstream on the Perdenales River and worked upstream on either side of the river back towards the Hwy 290 Bridge.

Both canine teams on the south side of the 290 bridge reported interest shown by their canines upstream. The single canine team on the north side of 290 also reported interest upstream.

Teams were brought in from the field and rested at noon. After convincing LE (law enforcement) to allow us to re-search an area previously called clear, a Jon boat was obtained to perform a more efficient water search with a certified water recovery canine unit.

A coastguard volunteer with swift water experience drove the boat. One support member also accompanied the team to assist with steering and safety of the boat. All members wore PFDs (personal floatation devices.) The boat was launched ¼ mile upstream from the Barrons Creek junction.

The canine unit showed no interest in the water prior to the Barrons Creek junction. Soon after passing the junction, the canine began to show animation and began tasting the water. Approximately ¼ of a mile past the junction, the canine offered an alert that for which GPS points were taken. River conditions were such that the team was unable to turn the boat around and do a systematic search of the area. This unit basically got one shot at any given location on the river. The canine continued to show interest in the direction from which the boat had come, diminishing with distance as the Hwy 290 Bridge was approached.

Upon return to IC (incident command), the GPS (global positioning system) points were given to the commanding officer. These points were relayed to the Texas Parks and Wildlife agent who was also kayaking the river daily assisting in the search for the body.

All handlers and dogs were retired for the day and returned again at 8 am the next morning for a second day of searching. Due to the interest shown upstream, the canine units were taken to the site where the vehicle was alleged to have entered the water and searched both sides of the banks. Upon arriving at the vehicle, all canines showed interest in the vehicle, especially in the rear area of the vehicle, but none offered alerts. Multiple articles of clothing were found strewn along the banks.

The dogs for the remainder of the search showed no other interest and the units were extracted. The dogs, due to a report of a strong odor, checked a second site of possible entry. No interest was shown. Cen-Tex stood down and returned home. Recovery of the body did not appear to have been a successful conclusion.

Buzzards and Butterflies

On Saturday, June 2, we received a report that a Texas Parks and Wildlife Department. Agent, kayaking on the Perdenales River, had utilized the GPS points provided by our canine unit and as the water had receded even more, recovered the body in the area where the canine alerted. The body was snagged in a tree that had been deeply submerged in the center area of the river, in a bend, approximately ¼ of a mile from the junction where Barrons Creek ties into the Perdenales River. The subject retained all of his clothing except one shoe.

In assessing any mission, honesty is integral to improvements that can be made for future missions, and in preparation. Based on the information imparted to the Cen-Tex handlers during the briefings, the following extrapolations were made:

Lessons learned:

1. Flash flood searches are inherently difficult due to a variety of conditions such as current, water levels, and water speed. Teams should be very careful in calling an area clear, even in a recovery mission. The area that actually contained the body was initially called clear by the first teams responding. This could have potentially resulted in a no recovery for the agency and family.

2. Possible explanations for the initial lack of detection by the first teams to respond could have been due to conditions. High, swift water is dangerous. It may have precluded the initial handlers from being able to get their canines in a position to detect the body. Unintentional handler interference due to concerns for their partner's safety could have also been a contributing factor for lack of detection.

3. Type of canines utilized may have also affected detection. There is currently no scientific peer reviewed information concerning decay timelines for bodies in water, though there is a great deal of anecdotal evidence to support the delay of decay in water. This may lead to a discussion of what type of dog is most appropriate for the early period of recovery for drowning victims based on environmental conditions. If decay is indeed slowed, where the scent picture may be more like that of a live person, vs. a cadaver, it might behoove us to utilize live find dogs who have experience with divers in water. Likewise, if conditions or time lend us to believe that the scent picture is more like that of a cadaver, utilizing water recovery trained cadaver dogs would be the logical explanation.

4. The handler working the canine on the boat was reticent to call an alert due to being unable to double check or triangulate the area for a stronger indication and ability to pinpoint the location. However, he did advise his teammates to GPS the alert and turned the GPS points of the alert into LE. In the end, it is up to LE to follow up on any alerts or areas of interest shown by our canines. It is up to us, the handlers, to be honest and report our findings. We are there for the victims; they deserve the best we can give.

5. Utilizing appropriate resources in an appropriate manner is of utmost importance. Experienced personnel navigated the boat and proved to be a great asset for this search. Only one canine unit certified to work off of a boat was present. Therefore, this was the unit deployed for the riverboat search. Utilizing a different canine would not have been the judicious decision and could have resulted in a missed recovery.

6. Communication and teamwork are of utmost importance. The units present for this search did so with professionalism and a sense of unity. The end result was a successful mission and closure for the family.

The Letter

By Christy Judah
Brunswick Search and Rescue, NC
K9 Bailey and K9 Gypsy

Five years of searching. The serial killers admitted to the killing. It was not their first one on this two-week nationwide crime spree. Every word they uttered was analyzed and scrutinized. Every witness reporting had a bit more information on the four-hour time frame they were known to be in "our" county. The videotape placed them in the south end of the county at a convenience store at 4:05 pm. They were back in the neighboring state by 8 pm that night before leaving the area for the central part of the U. S.

Every report was followed up. The vehicle was spotted near the hunting club. A major search effort turned up nothing. The vehicle was spotted in a housing development where a "shot" was reported in the woods at the back of the development. The search turned up gun shells, lots of them, but mostly old. The vehicle was spotted in the central part of the county on a dirt road. A necklace was found.

The killers described a certain type of road with a certain type of road sign. Only two areas of our county met those descriptive criteria. Both areas were searched. A ladies beret was found in one. Nothing was found in the other. The search area was literally 787 square miles - ROW (the rest of the world).

The killers provided just enough clues in their description of where they "left" the body to keep us on our toes for years. Training continued in many "hot" areas. Maps covered the floors of our homes. We just couldn't let it go. We had to bring her home. We often thought of the other young girl, in another state, who was yet another victim of their murderous spree.

The trial was held. Two killers at two death penalty trials had each defendant pleading guilty. The first-ever federal death penalty case without a body was conducted. Both ended with the death penalty verdict. The searchers had come face to face with the killers. Not a pleasant experience.

Fast-forward several years. The killers, now sitting on death row, reach out to the family and attorneys to offer to lead them to the location of the body, still not recovered. There were hints of the location of the body noting that it was in the adjoining state, some fifty miles from "our" search area. Was this an honest offer or passive-aggressive action for some unknown reason from mentally disturbed individuals? No one took the bait.

The killers remained on death row in a maximum-security prison. The body of the missing person remained undiscovered. The case was not yet closed in the hearts and minds of the searchers or the family.

Buzzards and Butterflies

The letter arrived. Quite unexpectedly, on a lazy Friday afternoon, the Chief opened the letter addressed to the Search Team to find a three-page letter from yet *another* killer "stationed" in the Midwest on the same cellblock as the two killers who had gone on their crime spree several years ago. Mentioning the killers by name, he identified himself as yet another death row inmate contacting us on behalf of the original killers. They were offering to send a detailed "map" of the location of the body.

A quick computer search found the writer of that letter, his bio and crimes. How did this volunteer searcher and canine handler become the intended recipient of a letter from a convicted killer? Maximum-security prisons were not a location listed in my personal address book. It was quite an uneasy feeling to hold those three pieces of paper in my hands.

The reality of the situation soon morphed into a dark haze when the realization emerged that we had been the subjects of a conversation by three convicted killers. They knew our name and address. Our team address and handler names had been posted on the World Wide Web and were also contained in the trial transcripts. It took precisely fifteen minutes for the team web site to be re-vamped to omit addresses and last names. It took precisely twenty minutes to realize that contact with these folks was unwise and dangerous. The letter was turned over to federal officials and the outcome of the offer is yet to be determined.

The team yearns for a conclusion to this case. The Clarice Starling/Hannibal connection is unsettling. Dr. Hannibal Lector. Brilliant. Cunning. Psychotic. In his mind lies the clue to a ruthless killer. The Silence of the Lambs has come into our home. Not a pleasant feeling. Is this case nearing resolution or not? Time will tell.

Incidental Voids Become a Clue

By Roxye Marshall
K9 Mandy
Brunswick Search and Rescue, NC

Certain suggestive behaviors can occur on and around water, just as they do on land. For example, a cadaver dog working in a storage lot may show interest at a bucket, box, or bin. These objects because of their characteristic structure can actually *capture, collect,* and *hold* wind driven scent. In a water recovery incident, be aware that a K9 might mimic this behavior on or around the water operative area.

In a real case scenario, it was learned that structural cavities within the boat's hull can produce these same results. These void, concave areas have the same ability to capture, collect, and hold wind driven scent. At this particular water recovery, the search boat had already been launched. Awaiting the arrival of the K9s, the boat had been pulled ashore, bow (front) first, and beached. Strong winds prevailed; blowing across the lake, toward the boat over it's stern (rear). As soon as the first K9 boarded the boat, interest was shown. Agitation and whining were exhibited as the K9 paced the deck of the boat and examined its hull. Eventually, the K9 focused her attention on the cavity located at the bow of the boat underneath the front deck. The second K9 on board also showed interest within the boat's hull. This K9 was so insistent upon searching the cavity beneath the cockpit that he deliberately shoved the captain's knee out of the way so he could get his nose into the void.

Corroboration of this information allowed us to successfully locate the victim. Aside from the interest shown on the water, the interest shown as the K9s boarded the boat was telling. While the boat was pulled ashore and parked, wind driven scent that had been blowing across the back (stern) of the boat was collecting in the interior cavities of the boat's hull. The victim was located less than 80 feet from the point where the search boat was being pulled ashore. Similar cross-contamination should always be considered when the canine shows interest or alerts in seemingly benign areas. Situations such as residue remaining from previous recoveries, or contamination on docks or other operational areas, including a shelter on shore can become a clue for the location of the ultimate missing person.

Hurricane Katrina and the World Trade Center Recovery Dogs

By Bruce Barton
Rescue International
c. 2008

There have been only a few real major disasters over the past 25 years where cadaver or recovery dogs (as a more socially acceptable term) have been deployed in a formal, large and responsive manor. The World Trade Center (WTC) was one of the largest if not probably the largest deployment of Recovery Dogs and supporting personnel. As soon as we all witnessed the towers and the Pentagon attacks we knew that our lives as handlers and as a recovery asset were going to change. Most did not know just how much.

The recovery operations at the WTC relied on the fast removal of the debris from Manhattan to the Freshkill landfill in Staten Island in as quick a manner as possible. Fireman Police, and construction workers scanned debris for human remains but even with cadaver dogs from many police agencies assisting, hundreds of pieces of human remains were loaded with debris onto trucks to be taken to Freshkill.

On Sept. 16, 2001, Bruce Barton, Director of Operations for Rescue International, received a call from the lieutenant in charge of the NYPD (New York Police Department) canine unit. He called because of previous personal conversations and offers made earlier during the week in New York City to provide cadaver dogs when needed. The Lt. asked if it was possible to get cadaver dogs to work the Fresh Kill Landfill in Staten Island. He advised that they had a good supply of dogs working ground zero but needed some to handle a request that had been waiting, for dogs at the landfill. Issues of having non-law enforcement dogs working at the site, as it was considered a crime scene, had to be addressed with the FBI and other agencies. After a few hours a second call

Buzzards and Butterflies

was received with approval of all parties to have the volunteer dog/handlers respond. RI (Rescue International) started to reach out to member units and resources.

By late Sunday afternoon RI responded with a team comprised of Karen Dashfield and Sophie from Northeast SAR and Michelle Will and K9 Louie, Bob Will and K9 KEA, John Valvardi and K9 Nemo from SE PA Specialty Dog Unit Accompanying them was a small overhead team, RI's Response Truck and Disaster Response Trailer staffed by members of Northeast SAR, and a second Disaster Response Trailer with support members from the East Penn SAR team. The first unit of the Task Force's Response arrived Sunday evening at the Freshkill Landfill.

The landfill site was a few hundred acres with many dozens of piles of rubble from the trade center. It was an eerie site as we came across the Verizono Bridge; we could see all the portable light towers on top of the only hill around. In fact it was not a hill but one of the largest piles of garbage in the country. The landfill had only been closed a few months. As we entered the site we were greeted with the smell of the landfill, something that we all grew to live with. The National Guard was set up to help support the operation with tents, generators, manpower and a canteen. As we pulled in we saw the work area, I think everyone thought, "What are we in for?" Can the dogs work with all of this going on around them? We found out quickly they can.

Four areas were set up where the trucks dumped their loads. A dozer or backhoe then spread out the load over the ground so it was only 12-18" tall. Then a few dozen white suited officers started to pick through the rubble looking for the flight recorders, any possible clues and any human remains. The site was being monitored for Haz-Mat (hazardous materials) and the major concern was the asbestos. All persons working the fields had to have full protective suites and respirators. Regretting it later, many people did not keep their respirators on all the time as it made communications with the dogs very hard. Some of these people have experienced long term health effects.

Search fields at Freshkill Landfill

Dog indicates on source

RI Disaster Support Trailer

Officers provided a friendly place for K9's to relive them self.

Note says FOR K9 USE ONLY

Conversations about the use of the dogs and how the hazards may affect them resulted in a decision that they can handle it much better than we can and that the levels of asbestos were very low. The levels were usually below human danger levels. This was an on going monitored concern for both dogs and the workers.

Upon arrival to the landfill, the Task Force Coordinator Bruce Barton reported to the NYPD command post. The NYPD had been finding about a 6-12 human remains per 12-hour shift. It was correctly felt that cadaver dogs could find many more body parts than the eyes of the workers.

By late Sunday night three dogs were working shifts at the site and finding numerous body parts. Over 100 items were found in the first 14 hours. Only 8 parts had been found in the 12-hour shift before, using only the eyes of searchers.

The first night was a learning experience for all the handlers, support and the canines. We learned that the dogs reacted differently to

Buzzards and Butterflies

different types of sources and many dogs that were experienced in cadaver were walking over large pieces of human remains that were coated in this thick dust and were lacking any signs of decay at 5 days old. I believed this was due to the cool weather and the coating of dust.

The first nights (Sunday 16th) searching also showed us the amount of scent that was in the area. A few dogs keep trying to work into the wind and out of the search fields. After watching one of the dogs that had lots of experience try to drag his handler off the field for the third time I walked out to the team and told them to let him work the breeze. K9 Kea took off with a mission right into the breeze and headed for the many piles of WTC debris that surrounded the recovery site that were awaiting a slow pause in deliveries that never seemed to come. As we approached the piles with KEA on lead you could see his change in posture. It was almost an apprehension of the site, possibly due to what turned out to be an area with numerous large sources, including a NYC EMS ambulance that had been flattened. In conjunction with the NYPD personnel, we recovered as many sources as possible over the next 18 hours.

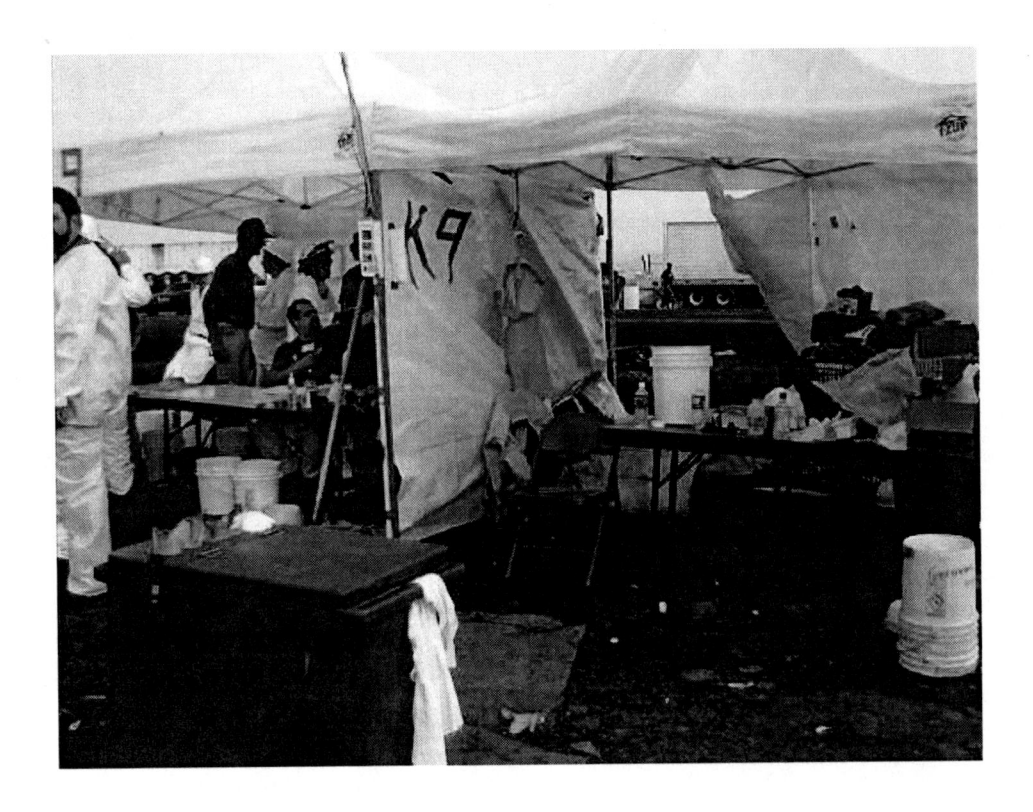

Command Tent

Handlers were briefed in the use of the protective gear and a system to check the rubble was developed by Bruce and the handlers. A pop up tent was placed next to the fields and equipped with a table, dry erase boards, satellite phone provided by MSV, a Davis electronic weather station, to monitor wind direction, and a bank of ICOM two-way radios.

Handlers worked shifts of 1 hour on and 1 hour off, with the final decision on working longer or shorter shifts up to the handlers. All dogs were to be on lead for safety. Dozens of dozers, backhoes and dump trucks worked the area along with a hundred and fifty plus officers in white Tyvek suites and facemasks.

The next day a meeting with the Incident Commander resulted in a request to keep the effort going 24/7 for what they expected to be as long as a few months, if possible? Bruce then went about the non-stop effort to bring in dozens of dog teams and support personnel. In all over 60 dogs and 300 plus people were brought in over the two weeks the task force was in operation. The Base of Operation was expanded over the next few days and was moved three times during the two-week stay.

Handlers work the piles of spread out debris from the WTC

CRTF Base of Operations end of week one with better tents and AT&T Mobile Cell site.

Now how do you find dozens of trained experienced cadaver dogs? RI had some dogs but nowhere near the numbers to handle a 24/7 operation. A call for more dogs started to go out to select teams and state groups. Not only did we need the dogs and handlers but also every dog team working the pile needed to have one or two support people to handle the body parts, plus we needed the support people to do the remains tracking, decontamination of the dogs and maintain the base camp. An overhead team for

Buzzards and Butterflies

each 12-hour shift was needed to keep track of the activities and a logistics team in NYC and PA worked to keep the shifts manned and equipped.

Donations of supplies from around the country came in to support the dogs. The NYPD provided meals in cooperation with the Red Cross and the National Guard. EZ-Up donated tents, Go America provided wireless computer service and ARCH Wireless provided two-way pagers for team leaders. Tempo Distributors provided the use of a photo ID system to make ID's for many of the 300-team members.

As we expanded the operation, we heard from the NYPD K9 unit that the American Humane Association had its Animal Rescue Truck in the city and it had been released from ground zero. A call to the AHA got us instant confirmation that the truck was on it's way back to NYC. The AHA - Animal Planet Rescue truck arrived Sept 26. This unique truck and trailer was an answer to our prayers for a way to better de-contaminate the dogs and support the logistic operation.

At the same time the Department of Health's Veterinarian Medical Assistance Team sent in shifts of veterinarians and technicians to staff the Canine Recovery Task Force's operation 24/7. This allowed pre and post shift physical checks of the dogs. It provided instant treatment of the minor injuries that occurred, and with the aid of the AHA staff, all canines were decontaminated in a tent with warm water in a tub. Before the AHA arrival decontamination was done with a small propane camper hot water heater supplied from a drum of water out in the open in the mud with only a trap. A dramatic difference was noticed in the response of the dogs to the warm water from the cold water used in the first days; and, again I noticed a positive response and willingness of many of the dogs to participate in the de-con process. De-Con training of K9 teams and support members is a must for team planning when responding to disaster, fire, or other incident that can expose the team to hazards or even just muddy.

CRTF Base of Operation with the American Human Association Rescue Trailer

These types of support units on a smaller scale have been identified as a priority need for Rescue International's supported responses and trainings. As a result of lessons learned RI has obtained and is equipping a 26 foot canine support and de-con trailer to support future responses and was used during Katrina operations.

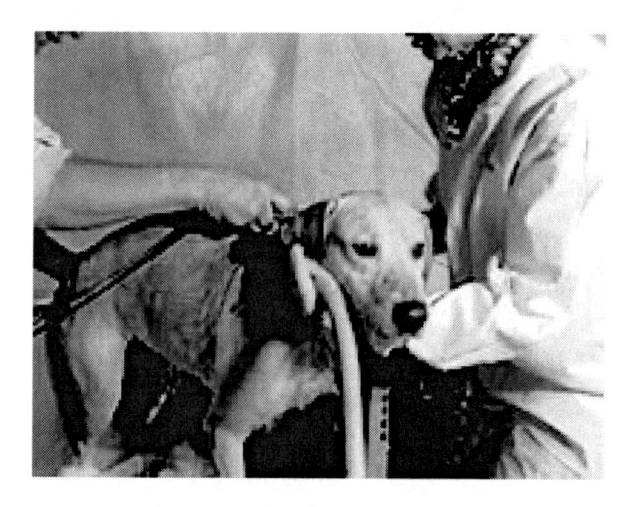

VMAT staff gives dog a warm De-Con bath   *Vet checks dog*

    The dogs were very effective. Some dogs were better than others but everyone gave it their all. Sources as small as a quarter to as large as a leg was found. Most of what the TF searched had been screened at Ground Zero loaded and reloaded up to four times and then looked at by dozens of sifters. With all that already done the canines still found over 500 items in two weeks of identification. Working with the DMORT team's doctors many handlers received advanced on-the-job training in the identification of human remains.

    A few handlers arrived on site and after a short time decided that the job was not for them and left. Some handlers worked a few hours and then pulled their dogs off the line, as they were not working very well. A lot of on-the-job training or re-training was done to get their dogs to understand what we were looking for. Cadaver is not always cadaver.

    The other important lesson was that many dogs trained for forensic level searches that had minimal exposure to large sources, were over whelmed with the stronger sources and experience difficulty in handling the mass contamination of the site and became frustrated. A number of the handlers withdrew from the mission. Some did on site training and then worked very well.

    The way a dog was trained affected how well the dogs worked. Many dogs trained for very funky smelly stuff blew by a lot of the less than week old items. A short introduction to the real stuff solved that problem for most dogs. Newer dogs were exposed to confirmed larger sources as there were found. This helped speed the learning process and focus the dogs on cadaver that was at the right point in the decay process.

    Training aids were on site to allow rewards, to test some less experienced dogs and to make them feel better about the surroundings by getting a quick find. On Saturday, September 30th, the Task Force received word from the NY City Office of Emergency Management that we were to shut down and pack up. FEMA and OEM had now taken a more direct role as they were paying the bills. The official reason was that a new system of conveyers and automated sifters was to be used that was not conducive to working with the dogs. Later they released the reason that dogs were not being used was due to health concerns for the dogs. This was never discussed with our veterinarians or us. Attempts to return to help failed.

Buzzards and Butterflies

We have all learned a lot at the expense of so many others. God bless the ones we have lost, their families and those now protecting us every day. My hat goes off to the NYPD, FBI, National Guard, and the NYC Sanitation Dept. for making an impossible job at the landfill work so well and for treating all of the CRTF members like the professionals they were.

Many of the lessons learned at the WTC recovery were to be used in the aftermath of Hurricane Katrina.

Katrina Disaster Recovery Dogs

By Bruce Barton
Rescue International Recovery Task Force
© 2008

The events of Hurricane Katrina resulted in many people being trapped or completely caught off guard by the water surge that swept over the Gulf Coast. Katrina resulted in many deaths and missing persons. Rescue International had resources deployed to New Orleans for water rescues and later recovery teams in the Slidell area of Louisiana, working under the local sheriffs offices, in the weeks right after the storm hit the coast. We spent a few days searching with the St Tammany Parish Sheriffs Dept and their K9 unit. This included checking dozens of houses along the coast and many small islands that were inland from the coastal houses were people were reported missing. The ability of a recovery dog to be transported by many different types of transportation became an important issue and needs to be done in training lessons. We must always expose our K9's and handlers to larger noisy environments, boats and trucks.

Recovery K9's have to be able to ride in all types of boats and work on all types of rubble piles.

Ebby and Bruce search debris piles from airboat and on a remote island

As operations wound down, RI's Recovery task force received an EMAC request thru the State of PA EMA for Cadaver/Recovery dogs to fill a request for assistance in Hancock County, Mississippi.

RI's CRTF responded with 4 dogs and was joined by 2 additional dogs from Appalachian Mountain Rescue Group in western Pennsylvania. Upon arrival to Hancock County we established a Base of Operation in the rear of the Vocational Technical School that was being used as the county Emergency Operations Center. We were first partnered up with members of the Rhode Island USAR (Urban Search and Rescue) team and later with Tennessee USAR team. They provided great support and logistic support to our K9 Teams as well as doing dozens of building searches for the county.

Daily duties included responding to reports of human cadaver smells, checking the hot zone pile where debris suspected of containing human remains was dropped. We did daily searches of that pile. This allowed removal crews in outer areas to clear areas faster as they did not have to wait for search teams to check the loads that smelled of what may have be human remains.

Nemo and John Valvardi from CRTF search large dump site in Waveland, MS

Most of our daily searches turned out to be calls to food items and refrigerators. We did not need the dogs after a few dozen of these calls but we always confirmed our suspicions with the dog. On a few calls the dogs found remains and the coroner was called. The ability to respond with a K9 team to these requests was critical to the removal operations as it allowed for a quick

Buzzards and Butterflies

release of suspect debris. It could tie up a few trucks and 5-8 people for hours every time they had to wait to make the removal. We hand 2-4 dogs working for most of the time we were in operation.

Working this type of debris on very large and unstable piles required a dog that was able to work slow and was very comfortable with the lay of the land, the many years of training classes and exercises paid off for many of the dogs with only a few minor cuts happening over the two months the recovery task force was operational in the Gulf coast. Repeated quick physical checks and soap and water decontamination of the dogs was done routinely and prevented additional complications form chemicals or hydrocarbons.

John checks Nemos paws after a quick De-Con wash with a battery powered hand sprayer and Dawn dish soap

Bob, Michelle and Dale prepare to search a housing development.   *Michelle takes a break with her pup at housing development*

178

Even with high temperatures basic PPE was required when searching, handlers had to hydrate the dogs and themselves regularly. One dog had to be treated in the early days for heat stroke because it became sick from drinking bad water and was repeatedly throwing up, a saline bolus, some medication for the vomiting and a days rest had her back on the job. The use of water additives that bait the dog's water worked very well for these conditions.

Dale from RRTF-1 and AMRG K9 team load into inflatable boat to search woods a mile away.

Crews worked 12-14 hour shifts with operations shutting down at night for safety and security reasons. Teams had to endure heat, a second hurricane that shut us down for a few days and a few reptiles. Team members reverted to rescue mode when the second hurricane water surge flooded some costal areas for a day or so. We were spared any serious damage and got back to Recovery operations quickly.

Some search areas required that we load the K9 teams into boats to access the debris fields deep in the woods and to works the many areas were bodies were expected to be underwater. Basic boating and water skills training for the K9 teams are a must for the advanced recovery dog as is basic water search training. If doing water recovery the same rule applies to do some of the training with larger fresh dead and cadaver decayed sources so dogs are use to larger sources of both fresh dead and cadaver type targets.

As word spread there were recovery dogs working in Hancock County a request went out for the dogs to respond to Waveland in Harrison County to check a few locations including a collapsed hotel.

K9's from the Recovery Task Force and USAR dogs from Tennessee Task Force 1 responded to the hotel to check the report of cadaver smells. Upon arrival the other handlers and myself inspected the site and found a strong cadaver smell. We worked four dogs on the site. All four dogs showed interest in the same section, some gave alerts, but in somewhat different areas of the same section. With the dogs not pinpointing due to the massive amount of scent I asked for a heavy-duty excavator to start removing the concert roof slab in the center of the area.

Buzzards and Butterflies

Ebby Alerts on underside of roof slab before it was removed

Ebby alerts just down wind on scent from body of security guard trapped in a collapsed hotel in Gulfport MS.

After the excavator removed some of the roof we worked dogs to check and try to pin point the location. Some dogs had problems with the large amount of scent from a full body source. It is important for handlers to work the dogs on larger training aids, as hard as it is to get larger sources it is critical to the advanced K9's training for recover operations. One thing that I did on Ebbys second run was to request that we clear the site to let it air a bit before working her to try to pin point the location. After a short break, we proceeded to work the site from the down wind side. She almost immediately went for the excavation site, did her classic circle around the site, and worked the cone right into one spot. She circled the spot again and then gave me a positive touch and the confirming natural look for approval. I rewarded Ebby then looked at the spot and saw all the clothes. That little devil on my shoulder started to say "well she was hitting on clothes" but after 28 years of working K9's and knowing her response to the other bodies we had found in the Gulf Coast and elsewhere, I just trusted my dog and said dig right here and lift that piece of concrete. As soon as the excavator started to move the concrete the county crew yelled to stop; they saw him.

I feel that it is always best to give yourself the very best chance you can have to find a subject or a source. Do not be afraid to ask to have the area cleared if practical and even ventilate a house to reduce the amount of by-stander scent or to reduce saturation in the structure. You can simulate this at most any Fire Burn Building that has exhaust fans to ventilate the building during training.

Over the next four weeks we rotated dog teams to cover the counties needs, bringing in dogs from across the country on two more EMAC requests for the county. Rescue International had teams of different types in the Gulf Coast for almost 3 months, rescued many, saving lives, helping agencies communicate and helping to bring closure to many families of the missing.

A special thanks goes out to all the CRTF handlers and support members that worked the response to Katrina and the WTC, donating there time for many days to find the missing and thanks to all the EOC staffers and USAR teams for making it all happen safely.

Closure

By Jim Ware
Brunswick Search and Rescue Team, NC
K9 Kinder and K9 Storm

The older couple sitting in their late-model sedan didn't catch my eye at first as I walked the banks of a trout stream along I-70 in western Pennsylvania looking for the remains of a young woman missing for more than a year.

It was a gray early spring morning with wind that chilled the sweat on our backs from hiking through dense underbrush and up steep embankments. Water that had leaked into boots while wading across a web of streamlets squished through socks and wrinkled toes.

State police investigators from the station at Washington, Pa., called in our dog team to assist them in their search for the woman's remains after a man fishing for trout found a woman's skull on a sandbar.

We were joined at the site by investigators, Allegheny County deputy coroners and a team of forensic anthropology students and their professor from Mercyhurst College.

Fishermen continued to cast for trout in the stream as we set out on our gruesome tasks, not knowing what we'd find or how we'd react.

Over the churning noise of water on rock, tractor-trailers roared by on I-70, barely 20 yards away. Police suspected a passing trucker she'd met in the bar where she worked had kidnapped the woman. The discovery of her skull in such close proximity to a major east-west highway bolstered their theory.

Now they wanted more evidence. And the woman's family wanted closure.

Buzzards and Butterflies

It was late afternoon on a day full of peaks and valleys. Bones found on a hillside brought coroner's officials and anthropologists running, only to be pronounced the remains of a deer. The German shepherd seemed to hit on a scent flowing downstream, but lost it in the frustrating, swirling confluence of streams.

Then the radio crackled with excitement: Somebody found bones – human bones.

Dog team members headed back to base to find an anthropology student painstakingly excavating a 1-square-foot segment of a gridded hillside within sight of the I-70 guardrail. He'd found what appeared to be the woman's rib cage.

Suddenly our search had a starting point. While the coroner's officials photographed the scene and began removing the remains, our team headed downstream again. One team member remembered seeing a swatch of material. It was her shirt. Another member wading through a creek stumbled across a lump that turned out to be her purse.

Each new discovery brought excitement to the ensemble of searchers, students and law enforcement officials.

In a makeshift parking lot within easy sight of the recovery activities, the older couple got out of their car. A detective wearing only wet socks on his bone-cold feet saw the couple emerge and hurried to them, pulled them close in a firm embrace and told them what they feared, but what they also wanted to hear: Their daughter was coming home.

Light was fading as the couple leaned against each other, and then settled into their car to watch every last detail of the recovery work.

Our work there was done. Team members were cold and hungry, and experiencing a roller coaster of emotions. Yet we, too, lingered – just a few parking spaces away from the woman's parents.

My mom never met a stranger. Neither had I. I tapped on the window of the car and the woman's mother rolled it down.

I don't know what I said or how I said it, but somehow it was the right thing. Eventually the conversation turned to the search dogs and the work they'd done that day. Would they like to meet one of the dogs?

I hurried back to where our team members were gathered and told our leader I needed to borrow her bloodhound Lucy. The team members who already couldn't believe I'd struck up a conversation with the woman's parents now shook their heads in disbelief as Lucy and I headed across the parking lot.

The bond between man and dog transcends its thousands-of-years-old hunter-scavenger roots. There is a kinship that somehow lets us share our emotions, that elicits a sympathetic response. Lucy was into licking faces that day.

Suddenly the emptiness, the need to hug that would never be fulfilled, had an outlet. The soft folds of Lucy's face and neck enveloped the mother's tears; sloppy wet hound kisses brought a smile.

In the overall picture of the day's search, our team mostly failed. The forensic anthropologists were the heroes. The remains of the couple's daughter would get a proper burial, away from foraging animals and the elements that had taken their toll the past year. Investigators no longer had a missing person case. Now they were looking for a murderer.

But our team left with the feeling that, somehow, we – and Lucy – helped the couple find more than their daughter's remains. Perhaps Lucy's hugs and kisses helped them take a healing step through grief toward that elusive stage known as closure.

Whatever it was that happened between searchers and the woman's family that grueling day along a lonely creek on a lonely stretch of highway, I know it changed my view of the value of victim recovery.

Since then I've been keenly aware of the watching, waiting families as my team members and I searched for their relatives on land and water.

I've held in my arms the miracle girl who survived a boating accident as I helped direct the search for her father's body. I've had distraught family members plead and drunken relatives demand that we find the remains of their loved ones.

"So that others may live" is the motto of many search and rescue organizations. The motto takes on a new significance when we consider what it means to the survivors of victims whose bodies we seek to recover.

Buzzards and Butterflies

APPENDIX

1. Sample HRD Evaluation Forms -Permission granted to duplicate for SAR team purposes only. Permission granted to alter form to meet the needs of the individual team.

Human Remains Detection Certification Sample Evaluator Form

Name of Handler:_____ Date:_____
Location:_____

Name of K9:_____
Name of
Evaluator:_____

Recommended for Certification (circle one): Yes No
Evaluator Signature:_____
Witness Signature:_____

Element	Required Skill	Completed	Did Not Complete	Retake Date y/n
		YES	NO	
Protocols	Handler followed all team protocols: see attached listing			
	Rabies Vaccination up to date			
	Training Records – Logs inspected and up to date			
	Transported in crate in vehicle			
	Minimum Four-foot lead and appropriate collar used and available			
	Appropriate water and food available			
	Plastic bags for clean up available			
	Apparent healthy canine			
	Ride quietly in motor vehicle			
	Ride quietly in boat			
	Load and unload easily, alone into a vehicle, on or off lead			
Obedience	*Recall from a group of dogs or other distractions, at least 20 feet away			
	Allows other handlers to transport & exercise the K9			
	*One minute sit			
	*Three minute down-stay			
	Heel on lead, loosely			
	*Stand for exam			
	*Comes when handler calls, distance 20 feet			

	No apparent signs of aggression			
	* May be done "on lead" for canines "worked" on-lead			
Agility	Ability to maneuver obstacle: off lead including at least one jump			
	Ability to maneuver obstacle: cat walk, at least five feet long X 4 ft. high			
	Ability to cross a narrow stream			
	Able to be loaded on a truck bed with other K9 teams			
Alerts/Indications	Handler demonstrates ability to work and control dog effectively in a variety of areas & conditions according to terrain & weather			
	K9 able to locate three out of four HRD samples hidden under natural or man-made debris, hanging 4 -5 ft above ground, buried at least 1-2 inches below ground level (with distracter disturbances in the general area), or covered lightly with leaf or brush			
	Handler describes search strategy to evaluators based upon terrain & weather conditions			
	Handler has ability recognize & describe when canine is not working effectively and compensate or remedy the situation			
	Handler describers the working posture of the K9 so as to be easily recognizable to the evaluators			
	K9 alerts in a passive alert to location of HRD sample within five feet of sample. Handler can readily identify the alert/indication of the canine prior to the test beginning in order for the evaluator to easily recognize the canine alert.			
	No false alerts/indications as called by handler, i.e. Handler denotes "wrong" location of sample			
Canine	Canine at least 12 months of age: DOB:			
	Willing to find and approach strangers			
	Eager to work in a variety of terrains, always under control of the handler			
	K9 finds three of four samples hidden in search area of one acre			
	K9 does not miss an obvious scent, even when tired			
	K9 able to find samples in a contaminated area			
	K9 able to work effectively with one or more members of a crew, including possibly a previously unknown person			
	K9 responsive to handler when off lead, if working off lead			
Canine First Aid	Handler shall have adequate basic canine first aide training			
	Handler describes how to take the temperature of			

		the K9 & is aware of normal temperatures and critical temperatures			
		Handler describes how to set a broken bone on a canine and demonstrates an appropriate technique			
	Equipment	Handler possesses the required equipment listed below: Dog food & water for 24 hours Collar & leash, at least four foot Harness for working; if needed Necessary medications K9 First Aide K9 including minimum items of: kling wrap, telfa 4 X 5 " pads, small bottle of betadine ointment, saline solution, splint, thermometer, large syringe for flushing, antibiotic spray or ointment, aspirin,; Muzzle is recommended, or materials/supplies to construct a muzzle.			
	Terrain	Combination of terrains to include light brush, trees, asphalt, dirt road, or field; approximately one acre in size			
	Scenario	Four samples are placed. One sample should be bone, one shall be blood, and the remaining two choice of evaluator.			
		Recognizable parameters available to define search area.			
		Samples may be manufactured HRD if requested and supplied by candidate in original container, sealed.			
	Sample Placement	Samples are placed in position no less than 30 minutes prior to the start of the exercise.			
	Timing	Test should be completed in a reasonable amount of time as determined by the evaluators, the terrain, weather conditions. Normally, test should be completed in two hours or less. Handler may request rest breaks, no more than 10 minutes per 20 minutes working time. Break time does not count toward total search time.			

Comments:

Evaluator Signature: Date:

HRD Water Recovery Certification Sample Evaluator Form

Name of Handler: _____ Date: _____
Location: _____

Name of K9: _____
Name of Evaluator: _____

Recommended for Certification (circle one): Yes   No
Evaluator Signature: _____

Witness Signature: _____

Element	Required Skill	Completed	Did Not Complete	Retake Date y/n
		YES	NO	
Protocols	Handler followed all team protocols			
	Rabies Vaccination up to date			
	Training Records – Logs inspected and up to date			
	Transported in crate in vehicle			
	Minimum Four foot lead and appropriate collar used and available			
	Appropriate water and food available			
	Plastic bags for clean up available			
	Apparent healthy canine			
	Ride quietly in motor vehicle			
	Ride quietly in boat			
	Load and unload easily, alone into a vehicle, on or off lead			
	Previously certified in at least one prior discipline: W, HRD, H2O, Tr			
Obedience	*Recall from a group of dogs or other distractions, at least 20 feet away			
	Allows other handlers to transport & exercise the K9			
	*One minute sit			
	*Three minute down-stay			
	Heel on lead, loosely			
	*Stand for exam			
	*Comes when handler calls, distance 20 feet			
	No apparent signs of aggression			
	* are optional for on-lead trailing canines, required for off lead trailers			
	Ability to cross a narrow stream			
	Able to be loaded on a truck bed with other K9 teams			
	*May be completed "on lead" for canines "working" on lead.			
Alerts/Indications	Handler demonstrates ability to work and control dog effectively in a variety of areas & conditions according to terrain & weather & size of boat or			

		water vessel			
		K9 able to locate two out of three HRD totally or partially submerged in a water location such as stream, waterway, pond, stream, dock, etc. within an accuracy of 15 feet.			
		Handler describes search strategy to evaluators based upon waters, currents, prevailing winds, search scenario, known clues & weather conditions			
		Handler has ability recognize & describe when canine is not working effectively and compensate or remedy the situation			
		Handler describers the working posture of the K9 so as to be easily recognizable to the evaluators			
		K9 alerts in a passive alert to location of HRD sample under water and can readily identify the alert/indication of the canine prior to the test beginning in order for the evaluator to easily recognize the canine alert while on the boat.			
		No false alerts/indications as called by handler. I.e. Handler calls wrong location for sample submerged or not within range allowed.			
	Canine	Canine at least 12 months of age: DOB:			
		Willing to find and approach strangers			
		Eager to work in a variety of terrains, always under control of the handler while on the boat			
		K9 finds two of three samples hidden totally or partially submerged or in water area of at least one acre			
		K9 does not miss an obvious scent, even when tired			
		K9 able to find samples in a contaminated area			
		K9 able to work effectively with one or more members of a crew, including possibly a previously unknown person			
		K9 responsive to handler when off lead, if working off lead			
	Canine First Aid	Handler shall have adequate basic canine first aide training			
		Handler describes how to take the temperature of the K9 & is aware of normal temperatures and critical temperatures			
		Handler describes how to set a broken bone on a canine and demonstrates an appropriate technique			
	Equipment	Handler possesses the required equipment listed below: Dog food & water for 24 hours Collar & leash, at least four foot Harness for working if needed Necessary medications			

	K9 First Aide K9 including minimum items of: kling wrap, telfa 4 X 5 " pads, small bottle of betadine ointment, saline solution, splint, thermometer, large syringe for flushing, antibiotic spray or ointment, aspirin; A muzzle is recommended or materials/supplies to construct a muzzle on hand.			
Terrain	Test sight may include a pond, waterway, stream, docks, shorelines, etc.			
Scenario	Three samples are placed. One sample should be bone, one shall be blood, and the remaining choice of evaluator. Scent machines may be used but if used shall be not visible (tubing) to searcher.			
	Recognizable parameters available to define search area.			
	Samples may be manufactured HRD if requested and supplied by candidate in original container, sealed.			
Sample Placement	Samples are placed in position no less than 30 minutes prior to the start of the exercise.			
Timing	Test should be completed in a reasonable amount of time as determined by the evaluators, the terrain, weather conditions. Normally, test should be completed in two hours or less.			

Comments

Evaluator Signature:
Date:

Date:

Human Remains Detection
Greater Houston Search Dogs
Recommended Guidelines for Mission Ready Status

Criteria and Setup

◆The handler/dog team must successfully complete five out six stations for certification in human remains detection.
◆The evaluators will choose 6 stations out of 9 scenarios. The handler will not know which station he or she is being tested on.
◆The dog may use either a passive or active indication.

Passive Indication – The dog indicates to the handler the positive scent source through passive means, such as a sit or a down.

Active Indication – The dog indicates to the handler the positive scent source through active means, such as barking.

◆The handler must be able to describe the dog's indication to evaluators.
◆The handler must "call" the dog's indication for a "find" to count. If the handler decides not to call what appears to be an indication by the dog, it will not count as an indication. Only the handler is qualified to interpret the dog's behavior on a distraction as opposed to its behavior on a positive scent source. Upon calling the indication, the handler has committed to declaring a "find". The dog may be rewarded.

◆The handler must effectively communicate to the evaluators that the dog has indicated a positive scent source.
◆The handler cannot assist the dog in the indication.
◆The handler will execute and communicate his/her search strategy to the evaluators. The handler will be able to identify factors influencing canine search strategies and search results: wind, water, temperature, convection, terrain, and time of day. He or she will understand the differences between hasty searches, efficient searches, thorough searches, and confinement tactics. The handler may choose to deviate from the strategy.
◆The handler must draw a map of one area searched, including the position of any positive scent sources, distractions, vegetation, and other pertinent information.

◆A debriefing will be conducted and should include a description of the weather and search conditions, search area covered, start and end times, findings and clues, POD, and, any other important information.

◆All tests will have a dog certified in human remains detection work the area to prove the test.
◆The cadaver materials used for this evaluation, referred to as the positive scent source, will be of human origin (e.g. blood, teeth, tissues, unbleached bone, body dirt, etc…). The positive scent source may be placed in a container (PVC pipe, jar, bag, etc…), attached to articles of

clothing, or attached to an instrument that might be used in a crime (knife, hammer, axe etc…). The types of materials used as well as the vehicles used to contain them will be determined by evaluators.
- ◆The safety of the dog is to be taken into account by the evaluator when selecting and placing articles and cadaver material.
- ◆The handler/dog team will be allowed a specific amount of time to search each test area. The handler will be given a five-minute warning. The handler may declare an area complete before the allotted time, but having done so may not re-enter the area later to re-search it.
- ◆Rural search areas will be approximately one acre per station with a minimum of 100' between each station.
- ◆All boundaries will be clearly marked by the evaluators.
- ◆Test will not be given in inclement weather or at night.
- ◆Dog should not eat the scent material or disturb the incident scene.
- ◆Handler must pass a written examination. (A SAR TECH I, II or III certification is an acceptable substitute).

Passed: ☐   Failed: ☐

- ◆Prior to testing, the handler must produce a training records log indicating success in blind problems over a period of six months.

Complete: ☐ Incomplete: ☐

- ◆Handler must have his or her pack complete according to the NASAR SAR Tech II Standards. Handler does not need to carry the pack during the tests.

Complete: ☐ Incomplete: ☐

- ◆Each testing area will be fresh and used only once per day.
- ◆Search area will be contaminated with human scent to prevent canine from trailing to the scent source.
- ◆Scent sources should be placed at least 20 minutes prior to search.
- ◆Two animal scent distractions will be utilized in the search area. (Surface and Bone station)
- ◆Canines may travel outside of border areas to compensate for wind and terrain.
- ◆The dog must be under the handler's control at all times. Failing to recall to the handler after exiting the search area will constitute a failure.
- ◆The handler, upon recognizing the dog's alert, should identify and mark the location of the scent source by placing a survey flag or wand into the ground or effectively communicate to the evaluator where the positive scent source is located.
- ◆The handler should finish searching the area after locating the scent source.
- ◆Any indication that handler identifies as a find, which is a negative scent source, will constitute a failure of that station.
- ◆The handler has 20 minutes to complete the each station with 10 minutes break in between.
- ◆Handler may choose to work sooner if requested and forfeit complete break. This time period does not include walking to the next station.
- ◆A flanker is not required for HRD tests.

Buzzards and Butterflies

◆A large source (approximately 1 lb) of various materials including tissue, blood, hair, bones, teeth and clothing will be utilized in one station.

Handler: _____ Evaluator #1 _____

Canine: _____ Evaluator #2 _____

Date: _____

Evaluation for Human Remains Detection
Greater Houston Search Dogs

The evaluation will consist of 6 stations in random order. The evaluators will choose 6 from the following. The handler/K9 team will not know which station he or she is being tested on.

◆Surface station (animal and human)
Surface station (large source (approximately 1 lb) of various materials including tissue, blood, hair, bones, teeth and clothing)
◆Buried station (6-24 inches deep)
◆Above surface station (hanging)
◆Vehicle search (line up of 6 cars)
◆Building search (building or warehouse at least 2000 square feet)
◆Trace evidence search (building or rural area less than 2000 square feet)
◆Bones on surface (animal and human)
◆Negative

Surface station:

The terrain should be rural with a mix of open area and trees. The search area will be approximately one acre. The cadaver scent material will be located on the surface but not readily visible to the dog and handler. It may be placed in a container or on the ground. The scent material will be placed at least 20 minutes prior to the test. A single animal scent distraction will be utilized in the search area. The dog must be able to distinguish the animal and human cadaver. The handler will place a survey flag within 36" of the scent source. The handler/dog team will have 20 minutes to complete the station.

Time placed: _____   Start time: _____   Finish time: _____

Passed: ☐   Failed: ☐

Surface station – Large source:

The terrain should be rural with a mix of open area and trees. The search area will be approximately one acre. Approximately 1lb of various materials including tissue, blood, hair, bones, teeth and clothing will be placed on the surface but not readily visible to the dog and handler. The scent material will be placed at least 20 minutes prior to the test. The handler will place a survey flag within 36" of the scent source. The handler/dog team will have 20 minutes to complete the station.

Time placed: _____   Start time: _____   Finish time: _____

Passed: ☐   Failed: ☐

Buried station:

The terrain should be rural with a mix of open area and trees. The search area will be approximately one acre. The cadaver scent material will be buried at least six inches but not more than 24 inches in porous soil and not readily visible to the dog and handler. Mixing debris such as leaves, branches, and rocks into the dirt can make porous soil. There will be four other blank holes dug in the search area (Note to evaluator: Special care must be taken when blank holes are dug so that they don't become contaminated with cadaver). The scent material will be placed at least 20 minutes prior to the test. The test shall not include known animal remains. The handler will place a survey flag within 36" of the scent source. The handler/dog team will have 20 minutes to complete the station.

Time placed: _____   Start time: _____   Finish time: _____

Passed: ☐   Failed: ☐

Above surface station (hanging):

The terrain should be rural with a mix of open area and trees. The search area will be approximately one acre. The cadaver scent material will be approximately three feet high and not readily visible to the dog and handler. The scent material will be placed at least one 20 minutes to the test. The search area shall not include known animal remains. The handler will place a survey flag within 60" of the scent source (Evaluators should take wind conditions into consideration). The handler/dog team will have 20 minutes to complete the station.

Time placed: _____   Start time: _____   Finish time: _____

Passed: ☐   Failed: ☐

Vehicle search

The terrain will be urban. The search area will be a parking lot with at least six vehicles. The handler will be allowed to direct the dog to search each vehicle. The handler/dog team must determine the vehicle with the positive scent source and the handler must determine which quadrant the material is located. The material will be placed out of site on the exterior or underside of the vehicle (wheel well, engine etc…).

Time placed: _____   Start time: _____   Finish time: _____

Passed: ☐   Failed: ☐

Building search

The terrain will be urban. The search area will be a building or warehouse at least 2000 square feet. The evaluator can determine whether to place the scent source on the exterior or interior. The handler will be allowed to direct the dog to search an area. The handler will place a survey flag within 36" of the scent source or verbally communicate a find to the evaluator.

Time placed: _____   Start time: _____   Finish time: _____

Passed: ☐   Failed: ☐

Trace evidence (Blood)

The terrain will be either urban or rural with a mix of open area and trees. The search area will be less than 2000 square feet. Trace evidence with blood will be placed on the surface but not readily visible to the dog and handler. The scent material will be placed at least 20 minutes prior to the test. The handler will place a survey flag within 36" of the scent source. The handler/dog team will have 20 minutes to complete the station.

Time placed: _____   Start time: _____   Finish time: _____

Passed: ☐   Failed: ☐

Bones on surface (Animal and human):

The terrain should be rural with a mix of open area and trees. The search area will be approximately one acre. **The HR bones will be placed on the surface and the animal bones will not be placed within 20' of the cadaver bones.** The scent material will be placed at least one hour prior to the test. The handler will place a survey flag within 60" of the scent source (Evaluators should take wind conditions into consideration). The handler/dog team will have 20 minutes to complete the station.

Time placed: _____   Start time: _____   Finish time: _____

Passed: ☐   Failed: ☐

Negative:

The terrain should be rural with a mix of open area and trees. The search area will be approximately one acre. The dog/handler team must call it within 20 minutes.

Start time: _____ Finish time: _____

Passed: ☐   Failed: ☐

Certified in Human Remains Detection: ☐

Not Certified in Human Remains Detection: ☐

_____ Evaluator #1 signature

_____ Evaluator #2 signature

_____ Handler's signature   _____ Date

Buzzards and Butterflies

Team:

Address:

Phone:

CONSENT AND RELEASE FOR PLACENTA DONATION

I, _____, the undersigned birth mother of a child born alive, acknowledge that I am over the age of 18 years and am capable of consenting to the donation of Placenta from my body.

I hereby release and donate to _____ Team, the Placenta to be used as a training aid for cadaver canines.

I agree to make this donation on the condition that I am not to be held responsible for any disease or hazard associated with the use or handling of this Placenta.

In turn, the _____ K9 unit agrees that the organization will not hold the undersigned or any medical staff or hospital responsible for any hazard resulting in the use of this tissue.

All Biohazard protocol and handling standards will be observed and instituted.

Signatures:

_____ Date_____
Mother

_____ Date_____
Witness

_____ Date _____
Witness

Team:

Address:

Phone:

CONSENT AND RELEASE FOR TEETH & TISSUE DONATION

I, _____, acknowledge that I am over the age of 18 years and am capable of consenting to the donation of tissue and teeth from my body.

I hereby release and donate to _____ Team the Tissue and Teeth to be used as training aids for cadaver canines.

I agree to make this donation on the condition that I am not to be held responsible for any disease or hazard associated with the use or handling of this tissue and teeth.

In turn, _____ members agree that the organization will not hold the undersigned or any medical staff or hospital responsible for any hazard resulting in the use of this tissue.

All Biohazard protocol and handling standards will be observed and instituted.

_____   Date_____
Donor Signature

_____   Date_____
Witness Signature

_____   Date_____
Witness Signature

Buzzards and Butterflies

Team:

Address:

Phone:

CONSENT AND RELEASE FOR TISSUE, BLOOD and / or FLUIDS DONATION

I, _____, acknowledge that I am over the age of 18 years and am capable of consenting to the donation of tissue, blood and / or fluids from my body.

I hereby release and donate to _____ Team, tissue, bone, materials / or Fluids to be used as training aids for cadaver canines.

I agree to make this donation on the condition that I am not to be held responsible for any disease or hazard associated with the use or handling of this tissue.

In turn, _____ team members agree that the organization will not hold the undersigned or any medical staff or hospital responsible for any hazard resulting in the use of this tissue.

All Biohazard protocol and handling standards will be observed and instituted.

_____   Date _____
Donor

_____   Date _____
Witness

_____   Date _____
Witness

Ground-Penetrating Radar Techniques to Discover and Map Historic Graves

Dr. Lawrence B. Conyers
DEPARTMENT OF ANTHROPOLOGY, UNIVERSITY OF DENVER,
2000 E. ASBURY ST., DENVER, CO 80208

ABSTRACT

Ground-penetrating radar is a geophysical technique that can be used to identify and map features commonly associated with historic graves, including intact or partially collapsed coffins and vertical shafts. Data are collected by moving radar antennas that transmit pulses of energy into the ground along parallel transects within grids, recording reflections of those pulses from significant discontinuities within the ground. Visual analysis of radar reflection profiles can be used to identify both coffins and the vertical shaft features commonly associated with human burials. Spatial analysis of the reflection amplitudes within a grid consisting of many profiles (when converted to depth using site-specific velocities) produces three-dimensional maps of these burial features. The identification and mapping of graves can identify remains for possible excavation and study, and the results can also be used for statistical and spatial analysis when integrated with historical records. If identified by these methods, previously unidentified graves can be preserved in areas threatened by construction or erosion.

Introduction

Locating, studying, and sometimes excavating historic period graves can produce a great deal of information about the past not otherwise available from archival documents or other datum sources. If the goal is to study skeletal remains for osteological or molecular studies, the first step must be identification of the graves of interest. Many historic cemeteries are poorly maintained and often threatened by erosion, development, and agricultural operations, making the identification of graves important if they are to be preserved. Sometimes unmarked graves need to be identified so that human remains may be removed if threatened by construction or even to make way for additional burials when cemeteries expand their boundaries or fill in areas that appear to be vacant. Geophysical techniques such as ground-penetrating radar (GPR) can be used to located unmarked graves and recover other information about historic period cemeteries.

GPR can often determine grave attributes such as depth of burial, grave size, type of caskets and their orientation; numbers of graves in certain locations; and the spatial distribution of graves within certain areas of a cemetery. This information can then be integrated with birth and death records, information found on headstones, or other historical documents to provide a database on the lives and behaviors of the individuals buried there. Often this information is not available by other means. Some Euro American cemetery characteristics such as the depth, orientation, and spatial distribution of grave shafts have changed over time. Often they reflect the economic background, ethnicity, and religious, social, or aesthetic values of both the dead and those doing the burying (Farrell 1980). Although in some cases these characteristics are well documented (Crissman 1994; Sloan 1995) they have not generally been applied to the study of specific communities or integrated with historic records, especially in older cemeteries where grave markers are moved or missing. GPR has the potential to precisely map these graves and add an important data layer to any historical study involving burials and burial practices.

Lacking geophysical means, finding historic graves using traditional probing or excavation methods has often been a "hit or miss" task for most archaeologists. Attempts to locate these subsurface features using visual analysis of surface soils or vegetation changes are also fraught with problems. Head- and footstones that were once present in many historic cemeteries are often deteriorated, relocated, or missing. Written documentation about grave locations is often incomplete, inaccurate, or absent. Falling trees can uproot underlying sediments as well as human remains; animals can burrow into graves; and the wood associated with coffins and surface markers quickly rots with little or no trace. Often there is little to assist researchers in locating graves other than vague memories about where burials were located or poorly drawn sketch maps. Archaeologists have attempted to locate graves by inserting probes in the ground in an attempt to detect soil changes, voids, or areas that might be less compacted (Killam 1990). Some have resorted to dowsing, with little success (Barrett and Besterman 1968; Reese 1985; Van Leusen 1998) or employed psychics (Goodman 1977), and a few have even attempted to use dogs, purported to have acute senses of smell, that are trained to sniff out human remains (Killam 1990). A more reliable method that has been used to locate and then map historic graves is the use of geophysical devices that can measure physical and chemical changes in the ground. These changes may be related to grave shafts, coffins, void spaces, and even the human remains themselves (Bevan 1991; Nobes 1999; Davenport 2001). The most common of these are magnetic gradiometry, electrical resistivity, GPR, and electromagnetic conductivity. Magnetic methods use passive devices that measure small changes in the Earth's magnetic field that are influenced by changes in soils and buried materials below the surface. These changes can result from the presence or absence of metal in coffins or even minute differences in soil and sediment types that exist between grave shafts and undisturbed adjacent materials. The other three most commonly used geophysical methods use tools that transmit energy into the ground and then measure how that energy is affected by changes in the ground related to the presence or absence of graves, grave goods, and soil changes. The resistivity method transmits an electrical current into the ground and measures the differences in voltage between the transmitting device and a recording device some distance away. When mapped spatially, changes in these resistance readings can be related to the presence or absence of graves. A similar method of energy transmittal is used in electromagnetic (EM) conductivity, where an EM field is induced into the ground and measurements are taken, which indicate how that field is affected by the underlying deposits. GPR is also an active method that transmits pulses of radar energy of differing frequencies into the ground and measures properties of the reflections derived from buried materials in the ground. All of these geophysical methods collect data along a series of transects within a grid, which can be interpreted individually as two-dimensional profiles or as a group to spatially map differences in ground conditions that might be related to the presence of graves. The differences in the readings within the grid, when mapped spatially, can often be related to burial phenomena, such as the presence or absence of artifacts associated with human remains or geological changes that can be related to grave shafts. The human remains themselves cannot generally be detected since there is not enough contrast between them and the surrounding material. GPR is one of the best methods to map graves because it is capable of measuring both physical and chemical changes in the ground in three dimensions; therefore, depth as well as the spatial distribution of graves can be determined (Bevan 1991; Davis et al. 2000). This can be accomplished because radar pulses are transmitted from a surface antenna and reflected off buried discontinuities. The returning pulses are measured in elapsed travel time. When time is converted to distance (using measurable velocities common to each site), depth in the ground can be readily determined. In addition, radar energy is readily reflected from any discontinuity in the ground, including soil compaction changes, mineralogical differences, sediment size distinctions, void spaces, and the type and concentration of associated artifacts. Amplitudes of the reflected waves can also be precisely measured, indicating differences in material properties within the ground, producing an additional measurement that is valuable in locating subtle buried features.

GPR systems are compact and easily transported to and from the field. A typical system consists of a radar control system and associated computer, antennas, and a power source (Figure 1). Grids of data (up to 40 x 40 m) can be collected in a day, depending on the transect spacing and the number and complexity of surface obstructions. Reflection data are= easily transferred from the GPR system to a laptop computer for immediate analysis, with preliminary results often available just hours after collection.

Grave Characteristics

Physical anthropologists have long concerned themselves with finding human remains, whether intentionally buried or covered and preserved by natural means. A large body of literature addresses the detection of human remains for forensic purposes, both anthropological and criminal (Imaizumi 1974; Boddington et al. 1987; Killam 1990). Addressed here is the use of GPR techniques to detect and map inhumations that were deliberate burials, usually in cemeteries, and not those that might have been the result of flood events, drowning, or other natural actions.

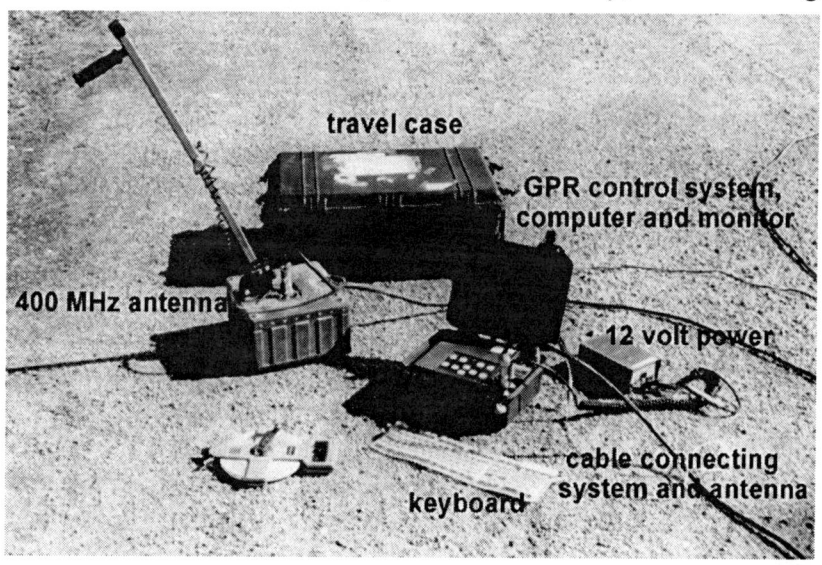

Most historic period Euro American burials in North America are primary interments, with and without coffins, placed horizontally, without changes in position since burial. There are, of course, many other deliberate burial types that were common throughout the world as well as North America. For example, secondary interments occurred where bones were collected after decomposition of the soft flesh and then reburied or where many individuals were buried in one grave, including ossuaries and other mass graves of this sort. In these cases, human remains are rarely in an articulated anatomical position and associated grave goods can be jumbled and are difficult to detect geophysically. Multiple interments are also common in military battlefield contexts where several bodies might be located in one grave. These can also be quite complex. Only those more common singular graves where human remains were buried once and not reinterred or highly disturbed are discussed here.

Figure 1 The Geophysical Survey System, Inc. GSSI. Subsurface Interface Radar SIR, model 2000 with antenna and carrying case. Photograph by author.

Each such grave has four distinct physical features that can potentially be imaged using GPR techniques: (1) the natural soil or substrate below and surrounding the grave shaft, (2) the buried coffin or human body and its associated artifacts, (3) the backfill used to fill in the vertical shaft, and (4) the surface layers of sediment or soil that have accumulated on that shaft after interment. Of these four features, the contact between the shaft and the surrounding material, coffins containing remains, and sometimes associated artifacts are what can be readily imaged using GPR. When human bodies, coffins, urns, or any other grave goods are placed in the ground, a vertical shaft is excavated through surface soils and underlying sediment or rock units, producing an aerially distinct and often recognizable feature that can be seen in GPR reflection profiles. During excavation of a grave, the natural substrate and surface soils are almost always placed on the ground nearby and then returned to the grave shaft after interment. The excavated material that is used to backfill the shaft is highly altered during this process, becoming less compact and more homogenized, losing any natural stratigraphy that might have existed prior to digging. Backfill material will then settle over time, sometimes leaving a natural depression on the surface but also producing settling structures within the shaft that can be distinctive.

If graves are placed in horizontally layered material, the backfill material can be quite apparent as the natural stratigraphy is disturbed during digging, and the zone of truncation is readily visible in profile. The backfill material lacks any natural stratigraphy and the interface between it and the surrounding material can be readily identified in both excavation faces and GPR reflection profiles (Figure 2). In areas where weathered bedrock is shallow or the ground is composed of gravelly or cobble-rich sediment, there can be a good deal of "clutter" in both the disturbed area of the grave shaft and the adjoining undisturbed material, making vertical definition of grave shafts much more difficult to discern. The same is true in homogeneous fine-grained soil and sediment that has little natural stratigraphy. In this case, little physical differentiation exists between shaft backfill and natural substrate.

In cases where individuals were placed in coffins or other containers, these will have deteriorated over time and partially or totally collapsed, producing subsurface and surface slump features. These surface depressions will often slowly fill in with sediment and soil will form, leveling the ground surface and making surface identification of these graves difficult. More substantial caskets constructed of oak or metal can remain intact for a much longer time, producing a noticeable void space in the ground that is readily detectable with GPR. The same is true for burial vaults made of brick or stone, which often preserve void spaces surrounding human remains for centuries. Burials within buildings, such as under the floors of churches or in small family shrines and mausoleums, will also preserve coffins and associated remains for a very long time. The void spaces beneath building floors are often distinctly visible on GPR profiles. The range of primary interment characteristics, soil and sediment differences, climate and soil chemistry factors, and many other variables often make challenging the detection and mapping of graves using GPR. Usually GPR will detect at least the contact between the vertical shaft backfill and the substrate and also the void spaces in completely or partially intact coffins. If there has been a good deal of post interment disturbance of burials due to human or animal and plant disturbance, normal grave features can be highly altered, making detection challenging by any method, including geophysics.

GPR Method

GPR data are acquired by transmitting pulses of radar energy into the ground from a surface antenna and reflecting that energy off buried objects, features, or bedding contacts. At a paired receiving antenna the elapsed time from when pulses are sent and then received back at the surface as well as the strength of that energy are measured and recorded. When collecting radar reflection data, surface radar antennas are moved along the ground in transects within a surveyed grid, and a large number of subsurface reflections, called traces, are collected along each line. Often GPR recording systems can be programmed to collect at a density of one trace, or even more, every 5 cm along the surface transects. When reflection traces are stacked together along one transect line, a reflection profile is created that illustrates a cross-section of the ground much like what might be visible in a trench wall (Figure 3). As radar energy moves through various materials in the ground, the velocity of the propagating waves will change depending on the physical and chemical properties of the material through which they are traveling.

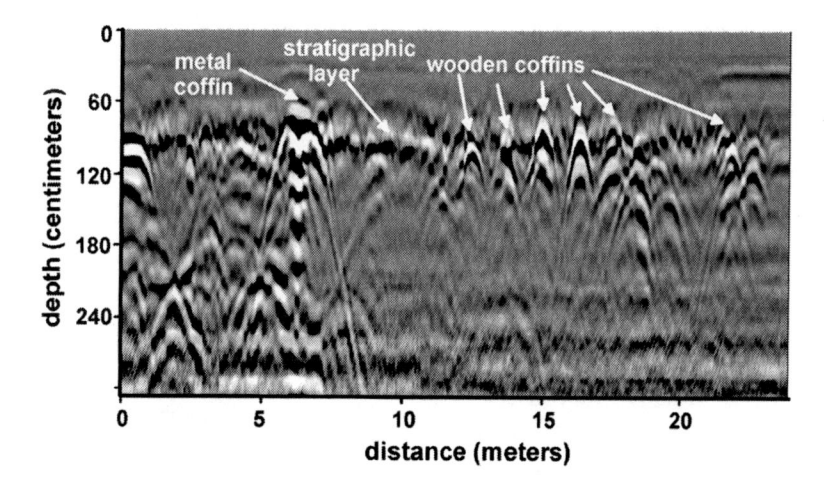

Figure 3. Reflective Profile with a cemetery with wooden coffins, interred between 1898 and 1921. One metal coffin is identifiable by the alternating strong reflections below it. Drawings by author.

(Conyers 2004:26). At each velocity change a portion of the propagating wave will be reflected back to the surface to be detected at a receiving antenna that is usually paired with the transmitting antenna. The remaining energy will continue into the ground until it is absorbed and dissipated. The greater the contrast in electrical (and to some extent magnetic) properties between any two buried materials at an interface, the stronger the reflected waves will be that travel back to the surface, and the greater the amplitude of recorded signals (Conyers 2004:49).

History of Ground-Penetrating Radar

Radar devices that transmit energy into the ground, as opposed to searching for objects in the air, were first experimented with in the 1920s to determine the depth of ice in glaciers (Stern 1929).

The ground-penetrating aspects of radar technology were then largely forgotten until the late 1950s when U.S. Air Force radar technicians on board airplanes noticed that their radar pulses, used to determine altitude, were penetrating glacial ice when flying over Greenland. A number of mishaps occurred because airborne radar analysts detected the bedrock surface below the overlying ice and interpreted the bedrock instead of the ice as the ground surface, resulting in crashes. In 1967, the first prototype GPR system (similar to those used today) was built by NASA and sent on a mission to the moon in an attempt to determine surface conditions prior to landing a manned vehicle (Simmons et al. 1972). One of the first archaeological applications of GPR was conducted at Chaco Canyon, New Mexico, in an attempt to locate buried walls at depths of up to one meter (Vickers et al. 1976). A number of experimental traverses were made, and the resulting reflection profiles were analyzed in the field. It was determined that some of the anomalous radar reflections represented the location of buried walls. These early studies at Chaco Canyon were followed by a number of GPR applications in historical archaeology that successfully located buried building walls and underground storage cellars (Bevan and Kenyon 1975). In these early studies what were described as radar "echoes" and "reverberations" were recognized as having been generated from the tops of buried walls.

Depth estimates were made, using approximate velocity measurements obtained from local soil characteristics.

FIGURE 2. A primary interment with distinct vertical shaft walls incising through naturally layered soil and sediment layers. (Photo by author).

These initial successes were followed by other GPR studies in the 1970s and 1980s that also successfully delineated buried walls, floors, house platforms, and other buried archaeological features. Most initial successes were primarily a function of the very dry matrix material surrounding those buried archaeological features that was almost "transparent" to radar energy propagation, allowing for deep energy penetration and producing relatively uncomplicated reflection records that were easy to interpret.

Throughout the late 1980s and early 1990s GPR continued to be used successfully in a number of archaeological contexts, mostly as what could be called "anomaly hunting" exercises. Unprocessed or partially processed GPR reflection profiles were viewed as paper records or on a computer screen as they were acquired. Interesting anomalous reflections, which could possibly have archaeological meaning, were then excavated. This type of acquisition and interpretation method led to mixed results, with some successes and notable failures, often leaving many archaeologists with the impression that GPR was a "hit or miss" method at best. In the early 1990s GPR manufacturers began to market systems that could collect reflection data as digital files, thereby storing large amounts of reflection data for later processing and analysis. About this same time, inexpensive and increasingly powerful personal computers were also becoming available that could process these digital data in ways that had not been previously possible. Recently, the application of two-dimensional computer simulation and three-dimensional processing techniques have shown that even radar data that does not yield immediately visible reflections when viewed in the field can still contain valuable reflection data when computer processed (Goodman 1994; Goodman et al. 1995; Conyers 2004:138). Computer enhancement of raw GPR reflection data and three dimensional visualization of buried sites is now becoming widespread as researchers increase their familiarity with some of the recent GPR computer-processing techniques (Conyers et al. 2002; Conyers 2004:150).

GPR has not commonly been used to map graves, as they are not usually aerially extensive, can be quite subtle features, and their characteristics vary greatly from site to site. Some notable exceptions are the historic cemeteries mapped by Bruce Bevan (1991) in the eastern and middle United States and those in permafrost in Norway (Davis et al. 2000). Somewhat less successful but nonetheless encouraging results were recently obtained at Texas and Hawaii military cemeteries (Buck 2003) and Maori burial grounds in New Zealand (Nobes 1999).

The success of GPR surveys in historical archaeology is largely dependent on soil and sediment mineralogy, clay content, ground moisture, depth of burial and surface topography, and the type of surface soils present. Electrically conductive or highly magnetic materials will quickly absorb radar energy and prevent its transmission into the ground. The best conditions for energy propagation are therefore dry sediments and soil, especially those without an abundance of clay, which can sometimes be very conductive.

The depth to which radar energy can penetrate the subsurface and the amount of resolution that can be expected in the subsurface are partially controlled by the frequency (and therefore the wavelength) of the radar energy transmitted (Conyers 2004:42). Standard GPR antennas propagate radar energy that varies in frequency from about 10 MHz to 1,000 MHz. Low frequency antennas (10–120 MHz) generate long wavelength radar energy that can penetrate up to 50 m into the ground in certain conditions but are capable of resolving only very large buried features. In contrast, the maximum depth of penetration of a 900 MHz antenna is about 1 m or less in typical materials. Its reflected waves are much shorter and can potentially resolve features with a maximum dimension of a few tens of centimeters. A tradeoff exists between depth of penetration and subsurface resolution. Most GPR surveys used to detect and map historic graves use antennas that range in frequency between 900 and 300 MHz, which produces good resolution data at depths between about 1 m and 3 m, respectively.

Data Collection and Data Analysis

To collect GPR reflections, paired antennas that generate the propagating radar waves and then record the resulting reflections are moved along the ground surface in transects, usually at a minimum of 10 m in length, with a transect spacing of 50 cm or less. Often a survey wheel is attached to the antennas, which will automatically record the horizontal location for all reflections that are recorded along each transect. Reflections that are received back at the surface from buried interfaces are usually recorded along many transects within a grid so that adequate spatial differentiation exists between burial features and natural soil and sediment substrate. Most stratigraphic layers, void spaces, and interfaces between coffins and backfill material, all of which are common to most historic graves, will reflect radar energy back to the surface.

The most efficient GPR collection method is to establish a grid across a survey area with reflection profile transects spaced between 25 cm and 1 m apart, depending on the subsurface resolution needed, the amount of ground to be covered, and the time budgeted for the survey. In GPR collection the elapsed time between pulse transmissions, its reflection from interfaces in the ground, and subsequent recording at the receiving antenna is measured for each reflection in each trace as well as the reflected wave's amplitude. The received reflections are then amplified, processed, and digitally recorded for immediate viewing on a computer screen and saved on some kind of storage medium for later post acquisition processing and display.

Distinct and often continuous horizontal reflections visible in reflection profiles are usually generated at a subsurface boundary such as a soil unit, stratigraphic layer, bedrock, or sometimes the water table (Figure 3). Reflections recorded later in time are those received from deeper in the ground. Hyperbolic shaped *point-source reflections* are generated from distinct *point features* in the subsurface, which in cemeteries are usually casket tops or sides and void spaces within intact or partially collapsed caskets. Similar hyperbolic reflections can also be produced by buried stones, tree roots, or tunnels created by burrowing animals, creating anomalous reflections that can often be confused with those of caskets. Point-source reflection hyperbolas occur because GPR antennas generate a transmitted radar beam that propagates from the surface into the ground in a conical pattern, radiating outward as it travels deeper in the ground (Conyers 2004:57). Some radar energy will be reflected from buried objects that are not directly below the antenna. Only when the antennas are directly on top of the buried object will the radar reflections be recording the exact location and depth of the object.

Reflection hyperbolas that are visible in reflection profiles (Figure 3) are generated because energy will be recorded from a buried point source prior to the antenna being directly on top of it, and antennas will continue to "see" the objects after they have passed. In the resulting hyperbola, only the apex denotes the actual location of the buried source. The arms of the hyperbola denote the reflected energy that traveled the oblique wave paths to and from the buried point source.

Metal- or lead-lined caskets produce both hyperbolic reflections and a series of distinct stacked reflections below the apex of the hyperbolas (Figure 3). This occurs because metal is a perfect radar energy reflector and almost all radar energy is reflected back to the surface from metal objects, which will then return back into the ground from the soil air interface, only to be reflected back again, often many times along these same pathways. This creates a series of stacked high-amplitude reflections, indicative of a significant amount of buried metal in the ground. Narrower hyperbolas lacking in multiple reflections below their apexes are usually wooden caskets or the remaining void spaces from collapsed caskets. Smaller hyperbolas are often generated from smaller caskets, such as those of child burials.

In some cemeteries without caskets or with deteriorated wooden caskets, little remains from the primary interment to reflect radar energy back to the surface,

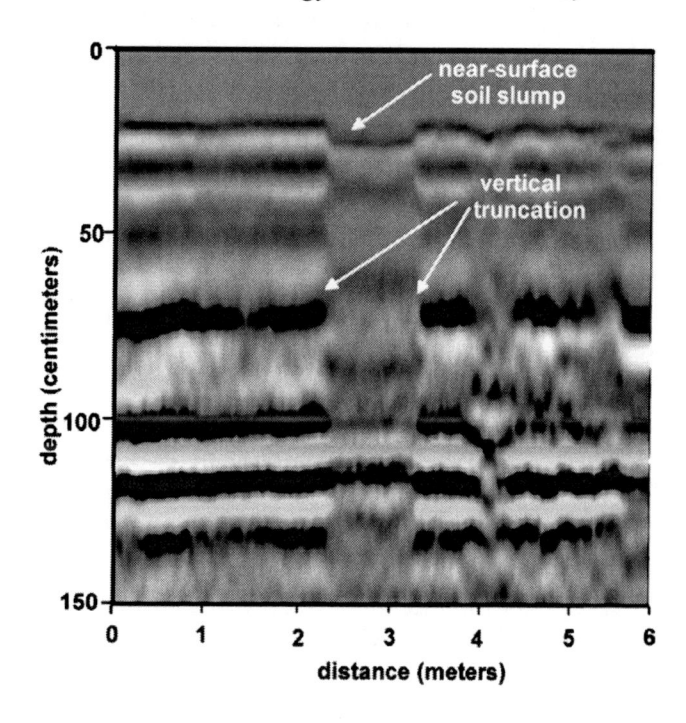

FIGURE 4. A likely grave shaft at the Chumash Indian Cemetery, La Purisima Mission, Lompoc, California. No casket is present, and any human remains at the bottom of the shaft are invisible in this reflection profile. (Drawing by author.)

and no distinctive hyperbolas will be generated. Bones or small amounts of metal from grave goods may still be present, but they are usually either too small or do not contrast enough either physically or chemically from the surrounding matrix to produce significant radar reflections. In these cases only the contact between vertical grave shaft and the natural substrate will be visible in reflection profiles as distinct truncation of the undisturbed adjoining material (Figure 4). Sometimes a near-surface slump of soil into the grave shaft can be discernible in reflection profiles.

Three-dimensional images are very useful in the analysis of historic cemeteries, which can be readily constructed from GPR reflection data when many profiles are collected in a grid. This mapping technique is accomplished by producing amplitude slice maps at defined horizontal layers within a grid of reflection data (Conyers 2004: 148). When abundant data are recorded along closely spaced transects in a grid and when good depth penetration of energy is obtained, a three-dimensional "cube" of reflections can be computer analyzed. The mapping of radar amplitudes is important because the degree of reflection, when mapped spatially, can show the distribution of physical and chemical differences in the ground that often are the product of buried grave goods and human remains. High-amplitude reflections often indicate substantial differences in coffin types, such as those composed partially or wholly of metal. Lower amplitudes can denote the location of wooden caskets.

The amplitude slice-map method is usually more precise and less time consuming than attempting to visually identify many reflections of importance in each reflection profile in a grid, as there can often be tens or even hundreds of potentially important reflections. Computer processing of these reflections compares digital data in a way the human brain cannot, producing complex databases, profiles, and maps of the spatial variation of both distinct and subtle reflections.

Amplitude slice maps are computer generated by comparing and spatially mapping all reflected wave amplitudes at defined depths in all profiles within a grid. Digital values of reflection amplitudes at each location in each profile are compared to those in adjacent profiles and then spatially interpreted, gridded, and mapped throughout a grid. The complete GPR database is then sliced horizontally in layers of any desired thickness and displayed to show the variation in reflection amplitudes at a sequence of depths in the ground. This produces images analogous to maps that might be constructed (but never would be, as it would be too time consuming) of all physical and chemical changes in arbitrary excavation levels within a very large standard excavation. The final product is a series of maps of certain layers in the ground, each of which illustrates the spatial distribution of both high- and low-amplitude reflections produced by caskets or other burial goods as well as other natural features

It is always interesting to compare maps of this sort to the location of existing headstones, especially in older cemeteries. In many cases the headstones have been moved over the years due to vandalism, natural processes, or other human-directed elements. The location of the GPR-mapped graves often correlates well with more recent graves, but sometimes there is little correlation with older graves as surface markers have been moved from their original locations (Owsley et al., this volume). It is also common to see distinct burials in portions of historic cemeteries where there are no markers or other documentation of graves at all. Actual depth in the ground for each amplitude time slice is determined by estimating the velocity of the radar energy in the specific soil and sediment types present at each site. This velocity can be highly variable from site to site and sometimes even vary within a GPR grid. It is affected by numerous physical and chemical variables of the ground and by compaction and moisture content. These velocities can be estimated using computer programs that "fit" the geometry of point-source hyperbolas to a known mathematical formula known for radar wave travel in certain media, which is a very accurate way to determine velocity (Conyers and Lucius 1996; Conyers 2004:99). Other, more sophisticated methods can be used if there are open excavations available or the actual depth to caskets is known and where both radar travel time and distance to known objects can be measured in the field. Time slices should always be converted to depth slices for archaeological interpretation, regardless of how velocity is determined.

Conclusion

If soil conditions are conducive to radar penetration and reflections from within the ground are obtained along many closely spaced transects within a grid, a number of grave features distinct grave features commonly visible are reflection hyperbolas from caskets and vertical shaft truncation planes. Other features common in cemeteries such as large rocks, tree roots, or animal burrows may be confused with caskets, and care must be taken to differentiate them, usually by mapping all reflections spatially.

Caskets will always produce spatially distinct reflection anomalies in the size of a human body, whether an adult or infant. Tree roots and burrows can be differentiated from human burials as they will produce elongated and sinuously shaped reflections. Individual rocks will almost always be visible in only one reflection profile and not on the parallel profiles, unless they are very large. The spatial distribution of these materials in the ground can be determined using amplitude slice maps and studied in real depth if the velocity of radar energy in the ground is obtained.

The other distinct grave elements that are visible in GPR data are the vertical planar surfaces of grave shafts that truncate surrounding sediment or soil layers. Often these features are the only clue to the location of graves if bodies were not placed in caskets or if caskets have subsequently collapsed and deteriorated. These types of features are less easily mapped using amplitude analysis and usually must be visually identified in reflection profiles and manually plotted on maps. Truncation surfaces are also only visible in reflection profiles if the undisturbed materials in the ground are stratified. A third, much less common, feature that is sometimes visible in reflection profiles consists of settling features in surface soils that can occur when grave backfill material compacts over time, allowing surface soils to become depressed. These features are sometimes visible in reflection profiles but, by themselves, would not be indicative of grave locations, as there can be other origins such as animal burrow collapse and the disintegration of rotting tree roots. The use of GPR as a grave-mapping tool can be a precursor to both invasive and noninvasive archaeological studies. Finding human remains that might be excavated for biological research or the analysis of grave goods is one very direct outcome of GPR mapping. Other types of studies not commonly used to date in archaeology would be the incorporation of GPR maps and information with historical records. This could potentially yield important information about changing burial practices over time and differences in ethnicity or economic background of the deceased, their survivors, and the communities in which the burials were located. The efficiency and accuracy of GPR techniques for historic cemetery mapping is just being realized and has the potential to add much to any historical study, whether it involves excavation of remains or noninvasive mapping of the graves alone.

References

BARRETT, WILLIAM, AND THEODORE BESTERMAN. 1968 *The Divining Rod: An Experimental and Psychological Investigation*. University Books, New Hyde Park, NY.

BEVAN, BRUCE W. 1991 The Search for Graves. *Geophysics* 56(9):1310–1319.

BEVAN, BRUCE, AND JEFFREY KENYON. 1975 Ground-Penetrating Radar for Historical Archaeology.

MASCA Newsletter 11(2):2–7. 11(2):2–7. BODDINGTON, A., A. N. GARLAND, AND R. C. JANAWAY (EDITORS). 1987 *Death, Decay, and Reconstruction: Approaches to Archaeology and Forensic Science*. Manchester, University Press, Manchester, England.

BUCK, SABRINA C. 2003 Searching for Graves Using Geophysical Technology: Field Tests with Ground-Penetrating Radar, Magnetometry, and Electrical Resistivity. *Journal of Forensic Science* 48(1):1–7.

CONYERS, LAWRENCE B. 2004 *Ground-Penetrating Radar for Archaeology*. AltaMira Press, Walnut Creek, CA.

CONYERS, LAWRENCE B., E. G. ERNENWEIN, AND LEIGHANN BEDAL 2002 Ground-Penetrating Radar (GPR) Mapping as a Method for Planning Excavation Strategies, Petra, Jordan. *Society for American Archaeology E-tiquity* 1 <http://e-tiquity.saa.org/Etiquity/title1.html> May 2002.

CONYERS, LAWRENCE B., AND JEFFREY LUCIUS. 1996 Velocity Analysis in Archaeological Ground-Penetrating Radar Studies. *Archaeological Prospection* 3(1): 25–38.

CRISSMAN, JAMES K. 1994 *Death and Dying in Central Appalachia: Changing Attitudes and Practices*. University of Illinois Press, Urbana.

DAVENPORT, G. CLARK 2001 Remote Sensing Applications in Forensic Investigations. *Historical Archaeology* 35(1): 87–100.

DAVIS, J. LES, J. ALAN HEGINBOTTOM, A. PETER ANNAN, S. ROD DANIELS, B. PETER BERDAL, TOM BERGAN, KIRSTY E. DUNCAN, PETER K. LEWIN, JOHN S. OXFORD, NOEL ROBERTS, JOHN J. SKEHEL, AND CHARLES R. SMITH 2000 Ground-Penetrating Radar Surveys to Locate 1918 Spanish Flu Victims in Permafrost. *Journal of Forensic Science* 45(1):68–76.

FARRELL, JAMES J. 1980 *Inventing the American Way of Death, 1830–1920*. Temple University Press, Philadelphia, PA.

GOODMAN, D., Y. NISHIMURA, AND J. D. ROGERS 1995 GPR Time-Slices in Archaeological Prospection. *Archaeological Prospection* 2(2):85–89.

GOODMAN, DEAN. 1994 Ground-Penetrating Radar Simulation in Engineering and Archaeology. *Geophysics* 50(2): 224–232.

GOODMAN, JEFFREY. 1977 *Psychic Archaeology: Time Machine to the Past.* Berkeley Publishing, New York, NY.

IMAIZUMI, MASATAKA. 1974 Locating Buried Bodies. *F.B.I. Law Enforcement Bulletin* 43(8):2–5.

KILLAM, EDWARD W. 1990 *The Detection of Human Remains.* Charles C. Thomas, Springfield, IL.

NOBES, DAVID C. 1999 Geophysical Surveys of Burial Sites: A Case Study of the Oaro Urupa. *Geophysics* 64(2):357–367.

REESE, K. M. 1985 Dowsing for Use in Archaeological Surveys. *Chemical and Engineering News* 63(2):124.

SIMMONS, G., D. W. STRANGWAY, L. BANNISTER, R. BAKER, D. CUBLEY, G. LA TORRACA, AND R. WATTS. 1972 The Surface Electrical Properties Experiment. In *Lunar Geophysics: Proceedings of a Conference at the Lunar Science Institute, Houston, Texas, 18–21 October 1971,* Z. Kopal and D. W. Strangway, editors, pp. 258–271. D. Reidel Publishing, Dordrecht, The Netherlands.

SLOAN, CHARLES DAVID. 1995 *The Last Great Necessity: Cemeteries in American History.* Johns Hopkins University Press, Baltimore, MD.

STERN, W. 1929 Versuch einer elektrodynamischen Dickenmessung von Gletschereis. *Ger. Beitr. zur Geophysik* 23: 292–333.

VAN LEUSEN, MARTIJN P. 1998 Dowsing and Archaeology. *Archaeological Prospection* 5(3):123–138.

VICKERS, ROGER, LAMBERT DOLPHIN, AND DAVID JOHNSON. 1976 Archaeological Investigations at Chaco Canyon Using Subsurface Radar. In *Remote Sensing Experiments in Cultural Resource Studies,* Thomas R. Lyons, editor, pp. 81–101. Reports of the Chaco Center, No. 1.
Chaco Center, National Park Service, and University of New Mexico, Albuquerque.

LAWRENCE B. CONYERS. DEPARTMENT OF ANTHROPOLOGY, UNIVERSITY OF DENVER,
2000 E. ASBURY ST., DENVER, CO 80208

Historical Archaeology, 2006, 40(3):64–73. Permission to reprint required.

Local Heroes

By Thomas Lynch

Some days the worst that can happen happens.
The sky falls or weather overwhelms or
The world as we have come to know it turns
Towards the eventual apocalypse
Long prefigured in all the holy books—
The end times of floods and conflagrations
That brings us to the edge of our oblivions.
Still, maybe this is not the end at all,
Nor even the beginning of the end.

Rather, one more in a long list of sorrows,
To be added to the ones thus far endured,
Through what we have come to call our history:
Another in that bitter litany
That we will, if we survive it, have survived.
Lord, send us in our peril, local heroes,
Someone to listen, someone to watch,
Someone to search and wait and keep the careful count
Of the dead and missing, the dead and gone
But not forgotten. Sometimes all that can be done
Is to salvage one sadness from the mass of sadnesses,
To bear one body home, to lay the dead out
Among their people, organize the flowers
And casseroles, write the obits, meet the mourners at the door,
Toll the bell, dig the hole, tend the pyre.

It's what we do. The daylong news is dire—
Full of true believers and politicos
Old talk of race and blame and photo ops.
But here brave men and women pick the pieces up.
They serve the living tending to the dead.
They bring them home, the missing and adrift,
They give them back to let them go again.
Like politics, all funerals are local.

Copyright 2005 by Thomas Lynch. Included by permission of Thomas Lynch.

Thomas Lynch is a poet and funeral director in Milford, Michigan. He's the author of "The Undertaking." "Wherever our spirits go or don't, ours is a species that has learned to deal with death—the idea of the thing—by dealing with the dead—the thing itself—in all the flesh and frailty of our human condition." In response to Hurricane Katrina, Lynch wrote *Local Heroes*.

****

Heart Thoughts

"Be kinder than necessary because everyone is fighting some kind of battle."

"Be fair and consistent. Make everyone feel welcomed and loved."

And for our departed partners......

"We have a secret, you and I, that no one else shall know. For who but I can see you lie each night in fire glow? And who but I can reach my hand before I go to bed, and feel the living warmth of you and touch your silken head? And only I walk woodland paths and see you ahead of me, your form racing with the wind so young again and free. And only I can see you swim in every creek we pass, and when I call, no one but I can see the bending grass."

"Always remember that you are never far apart if you look beyond the rainbow and listen with your heart. Our loved companions live on in the happy memories of times shared together."

Buzzards and Butterflies

Come and Sit a While......

I am your dog, and I have a little something that I'd like to whisper in your ear. I know that you humans lead busy lives. Some have to work, some have children to raise. It always seems that you are running here and running there, often much too fast,
often never noticing the truly grand things in life.

Look down at me now while you sit there at your computer. See the way my dark brown eyes look at yours? They are slightly cloudy now. That comes with age. The grey hairs are beginning to ring my soft muzzle. You smile at me: I see love in your eyes. What do you see in mine? Do you see a spirit? A soul inside, who loves you as no other could in the world? A spirit will forgive all trespasses of prior wrong doing for just a simple moment of your time?

That is all I ask; to slow down, if even only for a few minutes, to be with me. So many times you have been saddened by the words you read on that screen of others of my kind, passing. Sometimes we die young and oh so quickly, sometimes so suddenly it wrenches your heart out of your throat. Sometimes we age so slowly before your eyes that you may not even seem to know until the very end, when we look at you with grizzled muzzles and cataract-clouded eyes. Still the love is always there, even when we must take that long sleep,
to run free in a distant land.
I may not be here tomorrow: I may not be here next week. Someday you will shed the water from your eyes that humans do when deep grief fills their souls, and you will be angry with yourself that you did not have just 'one more day' with me.

Because I love you so, your sorrow touches my spirit and grieves me. We have NOW, together. So come, sit down here next to me on the floor and look deep into my eyes. What do you see? If you look hard enough and deep enough we will talk, you and I, heart to heart. Come to me not as 'alpha' or 'trainer' or even 'Mom or Dad'. Come to me as a living soul and stroke my fur and let us look deep into one another's eyes and talk. I may tell you something of the fun of chasing a tennis ball, or I may tell you something profound about myself, or even life in general. You decided to have me in your life
because you wanted a soul to share such things with.
Someone very different from you, and here I am.
I am a dog, but I am alive. I feel emotion, I feel physical senses, and I can revel in the differences of our spirits and souls. I do not think of you as a "dog on two feet" I know what you are and who you are. You are human in all your quirkiness, and I love you still.

Now, come sit with me on the floor. Enter my world and let time slow down if only for fifteen minutes. Look deep into my eyes and whisper into my ears. Speak with your heart, with your joy, and I will know your true self. We may not have tomorrow, but we do have today, and
life is oh so very short.

So please..... come sit with me now and let us share the precious moments we have together.
Love on behalf of canines everywhere,
Your dog.
(Author unknown).

Index

adipocere, 32, 59
age of scent sources, 68
Alert, 39, 40, 115, 116
Alexander, Ben, 164
American Indian Burials, 17
Amplitude Slice Map, 10
Amplitude slice maps, 208
APPENDIX, 184
AQUATIC BURIAL, 20
Autolysis, 31
Avalanche, 60, 80, 82, 84, 85, 86, 87, 149
Avalanche Rescue Pack, 87
Bahai Burial, 16
Bass, William, 33, 58
Behavior in Scent, 39
Bibliography, 219
Blackfeet, 18
Boats and Boat Operators, 108
Body Positioning, 16
Body Recovery Bag, 107
breathing, 50, 76
Burial Customs, 13
Burial Mounds, 13
Burial Statistics, 29
Butterflies, ii, 31, 36
Buzzards, ii, 31, 34
Canine Ethogram, 44
Caskets, 15
Categories of Behaviors, 45
Change of Behavior, 39
Closure, 181
Collecting Scent, 60, 64
Communication, 43
Concrete Samples, 60, 73
Contraband Substance Detector Dogs, 116
Conyers, Lawrence B., 199
Crime Scene Preservation, 124
Critical Incident Stress Management, 114
Cross-Trained, 126
Culberson, Nancy, 62
Decomposition Process, 31
Delbridge, Jim, ix, 70
detail method., 92
Divers, 108
Double - Blind, 40
Double Blind Problems, 68

Embalming, 31, 32
Emotions and Reactions to Death, 58
environment and soil conditions, 67
Evaluation for Human Remains Detection, 192
Factors Affecting Decomposition, 31
Family Interaction, 99
FEDERAL Case Law, 117
Final Response, 40
Findling, Amir, 151
flags, 11
Fleck, Terry, ix, 115, 116, 120
Floods, 111
Forensic anthropology, 33
Forensic entomology, 33
Forensic pathology, 33
Forensics, 2, 31
Freshkill, 169, 170, 171
Geophysicists, 8
Gibson, Patti, 148
Gilmore, Kim, ix, 80, 88, 98, 149
GPR, 7, 8, 10, 199, 200, 201, 202, 203, 204, 205, 206, 208, 209, 210
GPS, 1, 2, 11, 12, 77, 78, 88, 100, 102, 108, 133, 152, 153, 160, 161, 164, 165, 166
Grave Characteristics, 201
Grave wax, 32
Ground Penetrating Radar, 1, 7, 8
Ground Zero, 175
Hartell-DeNardo, Julia, ix, 43
Hazardous Materials, 111
HR/Shore, 110
HRD Water Recovery Certification Sample Evaluator Form, 187
Human Remains Detection, 190
Human Remains Detection Certification Sample Evaluator Form, 184
Human Scent Detector Dogs, 116
Illinois Mounds, 27
Indians inhabiting the Carolinas, 20
Indians of New York, 23
Infiltration, 91
INHUMATION, 20
Interest, 39
Irwin, K.T., 136
Jefferson, Jon, 33
Kaiser, 3

Katrina, 131, 174, 176, 213
Klamath and Trinity Indians of the Northwest, 21
Laidlaw, Bonnie, 148
Lakes and Quarries, 109
Land Search, 60
LAW, 115
Live Burial, 17
Local Heroes, 212
LOSS of a CONTRABAND "TRAINING AID, 123
Lynch, Thomas, 3, 212, 213
Magnetometer Maps, 7
Map, 11
Map Historic Graves, 199
Marshall, Roxye, ix, 69, 87, 124, 168
Martinez, Susan, ix, 39, 43
Massasauga Indians, 23
McNeil, Roy, 3
Mind and Heart, 57
Miss, 39
Mohawks of New York, 20
Mummification, 31, 32
Muscogulges of the Carolinas, 23
Natural Burials, 14
Navajos, 24
negative areas, 68, 70
NIMs, 60, 92
Peat Bog, 31
Pensacola Mounds, 28
Persians, 21
Peterson, Lacey, 135
Pima Indians, 22
Possession of Cadaver, 122
Possession of Contraband for K-9 Training Purposes, 120
Possession of Explosives, 121
Possession of Narcotics, 120
POSSESSION SOLUTIONS, 124
Preservation of the Body, 15
probe, 6, 7, 70, 76, 81, 86
Proofing, 60, 73
Ralston, Gene L., 107, 131, 133, 135
Rathe, Laura, 60, 73, 75
Reading the Dog, 39
Reasonable Suspicion, 116
Reliability, 40, 61
Research Facilities, 36
Rivers and Creeks, 109

Round Valley Indians of California, 24
Sanner, Carol, ix, 79, 80, 82, 85
Scent Article, 62
Scent Machines, 106
Scent Tube, 67
Search Strategies, 60
Selecting an HRD Dog, 41
Side Scan Sonar, 97, 108, 132
Sievert, Sharolyn, 145
Sioux, 17, 18
Skeletonization, 33
Slave Burials, 14
smoke bombs, 101
Soil Acidity/Moisture Meter, 6
Soil Composition, 5
soil pH, 6
Soil pH, 5
Soil Probes, 7
SOURCES of CONTRABAND TRAINING AIDS:, 123
Stakes, 7
STATE Case Law, 117
Storage of Scent Sources, 60
SWGDOG, 40, 41, 115, 220
Swiftwater, 110
Thermoclines, 97, 104
Tolhurst, Bill, 42
Tools, 6
Trained, Certified and Reliable, 116
Training Materials, 60, 61
Training Records, 61, 184, 187
Training Scenarios, 60, 70
Turner, Matthew, 7
Types of Water, 109
Unburied, 17
Videotaping, 128
Ware, Jim, ix, 77, 181
Water Search - Marking System, 106
Water Search - Reaching Device, 107
Water Search - Spotters, 104
Water Search Equipment & Supplies, 100
Water Search Training Techniques, 101
Water Searches, 5, 6, 26, 28, 56, 68, 83, 84, 86, 94, 97, 104, 125, 157, 159, 160, 163, 165, 171, 190, 192, 220
weather conditions, 68
Wood, Shelley, ix, 75
WTC, 169, 172, 173, 176

Bibliography

Antiq. of Southern Indians, 1873, pp 108-110.

Australian Museum Online. http://www.deathonline.net/decomposition/body_changes/rigor_mortis.htm

Bancroft. Nat. Races of Pac. States, 1874, vol. 1, p. 780.

Bartram. Bartram's Travels, 1791, pp. 515. Eleventh Annual Report of the Peabody Museum, Cambridge, 1878

Conyers, Lawrence B. University of Denver, Anthropology Department. lconyers@du.edu. http://mysite.du.edu/~lconyers/SERDP/surveyexamples2.htm

Culberson, Nancy, NC Search and Rescue Association.

Darwin, Charles. The Descent of Man.

Darwin, Charles. The Expressions and Emotions of Man.

Delbridge, Jim http://workingairedale.proboards78.com/index.cgi?board=searchandrescue&action

Fleck, Terry. Law Enforcement Officer, retired. Canine Legal Update Seminars. www.k9fleck.org.

GeoModel, Inc. http://www.geomodel.com/graves/

Gibbs, George. Schoolcraft's Hist. Indian Tribes of the United States Pt. 3, 1853, p. 140.

Grossman, F. E., Capt. Rep. Smithson. Inst., 1871, p. 414. USA.

Hartell, Julie. Canine Ethogram with Interpretation for Search Dogs.

Hoffman, W. J. U.S. Geological. Survey of Territories. for 1876, p. 473.

Holbrook, W. C. Amer. Natural, 1877, xi, No. 11, p. 688..

Jenkins, Jennifer. Oatley, Keith. Stein, Nancy. Human Emotions, A Reader.

L'incertitude des Signes de la Mort, 1740, tom 1, p. 430.

Martinez, Susan. Canine Ethogram with Interpretation for Search Dogs.

Peking Man World Heritage Site at Zhoukoudian. http://www.unesco.org/ext/field/beijing/whc/pkm-site.htm . World Heritage Patrimoine Mondial.

Platt, Kevin Holden. National Geographic Magazine. February 20, 2008. Ancestral Human Skull Found in China.

Putnam, F. W. Peabody Museum of Archeology, Cambridge, made to the Boston Society of Natural History, and published in Volume XX of its proceedings, October 15, 1878.

Ralston, Gene. Ralston & Associates an environmental consulting firm specializing in water-related services.

Scientific Working Group on Dog & Orthogonal Detector Guidelines. SWGDOG. www.fiu.edu/~ifri/SWGDOG.htm .

Simpson, Jacqueline (August 2005). "The Miller's tomb: facts, gossip, and legend". Folklore.

Simpson, Jacqueline (Jan.—Mar 1978). "The World Upside down Shall Be: A Note on the Folklore of Doomsday". The Journal of American Folklore 91 (359): 559-567.

Smith, C. J.; Peoples, M. B. Keerthisinghe, G. James, T. R. (1994). "Effect of surface applications of lime, gypsum and phosphogypsum on the alleviating of surface and subsurface acidity in a soil under pasture". Australian Journal of Soil Research 32 (5): 995-1008. ISSN 0004-9573.

Stansbury, George M., MD. Explorations of the Valley of the Great Salt Lake of Utah, 1852, p. 43. Surgeon, U. S. Army. Proc. Am. Ass. Adv. of Science, 1875, p. 288.

U. S. Department of Homeland Security. Federal Emergency Management Agency. Canine Search and Rescue Team - Land Cadaver Air Scent Standards. National Mutual Aid & Resource Management Initiative.

Vallortigara, Giorgio. "Asymmetric tail-wagging responses by dogs to different emotive stimuli." "Current Biology" (Volume 17, Issue 6, 20 March 2007, Pages R199-R201). Giorgio Vallortigara, a neuroscientist at the University of Trieste in Italy, and two veterinarians, Angelo Quaranta and Marcello Siniscalchi, at the University of Bari, also in Italy. (Reference for Canine Ethogram.)
Wikimedia http://en.wikipedia.org/wiki/Ground-penetrating_radar